THE VICTORIAN
——POET:——
Poetics and Persona

Edited by
JOSEPH BRISTOW

CROOM HELM
London • New York • Sydney

© 1987 Joseph Bristow
Croom Helm Ltd, Provident House,
Burrell Row, Beckenham, Kent BR3 1AT

Croom Helm Australia, 44-50 Waterloo Road,
North Ryde, 2113, New South Wales

Published in the USA by
Croom Helm
in association with Methuen, Inc.
29 West 35th Street,
New York, NY 10001

British Library Cataloguing in Publication Data

The Victorian poet: poetics and persona.
  — (World and word series).
  1. English poetry — 19th century —
History and criticism
  I. Bristow, Joseph
  821'.8'09   PR591

  ISBN 0-7099-3925-6
  ISBN 0-7099-3977-9 Pbk

Library of Congress Cataloging in Publication Data

ISBN 0-7099-3925-6
ISBN 0-7099-3977-9 Pbk

Typeset in 10pt Baskerville by Leaper & Gard Ltd, Bristol, England
Printed and bound in Great Britain by Mackays of Chatham Ltd, Kent

General Editor's Preface

The *World and Word* series, as its title implies, is based on the assumption that literary texts cannot be studied in isolation. The series presents to students, mainly of English literature, documents and materials which will enable them to have first-hand experience of some of the writing which forms the context of the literature they read. The aim is to put students in possession of material to which they cannot normally gain access so that they may arrive at an independent understanding of the interrelationships of literary texts with other writing.

There are to be twelve volumes, covering topics from the Middle Ages to the twentieth century. Each volume concentrates on a specific area of thought in a particular period, selecting from religious, philosophical or scientific works, literary theory or political or social material, according to its chosen topic. The extracts included are substantial in order to enable students themselves to arrive at an understanding of the significance of the material they read and to make responsible historical connections with some precision and independence. The task of compilation itself, of course, predetermines to a great extent the kind of connections and relationships which can be made in a particular period. We all bring our own categories to the work of interpretation. However, each compiler makes clear the grounds on which the choice of material is made, and thus the series encourages the valuable understanding that there can be no single, authoritative account of the relationships between word and world.

Each volume is annotated and indexed and includes a short bibliography and suggestions for further reading. The *World and Word* series can be used in different teaching contexts, in the student's independent work, in seminar discussion, and on lecture courses.

Isobel Armstrong
University of Southampton

Contents

Contents

Preface

The documents gathered together in this volume are designed to give readers a clear idea about the key issues at stake in Victorian poetry. The materials have been selected with a number of points in mind. Rather than focus the volume on the work of individual poets, such as Browning and Tennyson, the following chapters look at broader issues within Victorian poetic theory: the varying models of the poet; the role of emotion in poetry; the expression of sexual desire; questions of gender; and the debates on class and 'radical poetry'. Students may wish to follow up these general lines of enquiry by consulting the numerous reviews of Victorian poetry compiled in the *Critical Heritage* volumes on Arnold, Browning, Clough, Meredith, Swinburne, Tennyson and Wilde. The contents of this book have been chosen so as not to overlap with already available materials in those volumes and in Isobel Armstrong's *Victorian Scrutinies: Reviews of Poetry 1830 to 1870*, which focuses on Victorian debates about Browning, Tennyson, Clough and Arnold. It is a pity that only one woman is represented in the present study, particularly when the rise of the 'poetess' is so significant in Victorian letters. Periodical reviews of Victorian women's poetry are insufficiently critical to warrant reprinting. Essays by Victorian women on poetry are, as far as current research is concerned, scant indeed. But it is more than likely that there are writings by Victorian women on the poetry of their age waiting to be unearthed. A representative selection of Victorian women's poetry is to be found in the seventh volume of A.H. Miles's compendious *The Poets and the Poetry of the Age*, published in later editions as *The Poets and the Poetry of the Nine- teenth Century*. Unfortunately, this very useful anthology has been long out of print. There is certainly a need for a comprehensive anthology of women's poetry from the period, if only to demonstrate that significant work was produced by women other than Elizabeth Barrett Browning and Christina Rossetti. Given additional space, the chapters that follow would have included several more documents pertaining to working-class and radical Victorian poetry. One study to date deals with this often ignored area of writing — Martha Vicinus, *The Industrial Muse: A Study of Nineteenth-Century British Working-Class Literature* (London, Croom Helm, 1974), Chapters 3 and 4. Vicinus examines the work of the

'self-educated' (or, as the periodicals named them, 'uneducated')
poets, many of whom were centrally involved in Chartist
struggles.

Poetry as political propaganda (around the Corn Laws, in par-
ticular) and poetry as class consciousness-raising during the early
Victorian period preludes the institutionalization of poetry as an
educational tool with the advent of compulsory state education.
F.W. Robertson's rather patronising 1852 *Lectures on Poetry to the
Working-Classes* mark a half-way stage between the work of, say,
Ebenezer Elliott (the famous Sheffield 'Corn-Law Rhymer') and
Matthew Arnold's stodgy essay, 'The Study of Poetry' (1880) —
particularly revealing in its attempt to claim a 'future' for poetry
in the form of secular religion, a new faith enshrining the 'best'
moral qualities. Historians of English Studies have noted the
insidious (because still vestigially influential) development within
education of ideas about the moral 'relevance'-cum-'universal'-
validity of literature (in which poetry plays a key role).

Several of the essays presented here contained in their original
form inaccuracies of wording and oddities of punctuation. These
have all been corrected. Spelling is given in accordance with
house style. Likewise, Victorian reviewers are often casual when
citing their sources. Minor mistakes have been silently corrected.
A note has been given where the critic wrongly attributes his
source. Where in periodical publication the essays include
lengthy footnotes, these have been incorporated here into the
main text in square brackets. For ease of reference, additional
documentation (dates of poems, full names and so on) has also
been inserted in this way. Quotations have been checked against
volumes in the Oxford Standard Authors series or earlier Oxford
editions except in the following cases: *Arnold: The Complete Poems*,
2nd edn. eds Kenneth Allott and Miriam Allott (London,
Longman, 1979); *Swinburne's Collected Poetical Works* (London,
Heinemann, 1924); and *The Poems of Tennyson*, ed. Christopher
Ricks (London, Longman, 1969). All references to the works of
Shakespeare are to the *Riverside Shakespeare* (Boston, Houghton
Mifflin, 1974). It is the habit of Victorian reviewers to include particularly long quotations of poetry (as if to demonstrate which
sections of the poem should be seen as the most significant). In a
number of cases here, especially long citations have been
omitted. A note indicating which lines have been left out is given
in their place. It has not been possible to identify a number of
quotations, particularly where authors cite foreign sources in

translation. In a few instances, such as those to be found in Ruskin's article, it is clear that faulty memory has created lines of poetry which did not formerly exist.

Acknowledgements

A number of people have helped with translations from foreign languages: Ilse Geson (University of Southampton), Dr Barbara Garvin (University College London), Stuart Mason (Nene College) and Dr Ray Calcraft (University of Warwick). Professor Isobel Armstrong has been at all times helpful in giving advice on the selection of materials. The staff of Nene College library greatly assisted with inter-library loan requests.

Introduction

Victorian criticism of Victorian poetry

This book sets out to show that Victorian poetry has a wide range
— of critical contexts — contexts covering not just questions of
poetic form but ones which relate also to two challenging areas:
class and sexuality. This introduction aims to suggest, rather
than assert, how the critical documents presented here might be
used to inform our understanding of the poetry, and vice versa.
Connecting the poetry with the criticism, however, is complicated
by the fact that there is nothing coherently 'Victorian' about
either the one or the other, although certain continuities can
obviously be traced. What is more, both Victorian criticism and
Victorian poetry display a troubled awareness of this lack of
coherence. In this respect, it is worth pointing out that the key
question of early Victorian poetic theory is 'What is Poetry?' —
and that is why Chapter 1 takes this blunt enquiry up as its title.
The Victorians, particularly within the first decades of their era,
were at something of a loss to define and defend the role of the
poet, his poetry and indeed, his persona. The sections that follow
briefly examine major topics (and aspects of the major poets too)
to indicate what were urgent preoccupations: the Victorian
response to Romanticism; Victorian models of the poet; the dis-
placement of poetry by the novel; and the combined interests of
poets and critics in human emotions, psychology, and the idea (a
new one) of the 'individual'.

Victorian poetry was not without its problems (in terms of
style and subject-matter — hence the amount of conspicuous
experimentation), and it needs to be pointed out that the noticeable diversity of Victorian poetry has rendered it for some
modern readers (as it did for some Victorians) as inferior to that of
the Romantics. It is fair to say that the difficult passage from
Romanticism to Modernism through what might be tentatively
named as Victorianism has not been well charted by twentieth-
century criticism, largely because the Victorians have not been
understood as grappling critically with poetry, trying to find a
place for it in their culture, and, indeed, attempting to reformu-
late its purpose. This book, therefore, goes some way towards filling what remains as a gap in our knowledge by demonstrating

1

that Victorian criticism of Victorian poetry if pulling in different directions (towards, say, classicism on the one hand, and metaphorical ingenuity on the other) is all the more fascinating for that — fascinating because both the criticism and the poetry move out along lines that fractured Victorian culture. Poetry, as an art, was visibly breaking up in Victorian Britain, just as the nation seemed to be polarized (both in terms of class and gender) in the face of industrialization. But this is not surprising when the concept of 'Victorian Britain' has to be elasticated over some sixty or so years, a period of such length and social change that the word 'Victorian' loses any claim to specificity (a specificity implied, for example, in the false austerity enshrined in the idea of 'Victorian values'). Before going any further, then, it is worth pausing for a moment to consider what might be meant by both 'Romantic' and 'Victorian' — especially when there are renowned Romantic Victorians, Tennyson and the Brontës being the outstanding examples.

To the institution of English literature, those poets grouped as the Romantics possess an altogether more definite identity than the Victorians — and this is not necessarily a critical falsification. But 'Romantic' is none the less an ambiguous and misleading term, and the Victorians are largely to blame for this because they were responsible for inventing it and applying it in its commonly acceptable manner. 'Romanticism' confusingly describes both a set of aesthetic preoccupations and a historical period. Both are much debated and to make general statements about either compounds these historical and critical difficulties. The period 1790-1830 conveniently brings together a number of 'Romantic' poets whose biographies, aesthetic choices and actual works are closely interconnected. Moreover, the Romantics, unlike their Victorian heirs, produced a number of critical documents that spoke purposefully of a self-conscious project to make a break with eighteenth-century empiricism by focusing on the authenticity, autonomy and creativity of the poetic mind. Shelley's 'Defence' of poetry (published posthumously in 1840), Wordsworth's 'Prefaces' to *Lyrical Ballads* (1800, 1802), and Coleridge's *Biographia Literaria* (1817) all provide the modern student with the distinct sense that the Romantics share the same ideology (even if each poet had different political concerns), which, put as simply as possible, promotes poetry as a 'recreative' or transforming power. That is, poetry changes what it sees as it sees. Victorian critics frequently sustain this interest in the 'transfiguring' properties of the mind (see Sydney Dobell, passage 1.9), and a central Romantic term, imagination, is disseminated in much Victorian writing. Where, then, does Victorian criticism of poetry take off from its immediate predecessors? And, indeed, when the historical scope of the concept 'Victorian' is taken into consideration, what might 'Victorian poetry' define? These two questions need to be taken together.

Some, like Barbara Everett, would argue that Victorian poetry means only Tennyson and Browning; this is an arguably restrictive but none the less representative modern judgement:

> 'Art' is to a large extent the invention of the nineteenth century; and it may be said to explain why the Victorian period produced no really great poets, only two figures as considerable, in their different ways, as Browning and Tennyson are. The enormous expansion of the ordinary culture of the age could be assimilated with some directness into the developing form of the novel; but it left poetry with particular problems.[1]

Poetry was problematic for the Victorians partly because they were not, as they too well recognized, the Romantics. The stark stylistic contrast of Browning's and Tennyson's poetry was carefully examined by Walter Bagehot in 1864: he saw Tennyson as 'ornate', Browning as 'grotesque' and Wordsworth, by comparison, as 'pure'.[2] A multiplicity of styles and remarkable formal innovation distinguish the Victorian poets but their work can appear directionless. Tennyson was engaged with heterogeneous forms like the 'medley', and Browning took up a good deal of space with verse-novels (written late in his career). Browning's most discursive poetry was produced, for the most part, after his involvement with what he saw as a literary hybrid, the 'dramatic lyric' (his term for the form now usually known as the dramatic monologue. It is valuable to observe that the poetry by Browning least read today (that published after 1870) was most popular with Victorians. The trajectory of his career leads altogether away from that of Tennyson (made Poet Laureate in 1850). Even if both poets share roughly the same historical moment (their dates are almost identical), they diverge in every aspect of their work. Therefore, although the Victorians may have instituted the concept of 'Art' (on this, see George Henry Lewes, passage 1.5), as Everett says, 'Art' was not narrowly defined by either poets or critics of poetry — each had something of a competing definition, and, indeed, when it came to defining poets, Browning offered not one but *two* versions of poethood (passage 1.11). For Browning, perhaps more than most, the poet could be categorized according to certain tendencies which he named 'subjective' and 'objective' — a polarity that points up the contradiction that the poet, by 1852, had become. This redefinition of the poet according to tendencies rather than a single type can be seen as a symptom of the *loss* of identity of both the writer and his art.

Poetry, the individual, and emotion

Victorian poetry began in a vacuum. After the successive deaths of the major Romantics (bar Wordsworth, who lived until 1850), the decade that opened the Victorian era boldly declared the loss of the recently pre-eminent art now left to the likes of Felicia Hemans, Thomas Moore, Robert Montgomery and Joanna Baillie, among countless others.[3] It is true to say that ballads and 'parlour poetry' were exceptionally popular, especially in the work of the ever-multiplying number of 'poetesses', many of whom followed in the tradition of Hemans. But 'literary' (as opposed to 'parlour' and popular 'street-ballad') poetry was felt to be in decline when Victoria took the throne. During the 1830s, and indeed as late as the 1850s, it is particularly noticeable how periodical reviewers bemoan the supposedly moribund state of English poetry, looking out all the time for new talents to express the nascent Victorian 'spirit of the age'. William Bodham Donne, to take one example, when writing about the work of his fellow Cambridge Apostle, Richard Monckton Milnes, prefaces his commentary with these words:

> poetry is less plentifully supplied to us at present than it was a few years since, or, which comes to the same thing, everybody has agreed to say that such is the case, and every notice of a new writer is expected to begin with 'In the existing dearth of poetry', or some equivalent expression.[4]

The future of poetry was certainly unclear. As David J. DeLaura remarks: 'From about 1820, well into the 1850s, the continuous context for the discussion of poetry in England was a fear that it was nearly defunct, combined with sometimes wistful, sometimes extravagant hopes for its future.'[5] Indeed as late as 1849, when George Henry Lewes was reviewing the work of Browning, he said: 'In our day ... few men of remarkable powers have given any labour to poetry.'[6] By the middle of the century then, poetry was perceived as a marginal (as opposed to being a central) discourse, a relatively unimportant genre that did not appear to suit the needs and wants of the Victorians. How might the situation be remedied?

The essays of 1833 by John Stuart Mill provide a starting-point for examining how poetry was vital for its direct expression of feeling (see passage 1.3). For recent commentators, Mill's interests in the automatic translating of feeling into words in poetry look historically belated, coming, as they do, at the tail-end of Romanticism.[7] Herbert F. Tucker points out that when set alongside Browning's and Tennyson's monologues, and the ironic structure of those monologues, 'Mill's position' appears to be 'already its own absurd reduction.'[8] The poets, on the one hand, were fascinated by the duplicity of their speakers (such as Porphyria's Lover and Ulysses) while Mill and a number of theorists, on the other, were claiming that poetry expressed emotional truth: something sincere. In the monologue, irony operates to subvert the expressive ambitions of the Romantic ego (that is, the 'spontaneous overflow of powerful feelings' advanced by Wordsworth). Clearly enough, the first Victorian poets manufactured a poetic 'I' that no longer spoke as a subject guiding language at will but a speaker who was, instead, *subjected to* language. The monologue indicates how *language* speaks over against the speaker. This is one of the most significant advances made by Victorian poetry (mainly in the figure of Browning). Mill's essays are no less dispensable for illustrating how advanced the monologue (emerging in the 1830s) was for its time.

Mill, along with several other critics (passages 1.4, 1.5, 1.9 and 1.10) hold on to a notion of the private (confessional) poetic voice, a voice that, if expressing its feelings directly, is (perhaps obliquely) '*over*heard'. Therefore, if Mill's poet speaks truly of his feelings those feelings are very private, even secret. It is on this point that Mill's ideas appear to be more Victorian than Romantic. Victorian poetry, as much as its more popular counterpart the novel, made the individual seem more intricate, subtle and psychologically intriguing than ever before. Neither Tennyson nor Browning trades in stock characters and, to make a general point, their protagonists are distinguished by their eccentric fantasies. Mill and fellow utilitarian W.J. Fox were both interested in the theatrical and impersonating voice of poetry.[9] Dobell, likewise, emphasizes the poet's pre-eminent ability to produce 'an inexhaustible stock of men and women in the transmutable substance of his own character' (passage 1.9). This is a curious remark because it adheres to a Romantic ideal of authentic poetic identity while praising the poet's skill at producing an endless variety of characters. Personae are, therefore, seen as the infinite aspects of the great poet's genius and, moreover, the self is both personal *and* dramatic — and it is this multiple identity of the poet that marks out a Victorian difference from Romanticism. With this dramatic skill, the skill to proliferate the poet's identity into numerous personae, Victorian poetry managed to accommodate a startling range of themes — themes such as homicide, eroticism and irreligion — that other literary discourses found it difficult to take up. It is accurate to argue that the majority of early Victorian critics — like Mill and Alexander Smith (passage 1.4) — demanded sincere emotions in poetry (accompanied by simplicity of expression). However, while these critical requests were being made, the poets were directing their work into the darkest areas of the psyche, pushing on the limits of what was regarded as respectable. Browning's shockingly 'grotesque' style articulated many narratives which, in the words of Bishop Blougram (1855), teetered on the 'dangerous edge of things' (395). Tennyson's hero in *Maud* (1855) fuses together sexual love with military ambition in tones that render violence and tenderness as almost wholly interchangeable. In 1860, to put yet another case, D.G. Rossetti's 'Jenny' (a poem with a remarkable textual history — being exhumed in manuscript from his wife's grave) flew in the face of respectable morality by disclosing how those Victorian stereotypes, 'The Angel in the House' and the fallen woman, could only be kept distinct as long as they remained dependent (culturally, economically) upon one another. Examined together with the contents of Chapter 1, these risky poems demonstrate that the poets were working in a discourse that encountered the urgency of the Victorian 'double standard' well in advance of their critics. This was achieved by taking the initiative to express *real emotions*, ones not necessarily admitted to in public, to extremes, and, it is important to stress, usually by means of a persona. The persona — the dramatic voice — gave an extraordinary opportunity to the Victorian poet to explore what we know now to be forms of unconscious motivation.

The points raised above were particularly worrying to Matthew Arnold — one of the reactionary voices in this collection: 'The confusion of the present times is great, the multitude of voices counselling different things bewildering, the number of existing works capable of attracting a young writer's attention and of becoming his models, immense' (passage 1.8). Arnold sought as a remedy to this disunification a more reliable (because eternal) 'classical' account of poetry that would address itself to the 'great primary affections' — ones which 'subsist permanently in the race'. He did not want, as one of his contemporaries thought to be necessary, a '"a true allegory of the state of one's mind in a representative history"'. But even if rejecting something as prone to novelty and fashion as a 'representative history', Arnold nevertheless shares with his opponent a need for emotional truth. Arnold, it needs to be noted, had the Spasmodic poets in mind when he was writing in 1853 (in a 'preface' that shows severe doubts about his *own* writing too). The Spasmodics were a minor group of poets (Sydney Dobell was one) of epical ambitions who learnt much from Browning only to produce what read like awful parodies of that poet's *Paracelsus* (1835).[10] What the Spasmodics picked up on in their Victorian precursor was the extreme state of mind already referred to. This raises another point about the individuals, the dramatized personae, at the heart of Victorian poetry. They are men and women who bespeak an 'alien vision' (E.D.H. Johnson's phrase).[11] These characters are frequently withdrawn, isolated (one might say *privatized*) from the world of public affairs (for example, Browning's 'Pictor Ignotus' (1845) or Tennyson's 'Ulysses' (1830)). In the case of the Spasmodics, the individual is nothing other than a psychotic — Dobell's hero Balder murders his wife to save her from her madness. *Balder* (1854), in some respects, is a mammoth exploration into the eerie psychology of Browning's 'Porphyria's Lover' (1836). In response to this, Arnold wanted poets to seek out 'permanent passions' in direct proportion to 'excellent action[s]'. Arnold, then, wanted a different outlet for emotion.

Emotion was, for most poets, preferable to political action. Avrom Fleishman, in a stimulating series of 'notes' demanding a more historically informed understanding of poetry, observes that the genre at this time hardly registers any political activity (apart from momentary glances at the revolutions of 1848 and the later Italian struggles).[12] One could read these works, he argues, without apprehending that they were produced in the midst of the Industrial Revolution. (This point is open to some correction.) It can be inferred from this that the poets were relocating poetry away from, say, the 'language of common men' (Wordsworth) and revolution (Shelley) to an arena where the middle classes could reflect on their individuality — and their fantasies of a free and creative subjectivity. There is little sense of the major poetry of the 'Hungry Forties' (apart from that of Clough) taking the form of social critique, as many novels of that decade attempted to do. To sum up: in its concentration on individual states of mind, Victorian poetry found itself doing two things at once: first, it demanded greater attention to the uniqueness of human character in opposition to the stultifying forces of the 'march of mind' (industrial 'Progress' and the utilitarian values underpinning it) and, second, it discovered that this focus of interests (on the private self) actually evacuated it from the space it wished to occupy — the *centre* of culture. That Victorian poets wished to put their art at the centre of their culture is borne out by the fact that they wrote so obsessively about poetry (both Browning's *Sordello* (1840) and Barrett Browning's *Aurora Leigh* (1856) are fictional biographies of poets; Tennyson's early lyrics continuously turn to the poet and the peace of mind he needs — one such lyric is examined in the next section). Yet, in trying to put the individual — whether as poet or persona — forward as the most eminent cultural figure, poetry was none the less pushed to the *margins* of that culture (Alan Sinfield's significant observation).[13] The men and women dramatized by these poets are brought into public view in narratives which relate how *removed* they are from public experience.

If Chapter 1 guides Victorian poetic theory towards these preoccupations with emotion and the individual, the next two chapters examine, if more briefly, how subsequent decades, the 1860s and 1870s in particular, continued the effort (one that was never concerted) to restore poetry to its supposedly proper place. Alfred Austin, a poor poet but a sharp critic, pointed out that Victorian England could not foster 'great art' — 'artificiality ... self-consciousness ... feminine infirmities ... scepticism ... distracted aims', all militated against poetry, as if the genre were intrinsically vulnerable to external pressures (passage 2.1). There are all sorts of odd contradictions in Austin's writing, too many to be disentangled here, but one stands out in this context, and it concerns his attitude to gender. His previous sentence refers to both the age and its poetry as weakly feminine. To rectify this, what is required is 'manly concentration'. However, in his argument, poetry has succumbed to the conditions of its production, as if its weakness were *a priori*. The point to be made here is that all faith in art as triumphant in the face of adverse forces has been lost. If poetry has been marginalized, it has also been made effeminate. It is certainly within the 1860s through to the 1880s that the Victorians' interest in 'Art' is keenly associated with a negative femininity. Only a few ideas about the gendering of poetry can be offered here in relation to the contents that follow; and one topic that comes to mind is the treatment of sexuality by Browning and Tennyson and then the second generation of Victorian poets, the Pre-Raphaelites. Chapter 3 opens with an article by M.A. Stodart which instantly identifies poetry as a female domain — a 'proper sphere' for the many poetesses of the mid-nineteenth century (passage 3.1). The more poetry was identified with women, the less influential it became to the Victorians. Here it is necessary to point out that after her death in 1861, Elizabeth Barrett Browning declined in terms of her reputation. The 'poetess' — of which there were a great many — a woman who frequently wrote in a devotional mode — has long been regarded as a trivial if not laughable phenomenon, and only one modern anthology of women's poetry manages to reconsider critically the particular conditions in which Victorian women poets wrote.[14]

Austin declared that all Tennyson was interested in was 'woman, woman, woman', and one only has to turn to 'The Lady of Shalott' (1832, revised 1842) to recognize that the mysteries of woman were on Tennyson's mind from the earliest part of his career. His engagement with the complexity of Victorian sexual ideology discovers its bravest expression in *The Princess* (1847) where a case is made for the male protagonists to try to examine the femininity within them. Tennyson's effeminized hero, the Prince, clearly stands in opposition to the mainstream Victorian understanding of masculinity to be found, to cite a couple of examples, in the writings of the Christian Socialists (F.D. Maurice, Charles Kingsley and Thomas Hughes) and John Ruskin (notably *Sesame and Lilies* (1865)). But Tennyson was not quite such an unusual Victorian as he might appear. In this poem about the battle of the sexes, the hero still wins his lady, even if she has lived for some time as the feminist separatist leader of a women's university (she, the Princess, is depicted, at first, as manly). Tennyson examines the meaning of sexual difference from a radical right-wing position, using womanly men and manly women to reinforce, rather than eradicate, sexual divisions. (The poem is not, as some critics believe, in favour of androgyny.) As John Killham's highly detailed study of the poem indicates, Tennyson had a broad understanding of Victorian feminist controversies.[15] The poem is worth lingering with for a moment because it draws together an intense interest in sexual identity with class relations (this in itself is not a representative conjunction in Victorian poetry). *The Princess* has two narratives, one framing the other. The inset narrative tells of the romance between the effeminate hero and masculinized heroine. The outer narrative, however, concerns the benevolent attitude of the aristocracy towards the workers (in this case, skilled mechanics). The poem focuses much more, however, on the swapping of sexual identities (an interchange of gender roles that also reaches out to the narrative that frames it). Here, the mechanics and their inventions dwindle into insignificance (they are treated like children) while the aristocrats (who act paternalistically towards the workers *and* relate the framed narrative) act out bizarre sexual rituals. This poem, like many of Browning's monologues, established early in the Victorian period a long-lasting association between sexuality and poetry — which the contents of Chapter 3, in particular, all recognize. *The Princess* certainly anticipates the sexual risks taken by Swinburne and D.G. Rossetti. Sexual desire and poetic creativity are themes constantly entangled in Victorian poetry — from Coventry Patmore's lengthy (indeed overlong) and highly popular *The Angel in the House* (1854-63) (now a cliché of domestic wifedom) through to Swinburne's mythologized, sado-masochistic verses (in which the dominatrix is a recurrent figure). Victorian poetry manages, then, to maintain the contemporary stereotypes (often the obverse and reverse of each other) of the virgin/mother and the fallen woman. In Patmore, these are handled in a banal manner; in Clough, sexual love is given the full rein of male fantasy (as in '*Natura Naturans*' (1862)); in Meredith's *Modern Love* (1863), male sexuality finds its voice as one of jealous possessiveness; in the Pre-Raphaelites, perhaps unfairly taken as a whole, there is a really underrated sophistication and sensitivity to sexual relations between the classes and between women (in the sense of sisterly rather than lesbian).

In the 1860s, poetry was the focus of scandal. The majority of documents in Chapter 3 concern the 'fleshliness' that shocked the Victorian reading public. In the figure of Swinburne, Victorian poetry began to speak openly of the flesh. It was a breakthrough. Swinburne is of key importance because he became in the 1860s two things at once: first, the subject of controversy and second, the bright hope for the future of poetry. Even if some readers could not withstand the pulsation of desire in Swinburne's *Poems and Ballads* (1866), there were others who welcomed what was deemed to be a long-awaited revival of energy in mid-Victorian art, an art that had, perhaps, too deeply registered its loss with the world.

The passage from the earliest Pre-Raphaelite poetry to the interests of the 'aesthetic movement' of the 1880s is easy to trace, and out of that the decadent 1890s would produce in poetic form 'the Love that dare not speak its name' (Lord Alfred Douglas's phrase for homosexual desire). There is a large amount of male homosexual ('Uranian') poetry belonging to the late nineteenth century.[16] This writing on same-sex relations is light years away from the male working-class poets represented in Chapter 4; and the contrast between the 'fleshliness' of the 1860s (through to the sexual deviancy of the 1890s) with the struggles of working-class identification of the 1830s and 1840s casts into relief a number of the propositions put forward so far. By the late Victorian period, poetry was almost exclusively focused on sexual and emotional relationships and, it is reasonable to assert, it was a middle-class affair. Back in the 1830s, notably in the figure of Ebenezer Elliott, the Sheffield 'Corn-Law Rhymer', a strongly political grassroots poetry attracted attention in the periodicals, as did the work of several other self-taught poets (on these, see Kingsley, passage 4.3). Elliott's was a poetry for the masses; he campaigned for the repeal of the Corn Laws (lifted by Peel in 1846), a piece of legislation that provided the focus for Chartism and working-class organization. Elliott was the archetypal radical poet whom Kingsley would respond to in *Alton Locke* (1850), a novel that proselytizes on behalf of Christian Socialism. The radical poet was, by 1850, the stuff of novels — and his 'manliness' (idealized by the Christian Socialists) made little impact on a predominantly sensual poetry. Elliott, however, believed that poetry was 'impassioned truth' but it was a passion meant for the many and not the one. Chapter 1 opens with a passage by Keble who, using Coleridge's terms 'Imagination' and 'Fancy', appeals to poetry to exert a 'wonderful efficacy in soothing the emotions' (passage 1.1). Keble's is perhaps the position of greatest comfort offered in this collection; it is also the earliest (1829). For Arnold, writing in 1880, the same issue is at stake — 'In poetry ... the spirit of our race will find ... its consolation and stay' (passage 4.4) — but, then, fifty years later the consolations of poetry are deemed to belong to the *future*. The Victorians were not consoled by poetry. What Victorian poetry wanted and what was required of it remained, for the whole era, unresolved. 'The best poetry is what we want', declared Arnold. This is, in one respect, a statement of loss, and, in another, an optimistic view — either way Arnold is looking *beyond* the Victorian period, a time which has not produced classics, just individual styles. The styles were sufficiently individual for W.H. Mallock to reduce the work of each poet to that of a recipe (passage 2.2) — a not insignificant gesture with the rising popularity of cookery books. From Mallock's article, it is possible to see not only an immense dissatisfaction with Victorian poetry but, more specifically, a certain predictability and weakening femininity in that poetry. Finally — with Mallock and Austin in mind — criticism was gaining ascendancy over the poetry it read and judged. The future of poetry, as Arnold's article suggests, lies with the critics who will orient it to new locations, one of which would be the institutionalized study of English literature, where it would, in a variety of critical guises, operate to improve our feelings if not our whole concept of morality (in the work of F.R. Leavis, to give the chief example).

Victorian theories of the poet

Victorian criticism of poetry proceeds with two models of the poet in mind. These models are not, it needs to be said, mutually exclusive. The first is the poet as 'hero', propounded by Carlyle. The second is vaguer in formulation but has recently been identified by Sinfield as 'the poet of the margins'.[17] First of all, then, the hero, beloved by Browning (named as the 'Maker-see' in *Sordello*), and written about as follows by Barrett Browning in *Aurora Leigh*:

> What's this, Aurora Leigh
> You write so of the poets, and not laugh?
> Those virtuous liars, dreamers after dark,

12

Exaggerators of the sun and moon,
And soothsayers in a tea-cup?
                              I write so
Of the only truth-tellers now left to God,
The only speakers of essential truth,
Opposed to relative, comparative,
And temporal truths; the only holders by
His sun-skirts, through conventional gray glooms;
The only teachers who instruct mankind
From just a shadow on a charnel-wall
To find man's veritable stature out
Erect, sublime, — the measure of a man,
And that's the measure of an angel, says
The apostle. (1.854-69)

Here, the poet is certainly a Carlylean prophet: a *Vates*. Moreover, in this zealous passage, with its pliant syntax and speedy
movement, Barrett Browning beholds the poet as God's
messenger: the last species of 'truth-teller' on earth, someone
with greater capabilities than either the philosopher or scientist.
The poet is, in other words, the saviour of the secular age. In the
Romantic period, the poet was certainly divinely inspired. Now, a
generation later, the poet is God's emissary — an intermediary
between finite and infinite worlds. The extract has, of course, an
extraordinary urgency about it. The poet is the *last* of what is,
implicitly, a dying species. And Barrett Browning, practising
exactly what she preaches, takes to instructing her reader that she
knows that poets are invested with divine knowledge: it is this, she
avows, that makes them (and, one assumes, herself) so central to
culture. Her lines betray the fact that this is something of an illusion. In what is a not infrequent moment in Victorian poetry, her
writing discloses that the dynamic forces of industrial England
are in the process of undermining the role and purpose of her art.
In *Aurora Leigh*, she takes the following vatic opportunity to
remind her audience that poets still matter. She continues:

    Ay, and while your common men
Lay telegraphs, gauge railroads, reign, reap, dine,
And dust the flaunty carpets of the world
For kings and queens to walk on, or our president,
The poet suddenly will catch them up
With his voice like a thunder, — 'This soul,

This life, this work is being said in heaven,
Here's God down on us! what are you about?'
How all those workers start amid their work,
Look around, look up, and feel, a moment's space,
That carpet-dusting, though a pretty trade,
Is not the imperative labour after all. (1.869-80)

The point is strained, and even for its time, in being put forward
as a theory of poetry in the 1850s, is an idealistic one. The bewildering activity of Victorian society, all the 'labour' involved in
the construction of it, crowds out these impulsive lines. Barrett
Browning is clearly worried about the shift in values under the
'work' of capitalism. Poetry, as the last outpost of truth, is staked
out here to save the faith of the nation, to preach that there is
more in life than laying roads and building bridges. But the anxious
tone of this extract suggests that poetry has far less to offer the
Victorians than she is willing to believe. The passage illustrates
how difficult Barrett Browning found it to incorporate social and
political materials when her model of the poet was supposed to
stand *over and above* such mundane things as 'work'. These lines,
written in the wake of the controversial 'Condition-of-England
Question' (focused on the writings of Carlyle, Engels, Marx and
Macaulay), are trying to find a poetic solution to the social problems registered in her earlier poems such as 'The Cry of the
Children' (1844). Poetry was by the 1850s of diminished
importance. Barrett Browning and Browning himself refused to
acknowledge that their attempts to delineate the poet's profoundly prophetic and truth-telling role revealed that this was so.
If, then, they stand as major poets they hold a minority view of
their art. Only Emerson in this collection supports Carlyle's
beliefs — 'The Poet is the sayer, the namer, and represents
beauty. He is a sovereign, and stands at the centre' (passage 1.6).
To claim that the poet stood at the 'centre' was, to make a para-
dox of this, somewhat eccentric.

Arthur Hugh Clough is altogether more down to earth
(because so bitingly cynical). He is a marginal (but not necessarily minor) figure among Victorian poets, publishing his work
sporadically, and really gaining a reputation when his literary
remains appeared in 1862. It is to his credit that he could, as a
cultural 'outsider', one particularly suspicious of dominant
Victorian ideology (notably the practice of 'duty'), explode the
myth of the vatic poet promoted by the Brownings, Carlyle and

Emerson. 'Is it true, ye gods, who treat us', from his first volume, *Ambarvalia* (1849), puts forward this matter of hard fact with keen wit. The poem is worth quoting in full:

Is it true, ye gods, who treat us
As the gambling fool is treated,
O ye, who ever cheat us,
And let us feel we're cheated!
Is it true that poetical power,
The gift of heaven, the dower
Of Apollo and the Nine,
The inborn sense, 'the vision and faculty divine',
All we glorify and bless
In our rapturous exaltation,
All invention, and creation,
Exuberance of fancy, and sublime imagination,
All a poet's fame is built on,
The fame of Shakespeare, Milton
Of Wordsworth, Byron, Shelley,
Is in reason's grave precision,
Nothing more, nothing less.
Than a peculiar confirmation,
Constitution and condition
Of the brain and of the belly?
Is it true, ye gods who cheat us?
And that's the way you treat us?

Oh say it, all who think it,
Look straight, and never blink it!
If it is so, let it be so,
And we will all agree so;
But the plot has counterplot,
It may be, and yet be not.

Clough cites from Wordsworth's *The Excursion* (1814) (1.79) to indicate just how far the Victorians had moved away from Romantic ideologies. Categories of inspiration, imagination, divine 'power' — transcendent forces, in other words — are now, in an age of science, reducible to physiological conditions: the brain, the belly. Although Clough's tone implies that the 'gods' are, one way or another, dead for good, he is clearly concerned about the alternatives left for poetry. If 'invention', 'creation', 'fancy' and 'imagination' are no longer viable considerations in Victorian poetry, what might the art-form be about? On the one hand, the idea that poetry is simply a product of a number of bodily and mental processes seems rather crude, brutally deflating everything Romanticism had to offer. On the other hand, with the widespread advances in anatomy and psychology, Clough argues that poetry can all too easily be accepted as nothing more than a product of *human being*: cells, nerve-endings, the alimentary canal. This is a transitional poem, one which recognizes the mid-nineteenth-century disestablishment of traditional precepts about the creation of poetry. Clough's extraordinarily experimental canon of work, audacious in its use of hexameters (see *The Bothie-of-Tober-Na-Vuolich*, 1848), witnesses a sustained search for a new space that poetry may occupy. His intellectual career, which famously involves his refusal to assent to the Thirty-Nine Articles at Oxford, was fraught with endless self-examinations of conscience. He agonized over his religious beliefs and, closely connected with this, he changed his mind about the eroticism that prevails in his best-known poems. His impressive poetry thrives on these uncertainties — uncertainties about what can and might be said in a poetry deserted by the gods and abandoned to grey matter.

The 'gods' did not interest Browning so much as God himself. His 'Essay on Shelley' (passage 1.10) illustrates how his two kinds of poet — named 'subjective' and 'objective' — work along a calibrated scale between God and man. Both subjective and objective poets are heroes in their own right, and both approximate to the creative grandeur of the 'divine hand'. The Brownings were not the only writers of their day who claimed a religious function for poetry. The man who may well be the bestselling poet of the nineteenth century, Keble, lectured extensively on the obedience and devotion that 'sacred poetry' should exhibit (see passages 1.1 and 1.2).[18] Keble argues that this exhibition of love for God should be at all times modest (even deceitful), hiding true feeling by controlling spontaneity. Where Browning proposed a model of the 'Maker-see', one who spoke on behalf of God to the multitude (the Maker's seer, in other words), Keble, by contrast, offered an introspective model based on an idea of 'reserve' in poetry: '*Poetry is the indirect expression in words, most appropriately in metrical words, of some overpowering emotion, or ruling taste, or feeling, the direct indulgence of which is somehow repressed*'.[19] F. W. Robertson's rather patronizing 'Christian

Socialist' lectures on poetry to the working classes repeat many of
Keble's dicta (passage 4.2) (though it needs to be said, Carlyle,
the Christian Socialists' mentor on the 'Condition-of-England'
controversy, is clearly present also in Robertson's thoughts on
poetry). The devotional side of Victorian poetry persists well until
the end of the century, notably in the poems written by the many
'poetesses', the most eminent of whom, Christina Rossetti, had a
mystical interest in adventism, the afterlife and spiritual quest. In
a variety of forms, poetry stood as a kind of secular religion. By
1880, as is well-known, Arnold believed that 'the future of poetry'
was 'immense' because it could restore the values once preserved
by Christianity. As Chris Baldick's study of the emergence of
English studies demonstrates, poetry was allocated this
Arnoldian role in the designing of school curricula.[20] The spirit of
Keble, then, was never far away from the institutionalized study
of poetry. But the poets of school textbooks, even if censored carefully, were not accorded the prophetic status that Barrett
Browning believed to be their prerogative.

The alternative model of the poet, which can fairly be claimed
to dominate periodical reviews, is the more realistic of the two:
this is the secular 'poet of the margins' — the one theorized by
Mill, A.H. Hallam (returned to below) and, to an extent, Lewes
(passage 1.5). This is the poet divorced from politics, the one
whose duty is to aesthetics, pleasure, beauty — and not
prophecy, instruction and devotion. This particular model
(which is by no means a clear-cut type) found its major exponent
in Tennyson. The Poet Laureate may have been a national bard,
but he was certainly not a hero (in Carlyle's sense). Tennyson's
work easily accommodated a division of interests required by
many reviewers: that the poet spoke solely of private experience,
and not of the public domain. (But, as *The Princess* shows, he
reached out to public, 'contemporary' matters.) The opening
lines of his very early poem, 'The Poet's Mind' (1830), reveal
Tennyson's poet to be a reclusive, highly sensitive figure who
cannot endure challenges from lesser mortals. (It is worth noting
that Tennyson took adverse criticism badly.)

> Vex not thou the poet's mind
>   With thy shallow wit:
> Vex not thou the poet's mind;
>   For thou canst not fathom it.
> Clear and bright it should be ever,

Flowing like a crystal river;
Bright as light, and clear as wind. (1-7)

Tennyson's poet must not be contaminated or upset by external
influences: he is disengaged from public debate, thinking deeply,
clearly and immaculately in splendid isolation. He is part of the
natural elements, and yet also, perhaps conversely, sealed in his
own sanctum, safe on his 'holy ground' (9) from the encroach-
ments of the 'Dark-browed sophist' (8) — an intruder who is con-
temptuously 'foul with sin' (36). The poet demands respect, like a
priest, but he preaches nothing to command it.

Although Tennyson did not move in circles closely associated
with utilitarianism (that was Browning's terrain), there was a line
of thinking about poetry that draws together the work of W.J. Fox
with that of Mill and Tennyson's closest friend, Hallam. All
three critics share a utilitarian approach to poetry, in that poetry
is seen as instrumental to pleasure. (But it needs to be noted,
Bentham, the father of utilitarianism, was notoriously hostile to
poetry.)[21] Fox, Hallam and Mill in turn mark out stages whereby
the poet is completely divorced from the political realm. In detailing this movement in poetic theory, Sinfield states that 'poetry is
a valued part of the utilitarian world so long as it does not intrude
on the real conditions of life. It is *marginalized*.'[22] The poet's mind
must not be vexed, then, because it has to remain in its abstract
purity outside the social world. The poet may be pure, but he is
also vulnerable. Mill, after all, said that poetry was not 'eloquence' — it did not exist to persuade its audience. Poetry had to
please those who overheard it instead. It was not just that
Tennyson's poet had the quality to give pleasure to his readers
but that such pleasure could only come about if the public left
the poet to sing in solitude.

Throughout Mill's literary essays there is an emphatic wish to
divide poetry not just from the oratory of politics but from
another area once assigned to the genre: philosophical truth. In
his 1835 essay on Tennyson, Mill offered this warning:

It may not be superfluous to add that [Tennyson] ...
should guard himself against an error, to which philosophical speculations of poets are peculiarly liable — that of
embracing as truth, not the conclusions which are recommended by the strongest evidence, but those which have
the most poetical appearance.[23]

At not too great a distance from this view, Hallam designated Tennyson as a poet of 'sensation' (as opposed to one of philosophical 'reflection' — the terms were taken from Locke).[24] Although Tennyson was not entirely happy with the implications of his friend Hallam's definition (as 'The Palace of Art' (1832) demonstrates), his poetry often tended to the type of expressiveness advanced in Mill's essays. Poetry, Hallam argues, may be 'true' in its emotional representation but not in its logical analysis. Accordingly, he writes:

> though poetry encourages a wrong condition of feeling with respect to the discovery of truth, its enchantments tend to keep the mind within that circle of contemplative enjoyment, which is not less indispensably necessary to the exertions of a philosphic spirit. We may be led wrong by the sorcery; but that wrong is contiguous to the right.

In the same essay, Hallam states that 'pleasure is a constitution of every desire, so it must needs to be the only object desired'.[25] Here he is speaking of Epicurus, a figure of central importance to the aesthetic movement that emerged in the 1880s with Walter Pater as its leading theorist (see passage 3.8). Bentham's dictum that society should be geared towards 'the greatest happiness for the greatest number' can be seen in vestigial form in the pleasure-oriented writings of the Pre-Raphaelites. Of course, there are other precedents to be taken into account here, principally the idea of 'Art for Art's Sake' imported from German aesthetics quite early in the century.[26] (Generalizations of this sort need to be made with caution, especially in relation to the work of Morris, Swinburne and D.G. Rossetti, which ought not to be unhesitatingly conflated.) There are, of course, Romantic precedents for this focused interest in the pleasure-oriented qualities of poetry, notably in Coleridge. The famous fourteenth chapter of *Biographia Literaria* can be traced in both Mill's and Hallam's essays, as this extract shows:

> A poem is that species of composition which is opposed to works of science by proposing for its immediate object pleasure, not truth; and from all other species (having this object in common with it) it is discriminated by proposing to itself such delight from the whole as is compatible with a distinct gratification from each component part.[27]

Victorian critics seized on this. Mill and Hallam made what is an aspect of Coleridge's thinking about poetry the centre of their aesthetics.

In many respects, Mill and Hallam anticipate Ruskin's writings on the 'pathetic fallacy', which concerns the pleasure derived from the striking but essentially 'untrue' figures that characterize literary language (see passage 1.10). Ruskin's essay should not be misread as a simple statement about how poetry should not use metaphor, sticking instead to the literal truth (on this, consult Roden Noel, passage 1.12). The argument is quite complex, beginning with the proposition that there is something amiss in the enjoyment of apparently untruthful descriptions. He claims the 'pathetic fallacy' to be present when a figurative expression distorts the literal meaning. Most of the metaphors of this type that Ruskin selects attract attention to their metaphoricity. His essay attempts to analyse why these self-attending metaphors obtrude. Taking for granted that poets work with 'prophetic inspiration' (Carlyle's voice can be heard here), Ruskin offers the 'pathetic fallacy' as a form of Victorian sublime. Like the dizzying and vertiginous experiences that constitute the Romantic sublime, the pathetic fallacy is a product of violent, overpowering emotional states experienced when poets are 'submitted to influence stronger than they, and see in a sort untruly, because what they see is inconceivably above them'. The resulting 'untruth' in the form of a pleasing but deviant metaphor can be explained, then, as a symptom of the poet's encounter with the infinite. Even the finest poets, he says, are prone to such aberrations. These may be categorized as technical faults but they are as such because they originate in the highest forms of consciousness. Readers should, he says, treat such fallacies generously: 'as long as we see that the *feeling* is true, we pardon, or are even pleased by, the confessed fallacy of sight which it induces'. The poet's truth, therefore, must be inferred from these mistakes which can and do (even in classical writers) give pleasure.

Ruskin is, then, making an apparent wrong into a substantive right. He is correcting what might be mistaken for an error. His 'pathetic fallacy' denotes the inevitable inadequacy of poetry as a mode of representation. Like many of Ruskin's aesthetic definitions, such as the 'grotesque', this fallacy marks out a shortfall to be expected in all uses of language — a language premissed on imperfections, flaws and uncertainties. Read in this way, the 'pathetic fallacy' emerges as a theoretical proposition that is trying to recuperate poetry from its marginalized state. The scientific inaccuracy of poetry has to be converted into one of its prime virtues. But it is a virtue only in so far as it is not itself a higher truth. This line of analysis turns full circle to Browning's sceptical account of the poet who must 'approximate' towards (because never being able to represent) divine knowledge. What has been loosely termed in this essay the 'utilitarian' model of the poet is, in this respect, not so remote from Carlyle's *Vates* who, after all, had to struggle all the time to find forms appropriate to the age in order to mediate higher truths.[28] Victorian theories of the poet agree that great art is remote from perfect form, so much so that poetry cannot be expected to be successful in its aspirations to whatever intangible truths it searches after. Poets may be prophets — but limited ones. Poets may be sweet-sounding, but their song is not strong enough to bring about a revolution.

The two models of the poet offered here cannot, therefore, be diametrically opposed. Both are attempting to reconstruct the position of the poet — one demanding the poet's cultural centrality (the *Vates*), the other separating the poet from broader social concerns, and so relegating poetry, restricting it to its aesthetic duties. In the work of Lewes, the two models interestingly converge. Ranging across an immense number of English and European treatises on poetry, Lewes defines the art in terms of the two following propositions: that, first, '*Poetry is the phasis of a religious Idea*', and second, that '*Poetry is the metrical utterance of emotion*'. By the middle of the century, the first statement began to look like an unusable remnant of the past.

Isobel Armstrong's long introduction to *Victorian Scrutinies: Reviews of Poetry 1830 to 1870* illustrates in great detail the terms of critical discussion that prevail in the periodicals of the time. The early Victorians debated their poetry in a consistently humane and deeply *felt* vocabulary, although the values attached to such key terms as 'sympathy' and 'sincerity' were constantly redefined. This humanism, attending principally to particularities of poetic form and language, gathered strength as the grander claims of individual essays by the likes of Emerson and Carlyle lost their impetus. By the 1860s, it is uncommon to find a critic repeating the sentiments avowed by Emerson in 1840 that all language is 'fossil poetry'. Like critics after him, Emerson is fascinated by the metaphoric powers of poetry, but his claim that civilization began when man used metaphor in the naming of things (like Adam in Eden) is not a prime concern among the secular late Victorians.

Dobell, like Emerson, is committed to the fundamental importance of metaphor, but not as a 'primitive' or 'elementary' device. Rather, Dobell is considering Ruskin's 'Of Pathetic Fallacy' and rethinking it in terms which anticipate T.S. Eliot's notion (a variable one) of the 'objective correlative' — a poet, argues Dobell, 'must find an equivalent for his imagined facts ... The Poet requires his equivalent to be not a sign but a metaphor, *and the whole action of his mind in language is therefore to elevate it from the sign towards the metaphor.*' This concentration on the distinct language of poetry is unusual in Victorian poetic theory but, then, it is an article by a *poet*, even if a minor one. Ruskin, Noel, Emerson and Dobell are making points about language when most critics are considering the feelings expressed by it, and this fact goes some way towards explaining the prejudices against Browning's 'grotesque' (syntactically fractured, highly consonantal) style.

To return momentarily to Emerson, the phrase 'fossil poetry' is also noticeable in the way it uses a *scientific* item to explain a 'primitive truth' about signification. Victorian poetry and poetic theory tried to (but ultimately could not) take on board scientific vocabulary: it was a vocabulary that would, in any case, classify (as in the work of Alexander Bain and Charles Darwin) the emotions rather than express them. (It is worth remembering that the Romantics were successful in this. Erasmus Darwin's *Botanic Garden* (1789-91) was the most popular poem of the 1790s, and allusions to this fascinating work can be found in Keats, Shelley, Wordsworth and Blake.) By 1885, when W.J. Courthope published *The Liberal Movement in English Literature*, the Victorians were told that: 'Science and poetry are antagonistic forces, since the advance of science narrows the kingdom of imagination, which is the source of *creative* potential.'[29] Try as it might, Victorian poetry had not managed to assert itself as a primary discourse. Science, some readers believed, had usurped it. Likewise, the novel took one of the places formerly the preserve of poetry. H. Buxton Forman, writing in *Our Living Poets* (1871), said that 'if we go carefully into the popular-novel movement of the last few decades, we should find a very large share of what is properly poetic energy poured away into pages of work that cannot possibly survive the rush of these times of impetuous production'.[30] Would the poem survive in an age of mechanical reproduction? The poem was certainly squeezed out by this double-edged assault by science on the one hand, and the novel on the other.

Against this background, Oscar Wilde's statement of 1890 stands not as a piece of dry cynicism but as a historically accurate observation:

> In England, the arts that have escaped best are the arts in which the public take no interest. Poetry is an instance of what I mean. We have been able to have fine poetry in England because the public do not read it, and consequently do not influence it. The public like to insult poets because they are individual, but once they have insulted them, they leave them alone.[31]

Again, like his elder Victorians, Wilde sets about recuperating poetry, this time by making a virtue of its marginal status. Here, the very fact that poetry has been removed to an uninfluential sphere becomes the basis of its value. Untouched by time, poetry in this account speaks of better things than a scientific world. It is prized because it is so delightfully anachronistic.

The connections made in this Introduction may seem slightly tenuous (because they are offered as *general* points) but they do mark out a developing movement that localized poetry in a realm of feeling. That was by the end of the century its only place. The liberal humanism that guided the early years of English studies defined poetry in the Victorian terms that were its immediate antecedents. These were the assumptions that, in 1890, deemed poetry to be set apart from its immediate context, and that made it something of a refuge, to invoke Arnold, from 'the strange disease of modern life' ('The Scholar-Gypsy', 1853 (203)). In more ways than one Browning could not, when he died in 1889, speak as a prophet or *Vates* for his age. It was not the job of poets to do so any longer.

Notes

1. *Poets in Their Time: Essays on Poetry from Donne to Larkin* (London, Faber and Faber, 1986), p. 164.
2. 'Wordsworth, Tennyson, and Browning; or Pure, Ornate, and Grotesque Art in English Poetry', *The National Review*, 19 (1864), 27-67, reprinted in *English Critical Essays: Nineteenth Century*, ed. Edmund D. Jones (London, Oxford University Press, 1947), pp. 368-420.
3. These four writers form a representative sample of popular poets

of the 1820s and early 1830s. Felicia Hemans (1793-1835) is a vital influence on nineteenth-century women's poetry, notably that of Elizabeth Barrett, who dedicated a poem to Hemans in 1844. Thomas Moore (1779-1852) is best known for *Lalla Rookh* (1817), which went into many editions during the first half of the century. Robert Montgomery (1807-55) is remembered for *The Omnipresence of the Deity* (1828), which reached twenty-eight editions by the time of his death. Joanna Baillie (1762-1851), mostly appreciated for her dramas, was at the height of her fame in the 1830s. A volume of light verse, *Metrical Legends*, appeared in 1821. The passage of Victorian poetry can be traced by consulting *The Poets' Poetry of the Nineteenth Century*, ed. Alfred H. Miles (12 vols, London, Routledge, 1891-1907). For the extent of current research on Victorian poetry, see *The Victorian Poets: A Guide to Research*, 2nd edn, ed. Frederick E. Faverty (New York, MLA, 1968). The journal, *Victorian Poetry* (University of West Virginia), publishes an annual survey of research in the field. There are, to date, two full-length studies of the trajectory of Victorian criticism of poetry: Isobel Armstrong, *Victorian Scrutinies: Reviews of Poetry 1830 to 1870* (London, Athlone Press, 1972) (this book covers debates around the work of Tennyson, Arnold, Clough and Browning); and Alba H. Warren Jr, *English Poetic Theory, 1825-1865* (Princeton NJ, Princeton University Press, 1950). Warren usefully summarizes major Victorian essays by Newman, Keble, Browning and E.S. Dallas (author of *Poetics*, 1852), among others. (It has not been possible in this study to take a short enough extract from Dallas's important tract on poetry.) Carol T. Christ's *Victorian and Modern Poetics* (Chicago, University of Chicago Press, 1984) traces the Victorian background to the poetic theories of Yeats, Eliot and Pound. The Select Bibliography lists further documents for consultation.

4. 'Poems of Richard Monckton Milnes', *British and Foreign Review*, 7 (1838), 678. There are plenty of quotations of this sort to be found in early Victorian reviews of poetry.

5. 'The Future of Poetry: A Context for Carlyle and Arnold' in *Carlyle and His Contemporaries: Essays in Honour of Charles Richard Sanders*, ed. John Clubbe (Durham, NC, Duke University Press, 1976), p. 148. DeLaura's essay is one of the most useful surveys of Victorian criticism of poetry.

6. 'Robert Browning and the Poetry of the Age', *British Quarterly Review*, 6 (1849), 493.

7. The point is made by Marilyn Butler, *Romantics, Rebels and Reactionaries: English Literature and Its Background 1760-1830* (London, Oxford University Press, 1981), p. 8.

8. Herbert F. Tucker, 'Dramatic Monologue and the Overhearing of Lyric' in *Lyric Poetry: Beyond New Criticism*, eds Chaviva Hošek and Patricia Parker (Ithaca, NY, Cornell University Press, 1985), pp. 228-9.

9. W.J. Fox's essays have not been reprinted here. His well-known review of Tennyson's *Poems, Chiefly Lyrical* (1830), which first appeared in *The Westminster Review*, 14 (1831), 210-24, is reprinted in Isobel Armstrong, *Victorian Scrutinies: Reviews of Poetry 1830-1870* (London, Athlone Press, 1972), pp. 71-83. Fox was an early sponsor of Robert Browning and two other reviews by Fox are important in this respect, one of *Pauline; a Fragment of a Confession*, NS 7 (1833), 252-62 and 'Local

Logic', *Monthly Repository*, NS 7 (1833), 421.

10. For the Spasmodics (Philip James Bailey, Alexander Smith and Sydney Dobell) see Mark A. Weinstein, *William Edmonstoune Aytoun and the 'Spasmodic Controversy'* (New Haven, Yale University Press, 1968).

11. E.D.H. Johnson, *The Alien Vision of Victorian Poetry* (Princeton, NJ, Princeton University Press, 1952). This book, if old-fashioned in some respects, remains as a pioneering study of the dominant mood of estrangement in Victorian poetry.

12. 'Notes for a History of Victorian Poetic Genres', *Genre*, 18 (1985), 365.

13. *Alfred Tennyson* (Oxford, Basil Blackwell, 1986), pp. 11-21.

14. See Cora Kaplan, ed., *Salt and Bitter and Good: Three Centuries of English and American Women Poets* (London, Paddington Press, 1975). This excellent anthology is to be reprinted by Virago Press.

15. *Tennyson's 'The Princess': Reflections of an Age* (London, Athlone Press, 1958). Killham's study deals wih the massive range of sources used by Tennyson in this poem.

16. The best selection of homosexual and self-consciously 'Uranian' poetry is to be found in Brian Reade, ed., *Sexual Heretics: Male Homosexuality in English Literature 1850-1900* (London, Weidenfeld and Nicolson, 1969). Reade includes sections of Tennyson's *In Memoriam* (1850) in this 'homosexual' context. The question of same-sex love in Tennyson's writing has recently been reassessed by Sinfield, *Alfred Tennyson*, pp. 127-32.

17. Sinfield, *Alfred Tennyson*, pp. 11-21.

18. Keble's *The Christian Year* appeared in 1840 and sold 379,000 copies by 1873. For details of this and other sales figures for Victorian poetry, see Richard D. Altick, *The English Common Reader: A Social History of the Mass Reading Public, 1800-1900* (Chicago, Chicago University Press, 1957), pp. 386-7.

19. From an essay on Lockhart's *Life of Scott* that appeared in the *British Critic* in 1838. See *Occasional Papers and Reviews* (Oxford, 1877), p. 6. The italics are Keble's. G.B. Tennyson documents the course of Keble's poetics within the Tractarian movement in *Victorian Devotional Poetry: The Tractarian Mode* (Cambridge, Mass., Harvard University Press, 1981).

20. Chris Baldick, *The Social Mission of English Criticism, 1848-1932* (Oxford, Clarendon Press, 1983), pp. 1-85.

21. Bentham's renowned statement runs as follows: 'between poetry and truth there is a natural opposition: false morals, fictitious nature', *The Works of Jeremy Bentham* (Edinburgh, William Tait, 1843) II, p. 253. The remark is made in an essay entitled 'The Rationale of Reward' (1825).

22. Sinfield, *Alfred Tennyson*, p. 19.

23. *The Collected Works of John Stuart Mill*, eds John H. Robson and Jack Stillinger (12 vols, Toronto, University of Toronto Press, 1969) I, p. 417.

24. This point is made by W. David Shaw, 'Rites of Passage: "The Lady of Shalott" and "The Lotos-Eaters"' in *Tennyson: A Collection of Critical Essays*, ed. Elizabeth A. Francis (Englewood Cliffs, NJ, Prentice-

Hall, 1980), p. 19. Shaw refers Hallam's categories to Locke's *An Essay Concerning Human Understanding* (1790), book 2, chapter 7. Shaw's commentary originally appears in *Tennyson's Style* (Ithaca, NY, Cornell University Press, 1976).

25. 'Essay on the Philosophical Writings of Cicero', *The Writings of Arthur Hallam*, T.H. Vail Motter (New York, MLA, 1943), pp. 50-1.

26. The importation of German aesthetics into English intellectual thought is discussed by Peter Allen Dale, *The Victorian Critic and the Idea of History* (Cambridge, Mass., Harvard University Press, 1977), and Rosemary Ashton, *The German Idea: Four English Writers and the Reception of German Thought, 1800-1860* (Cambridge, Cambridge University Press, 1980).

27. *Biographia Literaria*, ed. George Watson (London, Dent, 1975), p. 172.

28. Carlyle's theory of the *Vates* relies on a blend of secondhand ideas (often misconstrued in translation) that he picked up from Schiller and Fichte. On the complexities of the 'Divine Idea' and its different manifestation in poetry from one age to another, see 'The State of German Literature' (1827), *Critical and Miscellaneous Essays* (5 vols, London, Chapman and Hall, 1899), I.

29. *The Liberal Movement in English Literature* (London, John Murray, 1885), p. 25.

30. *Our Living Poets: An Essay in Criticism* (London, Tinsley Brothers, 1871), pp. 3-4.

31. 'The Soul of Man under Socialism', *The Complete Works of Oscar Wilde* (London, Collins, 1966), p. 109.

1

'What is Poetry?'

Passage 1.1

(from John Keble, 'Sacred Poetry', Quarterly Review, 1825. Compare with passages 1.2 and 4.3, also by Keble. For a fully documented critical account of this article and the place of Keble's poetics within the Tractarian movement, consult G.B. Tennyson, Victorian Devotional Poetry: The Tractarian Mode, Cambridge, Mass., 1981)

If then, in addition to the ordinary difficulties of poetry, all these things are essential to the success of the Christian lyrist — if what he sets before us must be true in substance, and in manner marked by a noble simplicity and confidence in that truth, by a sincere attachment to it, and entire familiarity with it — then we need not wonder that so few should have become eminent in this branch of their art, nor need we have recourse to the disheartening and unsatisfactory solutions which are sometimes given of that circumstance.

'Contemplative piety', says Dr Johnson [in his 'Life of Waller' in *Lives of the Poets*, 1779-81], 'or the internal intercourse between God and the human soul, cannot be poetical. Man, admitted to implore the mercy of his Creator, and plead the merits of his Redeemer, is already in a higher state than poetry can confer.'

The sentiment is not uncommon among serious, but somewhat fearful, believers; and though we believe it erroneous, we desire to treat it not only with tenderness, but with reverence. They start at the very mention of sacred poetry, as though poetry were in its essence a profane amusement. It is, unquestionably, by far the safer extreme to be too much afraid of venturing with the imagination upon sacred ground. Yet, if it be an error, and a practical error, it may be worth while cautiously to examine the grounds of it. In the generality, perhaps, it is not so much a deliberate opinion, as a prejudice against the use of the art, arising out of its abuse. But the great writer just referred to has endeavoured to establish it by direct reasoning. He argues the point, first, from the nature of poetry, and afterwards from that of devotion.

> The essence of poetry is invention; such invention as, by producing something unexpected, surprises and delights. The topics of devotion are few.

It is to be hoped that many men's experience will refute the latter part of this statement. How can the topics of devotion be few, when we are taught to make every part of life, every scene in nature, an occasion — in other words, a topic — of devotion? It might as well be said that connubial love is an unfit subject for poetry, as being incapable for novelty, because, after all, it is only ringing the changes upon one simple affection, which every one understands. The novelty there consists, not in the original topic, but in continually bringing ordinary things, by happy strokes of natural ingenuity, into new associations with the ruling passion.

> There's not a bonny flower that springs
>   By fountain, shaw, or green;
> There's not a bonnie bird that sings
> But minds me of my Jean.
>   [Robert Burns, 'I Love My Jean', 1788 (13-16)]

Why need we fear to extend this most beautiful and natural sentiment to 'the intercourse between the human soul and its Maker', possessing, as we do, the very highest warrant for the analogy which subsists between conjugal and divine love?

Novelty, therefore, sufficient for all the purposes of poetry, we may have on sacred subjects. Let us pass to the next objection.

> Poetry pleases by exhibiting an idea more grateful to the mind than things themselves afford. This effect proceeds from the display of those parts of nature which attract, and the concealment of those which repel, the imagination; but

religion must be shown as it is, suppression and addition equally corrupt it; and, such as it is, it is known already.

A fallacy may be apprehended in both parts of this statement. There are, surely, real landscapes which delight the mind as sincerely and intensely as the most perfect description could; and there are family groups which give a more exquisite sensation of domestic happiness than anything in Milton, or even Shakespeare. It is partly by association with these, the treasures of the memory, and not altogether by mere excitement of the imagination, that poetry does her work. By the same rule sacred pictures and sacred songs cannot fail to gratify the mind which is at all exercised in devotion; recalling, as they will, whatever of highest perfection in that way she can remember in herself, or has learned from others.

There again, it is not the religious doctrine itself, so much as the effect of it upon the human mind and heart, which the sacred poet has to describe. What is said of suppression and addition may be true enough with regard to the former, but is evidently incorrect when applied to the latter: it being an acknowledged difficulty in all devotional writings, and not in devotional verse only, to keep clear of the extreme of languor on the one hand, and debasing rapture on the other. This requires a delicacy in the perception and enunciation of truth, of which the most earnest believer may be altogether destitute. And since, probably, no man's condition, in regard to eternal things, is exactly like that of any other man, and yet it is the business of the sacred poet to sympathize with all, his store of subjects is clearly inexhaustible, and his powers of discrimination — in other words, of suppression and addition — are kept in continual exercise.

Nor is he, by any means, so straitly limited in the other and more difficult branch of his art, the exhibition of religious doctrine itself, as is supposed in the following statement:

Whatever is great, desirable, or tremendous, is comprised in the name of the Supreme Being. Omnipotence cannot be exalted; infinity cannot be amplified; perfection cannot be improved.

True: all perfection is implied in the name of GOD; and so all the beauties and luxuries of spring are comprised in one word. But is it not the very office of poetry to develop and display the particulars of such complex ideas? in such a way, for example, as the idea of GOD's omnipresence is developed from the 139th Psalm? and thus detaining the mind for a while, to force or help her to think steadily on truths which she would hurry unprofitably over, how strictly soever they may be implied in the language which she uses. It is really surprising that this great and acute critic did not perceive that the objection applies as strongly against any kind of composition of which the Divine Nature is the subject, as against devotional poems.

We forbear to press the consideration that, even if the objection were allowed in respect of natural religion, it would not hold against the devotional composition of a Christian; the object of whose worship has condescended also to become the object of description, affection, and sympathy, in the literal sense of these words. But this is, perhaps, too solemn and awful an argument for this place; and therefore we pass on to the concluding statement of the passage under consideration, in which the writer turns his view downwards, and argues against sacred poetry from the nature of man, as he had done before from the nature of GOD.

> The employments of pious meditation are faith, thanksgiving, repentance and supplication. Faith, invariably uniform, cannot be invested by fancy with decorations. Thanksgiving, the most joyful of all holy effusions, yet addressed to a Being without passions, is confined to a few modes, and is to be felt rather than expressed.

What we have said of the variations of the devout affections, as they exist in various persons, is sufficient, we apprehend, to answer this. But the rest of the paragraph requires some additional reflection:

> Repentance, trembling in the presence of the Judge, is not at leisure for cadences and epithets.

This is rather invidiously put, and looks as if the author had not entire confidence in the truth of what he was saying. Indeed, it may well be questioned; since many of the more refined passions, it is certain, naturally express themselves in poetical language. But repentance is not merely a passion, nor is its only office to tremble in the presence of the Judge. So far from it, that one great business of sacred poetry, as of sacred music, is to quiet and sober the feelings of the penitent — to make his compunction as much of 'a reasonable service' as possible.

To proceed:

> Supplication of man may diffuse itself through many topics of persuasion: but supplication to God can only cry for mercy.

Certainly, this would be true, if the abstract nature of the Deity were alone considered. But if we turn to the sacred volume, which corrects so many of our erring anticipations, we find there that, whether in condescension to our infirmities, or for those wise purposes, we are furnished with inspired precedents for addressing ourselves to God in all the various tones, and by all the various topics, which we should use to a good and wise man standing in the highest and nearest relation to us. This is so palpably the case throughout the scriptures, that it is quite surprising how a person of so much serious thought as Dr Johnson could have failed to recollect it when arguing on the subject of prayer. In fact, there is a simple test, by which, perhaps, the whole of his reasoning on Sacred Poetry might be fairly and decisively tried. Let the reader, as he goes over it, bear in mind the Psalms of David, and consider whether every one of his statements and arguments is not there practically refuted.

It is not, then, because sacred subjects are peculiarly unapt for poetry, that so few sacred poets are popular. We have already glanced at some of the causes to which we attribute it — we ought to add another, which strikes us as important. Let us consider how the case stands with regard to books of devotion in *prose.*

We may own it reluctantly, but must it not be owned? that if two new publications meet the eye at once, of which no more is known than the one is what is familiarly called a *good book,* the other a work of mere literature, nine readers out of ten will take up the second rather than the first? If this be allowed, whatever accounts for it will contribute to account also for the comparative failure of devotional poetry. For this sort of coldness and languor in the reader must act upon the author in more ways than one. The large class who write for money and applause will of course be carried, by the tide of popularity, towards some other subject. Men of more sincere minds, either from true or false delicacy, will have little heart to expose their retired thoughts to the risk of mockery or neglect; and, if they do venture, will be checked every moment, like an eager but bashful musician before a strange audience, not knowing how far the reader's feelings will harmonize with their own. This leaves the field open, in a great measure, to harder and more enthusiastic spirits; who offending continually, in their several ways, against delicacy, the one by wildness, the other by coarseness, aggravate the evil which they wished to cure; till the sacred subject itself comes at last to blame due to the indifference of the reader and the indiscretion of the writer.

Such, we apprehend, would be a probable account of the condition of sacred poetry, in a country where religion was coldly acknowledged, and literature earnestly pursued. How far the description may apply to England and English literature, in their various changes since the Reformation — how far it may hold true of our own times — is an inquiry which would lead us too far at present; but it is surely worth considering. It goes deeper than any question of mere literary curiosity. It is a sort of test of the genuineness of those pretensions, which many of us are, perhaps, too forward to advance, to a higher state of morality and piety, as well as knowledge and refinement, than has been known elsewhere or in other times.

Those who, in spite of such difficulties, desire in earnest to do good by the poetical talent, which they happen to possess, have only, it should seem, the following alternative. Either they must veil, as it were, the sacredness of the subject — not necessarily by allegory, for it may be done in a thousand other ways — and so deceive the world of taste into devotional reading —

> Succhi amari intanto ei beve,
> E dall' inganno sua vita riceve —
> [Meanwhile he drinks bitter juices
> And he receives his life from the deceit][1]

or else, directly avowing that their subject as well as purpose is devotion, they must be content with a smaller number of readers; a disadvantage, however, compensated by the fairer chance of doing good in each.

Passage 1.2

(from *John Keble*, Keble's Lectures on Poetry, 1832-1841, *trans. Edward Kershaw Francis, 1912. Keble's lectures were originally delivered in Latin at the University of Oxford. A further extract from these lectures is given in Passage 4.3*)

To begin with, then we are all so framed by nature that we experience great relief, when carried away by any strong current of thought or feeling, if we are at last able, whether by speech or gesture or in any other way, to find an expression for it. This is most clearly seen in the case of those who, even when alone, utter and croon to themselves, under the influence of strong emotion. Illustrations are to be found again and again in Tragedy: where nothing is commoner than to represent the most important characters detailing their deeds and their schemes aloud to themselves. And such freedom (though too often abused) would assuredly not be tolerated on any terms, were not the audience conscious from their own experience of a certain natural propriety therein.

What need to spend time on this? In all languages, those common forms of lament, of exclamation, even of cursing, do not they all point the same way? Such curses are indeed impious and profane, the utterance of depraved and wicked men, but at least they serve to demonstrate how relevant to the stay of passion and speech and expression, yielding outlet as it were to the spirit.

But such utterance was suitable only in men uncivilized and scarcely removed from savagery: they would, almost like wild beasts, shout out aloud with every uncouth outcry, at once and in any way, whatever came into their minds. Yet there lingers, I believe, even in the most abandoned a higher and better instinct, which counsels silence as to many things: and, if they are willing to obey the instinct, they will rather die than declare openly what is in their mind. We may note too that men so wrought upon — I mean, for instance, by vanity, grief, and other like human emotions — very often exhibit excessive shamefacedness, being over-quick and sensitive in their sense of shame as in everything else: especially such as 'live the lives of freeborn citizens in a happy country, conditions which', as Cicero justly notes of the citizens of Rome, 'give men's minds a more delicate sensibility' [*Letters*, 5:21].

Not very far removed from these, yet not exactly the same,

appears clearly to be the case of lofty souls in whom, as in the youthful Nisus of Virgil,

> The restless mind is bent on some great emprise.
>> [Virgil, *Aeneid*, trans. John Conington (9.186)]

Some great emprise — something that is great, yet still vague and undecided, of which the outline and the details have yet to be filled in. All recognize this experience whose minds have at any time been overwhelmed in pondering, more closely than of wont, on the vicissitudes of human affairs, on the marvellous ordered symmetry of the universe, or last of all, on the holy vision of true and divine goodness.

The mind indeed, oppressed and overcome by a crowd of great thoughts, pressing in upon it at one and the same time, knew not where to turn, and sought for some such relief and solace for itself as tears give to the worn-out body. And thus to feel the same craving as is ascribed to men torn by violent passion; but there was this difference, the latter shrunk, through shame, from any speech: the former feeling of higher and nobler, and therefore is neither able nor willing to be expressed in the speech of daily life.

I say therefore that the Almighty power, which governs and harmonizes, not heaven and earth only, but also the hearts of men, has furnished amplest comfort for sufferers of either kind in the gift of poetry. I will not now take pains to consider what poetry fully means: even were I able to define it exactly, this is not the fitting opportunity: there are two points only, and points which no one will traverse, which it should wish to be allowed to assume as axiomatic; the first, that poetry, of whatever kind, is, in one way or other, closely associated with measure and a definite rhythm of sound; the second, that its chief aim is to recall, to renew, and bring vividly before us pictures of absent objects: partly it has to draw out and bring to light things cognate or similar to each other it represents, however slight the connexion may be; partly it has to systematize and explain the connexion between them: in a word, it is the handmaid to Imagination and Fancy. In both of these processes it exhibits, assuredly, wonderful efficacy in soothing men's emotions and steadying the balance of their mind. For while we linger over language and rhythm, it occupies our minds and diverts them from cares and troubles: when, further, it gives play to Imagination, summons before us the past, forecasts the future, in brief, paints all things in the hues which the mind itself desires, we feel that it is sparing and merciful to the emotions that seethe within us, and that, for a while, we enjoy at least that solace which Dido once fruitlessly craved, to her woe:

> a transient grace
> To give this madness breathing-space
>
> [*Aeneid* (4.433)]

But how can the needs of modest reserve, and that becoming shrinking from publicity before noticed, be better served than if a troubled or enthusiastic spirit is able to express its wishes by those indirect methods best known to poets? At all events, it is remarkable how felicitous are the outlets which minds moved by strong excitement, and aspiring by a kind of blind impulse to high ideals, have sometimes found for themselves, by following the leadings of measure and rhythm, as they first offered, like a labyrinthine clue. They needed, in part, some clue to guide them amid a thousand paths to take the right, and this clue, as every one can see, scansion and measure, simply in themselves, are well able to supply.

Passage 1.3a

*(from John Stuart Mill, 'Thoughts on Poetry and Its Varieties' in Dis*sertations and Discussions: Political, Philosophical, and Histori-*cal, 2nd edn, 1867. This essay amalgamates, in revised form, two essays which appeared in* The Monthly Repository, *1833: 'What is Poetry?' and 'The Truth of Poetry')*

In limiting poetry to the delineation of states of feeling, and denying the same where nothing is delineated but outward objects, we may be thought to have done what we promised to avoid — to have not found, but made a definition, in opposition to the usage of language, since it is established by common consent that there is a poetry called descriptive. We deny the charge. Description is not poetry because there is such a thing as a didactic poem. But an object which admits of being described, or a truth which may fill a place in a scientific treatise, may also furnish an occasion for the generation of poetry, which we thereupon choose to call descriptive or didactic. The poetry is not in the object itself, nor in the scientific truth itself, but in the state of mind in which the one and the other may be contemplated. The mere delineation of the dimensions and colours of external objects is not poetry, no more than a geometrical ground-plan of St Peter's or Westminster Abbey is painting. Descriptive poetry consists, no doubt, in description, but in description of things as they appear, not as they are; and it paints them not in their bare and natural lineaments, but seen through the medium and arrayed in the colours of the imagination set in action by the feelings. If a poet describes a lion, he does not describe him as a naturalist would, nor even as a traveller would, who was intent upon stating the truth, the whole truth, and nothing but the truth. He describes him by imagery, that is, by suggesting the most striking likenesses and contrasts which might occur to a mind contemplating the lion, in the state of awe, wonder, and terror, which the spectacle naturally excites, or is, on the occasion, supposed to excite. Now this is describing the lion professedly, but the state of excitement of the spectator really. The lion may be described falsely or with exaggeration, and the poetry be all the better; but if the human emotion be not painted with scrupulous truth, the poetry is bad poetry, *ie* is not poetry at all, but a failure.

Thus far our progress towards a clear view of the essentials of poetry has brought us very close to the last two attempts at a definition of poetry which we happen to have seen in print, both of them by poets and men of genius. The one is by Ebenezer Elliott, the author of 'Corn-Law Rhymes', and other poems of still greater merit.[2] 'Poetry', says he, 'impassioned truth.' The other is by a writer in Blackwood's Magazine, and comes, we think, still nearer the mark. He defines poetry, 'man's thoughts tinged by his feelings.'[3] There is in either definition a near approximation to what we are in search of. Every truth which a human being can enunciate, every thought, every outward impression, which can enter into his consciousness, may become poetry when shown through any impassioned medium, when invested with the colouring of joy, or grief, or pity, or affection, or admiration, or reverence, or awe, or even hatred or terror: and, unless so coloured, be it as interesting as it may, is not poetry. But both these definitions fail to discriminate between poetry and eloquence. Eloquence, as well as poetry, is impassioned truth; eloquence, as well as poetry, is thoughts coloured by feelings. Yet common apprehension and philosophic criticism alike recognize a distinction between the two: there is much that every one would call eloquence, which no one would think of classing as poetry. A question will sometimes arise, whether some particular author is a poet; and those who maintain the negative commonly allow, that though not a poet, he is a highly eloquent writer. The distinction between poetry and eloquence appears to us to be equally fundamental with the distinction between poetry and narrative, or between poetry and description, while it is still farther from having been satisfactorily cleared up than either of the others.

Poetry and eloquence are both alike the expression or utterance of feeling. But if we may be excused the antithesis, we should say that eloquence is *heard*, poetry, is *over*heard. Eloquence supposes an audience; the peculiarity of poetry appears to us to lie in the poet's utter unconsciousness of a listener. Poetry is feeling, confessing itself to itself in moments of solitude, and embodying itself in symbols, which are the nearest possible representations of the feeling in the exact shape in which it exists in the poet's mind. Eloquence is feeling pouring itself out to other minds, courting their sympathy, or endeavouring to influence their belief, or move them to passion or to action.

All poetry is of the nature of soliloquy. It may be said that poetry which is printed on hot-pressed paper and sold at a bookseller's shop, is a soliloquy in full dress, and on the stage. It is so; but there is nothing absurd in the idea of such a mode of soliloquizing. What we have said to ourselves, we may tell to others afterwards; what we have said or done in solitude, we may voluntarily reproduce when we know that other eyes are upon us. But no trace of consciousness that any eyes are upon us must be visible in the work itself. The actor knows that there is an audience present; but if he act as though he knew it, he acts ill. A poet may write poetry not only with the intention of printing it, but for the express purpose of being paid for it; that it should *be* poetry, being written under such influences, is less probable; not, however, impossible; but not otherwise possible than if he can succeed in excluding from his work every vestige of such lookings-forth into the outward and every-day world, and can express his emotions exactly as he has felt them in solitude, or as he is conscious that he should feel them though they were to remain for ever unuttered, or (at the lowest) as he knows that others feel them in similar circumstances of solitude. But when he turns round and addresses himself to another person; when

the act of utterance is not itself the end, but a means to an end —
viz by the feelings he himself expresses, to work upon the feelings,
or upon the belief, or the will, of another — when the expression
of his emotions, or of his thoughts tinged by his emotions, is
tinged also by that purpose, by that desire of making an
impression upon another mind, then it ceases to be poetry, and
becomes eloquence.

Passage 1.3b

*(from John Stuart Mill, 'Thoughts on Poetry and Its Varieties', 1867
[1833]. Compare Passage 1.3a, also from Mill's essay)*

One may write poetry, and not be a poet; for whosoever writes
out truly any human feeling, writes poetry. All persons, even the
most unimaginative, in moments of strong emotion, speak
poetry; and hence the drama is poetry, which else were always
prose, except when a poet is one of the characters. What is poetry,
but the thoughts and words of emotion spontaneously embodying itself? As there are few who are not, at least for some moments
and in some situations, capable of some strong feeling, poetry is
natural to most persons at some period of their lives. And any one
whose feelings are genuine, though but of the average strength,
— if he be not diverted by uncongenial thoughts or occupations
from the indulgence of them, and if he acquire by culture, as all
persons may, the faculty of delineating them correctly — has it in
his power to be a poet, so far as a life passed in writing
unquestionable poetry may be considered to confer that title. But
ought it to do so? yes, perhaps, in a collection of 'British Poets'.
But 'poet' is the name also of a variety of man, not solely of the
author of a particular variety of book: now, to have written whole
volumes of real poetry is possible to almost all kinds of characters,
and implies no greater peculiarity of mental construction than to
be the author of a history or a novel.

Whom, then, shall we call poets? Those who are so constituted, that emotions are the links of association by which their
ideas, both sensuous and spiritual are connected together. This
constitution belongs (within certain limits) to all in whom poetry
is a pervading principle. In all others, poetry is something
extraneous and superinduced: something out of themselves,

foreign to the habitual course of their everyday lives and characters; a world to which they may make occasional visits, but
where they are sojourners, not dwellers, and which, when out of
it, or even when in it, they think of, peradventure, but as a
phantom-world, a place of *ignes fatui* [false fires; will-o'-the-wisp]
and spectral illusions. Those only who have the peculiarity of
association which we have mentioned, and which is a natural
though not an universal consequence of intense sensibility,
instead of seeming not themselves when they are uttering poetry,
scarcely seem themselves when uttering anything to which poetry
is foreign. Whatever be the thing which they are contemplating, if
it be capable of connecting itself with their emotions, the aspect
under which it first and most naturally paints itself to them, is its
poetic aspect. The poet of culture sees his object in prose, and
describes it in poetry; the poet of nature actually sees it in poetry.

This point is perhaps worth some little illustration; the rather,
as metaphysicians (the ultimate arbiters of all philosphical criticism), while they have busied themselves for two thousand years,
more or less, about the few universal laws of human nature, have
strangely neglected the analysis of its diversities. Of these, none
lie deeper or reach further than the varieties which difference of
nature and of education makes in what may be termed the
habitual bond of association. In a mind entirely cultivated, which
is also without any strong feelings, objects, whether of sense or of
intellect, arrange themselves in the mere casual order in which
they have been seen, heard, or otherwise perceived. Persons of
this sort may be said to think chronologically. If they remember a
fact, it is by reason of a fortuitous coincidence with some trifling
incident or circumstance which took place at the very time. If
they have a story to tell, or testimony to deliver in a witness-box,
their narrative must follow the exact order in which the events
took place: *dodge* them, and the thread of association is broken;
they cannot go on. Their associations, to use the language of
philosophers, are chiefly of the successive, not the synchronous
kind, and whether successive or synchronous, are mostly casual.[4]

To the man of science, again, or of business, objects group
themselves according to the artificial classifications which the
understanding has voluntarily made for the convenience of
thought or of practice. But where any of the impressions are vivid
and intense, the associations into which these enter are the ruling
ones: it being a well-known law of association, that the stronger
the feeling is, the more quickly and strongly it associates with any

object or feeling. Where, therefore, nature has given strong feelings, and education has not created factitious tendencies stronger than the natural ones, the prevailing associations will be those which connect objects and ideas with emotions, and with each other through the intervention of emotions. Thoughts and images will be linked together, according to the similarity of the feelings which cling to them. A thought will introduce a thought by first introducing a feeling which is allied with it. At the centre of each group of thoughts or images will be found a feeling; and the thoughts or images will be there only because the feeling was there. The combinations which the mind puts together, the pictures which it paints, the wholes which imagination constructs out of the materials supplied by fancy, will be indebted to some dominant feeling, not as in other natures to a dominant thought, for their unity and consistency of character — for what distinguishes them from incoherencies.

The difference, then, between the poetry of a poet, and the poetry of a cultivated but not naturally poetic mind, is, that in the latter, with however bright a halo of feeling the thought may be surrounded and glorified, the thought itself is always the conspicious object; while the poetry of a poet is feeling itself, employing thought only as the medium of its expression. In the one, feeling waits upon thought; in the other, thought upon feeling. The one writer has a distinct aim, common to him with any other didactic author; he desires to convey the thought, and he conveys it clothed in the feelings which it excites in himself, or which he deems most appropriate to it. The other merely pours forth the overflowing of his feelings; and all the thoughts which those feelings suggest are floated promiscuously along the stream.

It may assist in rendering our meaning intelligible, if we illustrate it by a parallel between the two English authors of our own day who have produced the greatest quantity of true and enduring poetry, Wordsworth and Shelley. Apter instances could not be wished for; the one might be cited as the type, the *exemplar*, of what the poetry of culture may accomplish; the other as perhaps the most striking example ever known of the poetic temperament. How different, accordingly, is the poetry of these two great writers. In Wordsworth, the poetry is almost always the setting of a thought. The thought may be more valuable than the setting, or it may be less valuable, but there can be no question as to which was first in his mind: what he is impressed with, and

what he is anxious to impress, is some proposition, more or less
distinctly conceived; some truth, or something which he deems as
such. He lets the thought dwell in his mind, till it excites, as is the
nature of thought, other thoughts, and also such feelings as the
measure of his sensibility is adequate to supply. Among these
thoughts and feelings, had he chosen a different walk of authorship (and there are many in which he might equally have
excelled), he would probably have made a different selection of
media for enforcing the parent thought: his habits, however,
being those of poetic composition, he selects in preference the
strongest feelings, and the thoughts with which most of feeling is
naturally or habitually connected. His poetry, therefore, may be
defined to be, his thoughts, coloured by, and impressing themselves by means of, emotions. Such poetry, Wordsworth has
occupied a long life in producing. And well and wisely has he so
done. Criticisms, no doubt, may be made occasionally both upon
the thoughts themselves, and upon the skill he has demonstrated
in the choice of his media: for, an affair of skill and study, in the
most rigorous sense, it evidently was. But he has not laboured
in vain: he has exercised, and continues to exercise, a powerful,
and mostly highly beneficial influence over the formation
and growth of not a few of the most cultivated and vigorous
of the youthful minds of our time, over whose heads poetry
of the opposite description would have flown, for want of
an original organization, physical and mental, in sympathy
with it.

On the other hand, Wordsworth's poetry is never bounding,
never ebullient; has little even of the appearance of spontaneous-
ness: the well is never so full that it overflows. There is an air of
calm deliberateness about all he writes, which is not characteristic of the poetic temperament: his poetry seems one thing, himself another; he seems to be poetical because he wills to be so, not
because he cannot help it: did he will to dismiss poetry, he need
never again, it might almost seem, have a poetical thought. He
never seems *possessed* by any feeling; no emotion seems ever so
strong as to have entire sway, for the time being, over the current
of his thoughts. He never, even for the space of a few stanzas,
appears entirely given up to exultation, or grief, or pity, or love, or
admiration, or devotion, or even animal spirits. He now and then,
though seldom, attempts to write as if he were; and never, we
think, without leaving an impression of poverty: as the brook
which on nearly level ground quite fills its banks, appears but a

thread when running rapidly down a precipitous declivity. He
has feeling enough to form a decent, graceful, even beautiful
decoration to a thought which is in itself interesting and moving;
but not so much as suffices to stir up the soul by mere sympathy
with itself in its simplest manifestation, nor enough to summon
up that array of 'thoughts of power' which in a richly stored mind
always attends the call of really intense feeling. It is for this reason, doubtless, that the genius of Wordsworth is essentially
unlyrical. Lyric poetry, as it was the earliest kind, is also, if
the view we are now taking of poetry is to be correct, more
eminently and peculiarly poetry than any other: it is the poetry
most natural to a really poetic temperament, and least
capable of being successfully imitated by one not so endowed
by nature.

Shelley is the very reverse of all this. Where Wordsworth is
strong, he is weak; where Wordsworth is weak, he is strong. Culture, that culture by which Wordsworth has reared from his own
inward nature the richest harvest ever brought forth by a soil of so
little depth, is precisely what was wanting to Shelley: or let us
rather say, he had not, at the period of his deplorably early death,
reached sufficiently far in that intellectual progression of which
he was capable, and which, if it has done so much for greatly
inferior natures, might have made of him the most perfect, as he
was already the most gifted, of our poets. For him, the voluntary
mental discipline had done little: the vividness of his emotions
and of his sensations had done all. He seldom follows up an idea;
it starts to life, summons from the fairy-land of his inexhaustible
fancy some three or four bold images, then vanishes, and straight
he is off on the wings of some casual association into quite
another sphere. He had scarcely yet acquired the consecutiveness
of thought necessary for a long poem; his most ambitious compositions too often resemble the scattered fragments of a mirror;
colours brilliant as life, single images without end, but no picture.
It is only when under the overruling influence of some state of
feeling, either actually experienced, or summoned up in the vividness of reality by a fervid imagination, that he writes as a great
poet; unity of feeling being to him the harmonizing principle
which a central idea is to minds of another class, and supplying
the coherency and consistency which would else have been wanting. Thus it is in many of his smaller, and especially his lyrical
poems. They are obviously written to exhale, perhaps to relieve, a
state of feeling, or of conception of feeling, almost oppressive from

its vividness. The thoughts and imagery are suggested by the feeling, and are such as it finds unsought. The state of feeling may be either of soul or of sense, or oftener (might we not say invariably?) of both: for the poetic temperament is usually, perhaps always, accompanied by exquisite senses. The exciting cause may be either an object or an idea. But whatever of sensation enters into the feeling, must not be local, not of a part only. Like the state of sensation produced by a fine climate, or indeed like all strongly pleasurable or painful sensations in an impassioned nature, it pervades the entire nervous system. States of feeling, whether sensuous or spiritual, which thus possess the whole being, are the fountains of that which we have called the poetry of poets; and which is little else than a pouring forth of the thoughts and images that pass across the mind while some permanent state of feeling is occupying it.

To the same original fineness of organization, Shelley was doubtless indebted for another of his rarest gifts, that exuberance of imagery, which when unrepressed, as in many of his poems it is, amounts to a fault. The susceptibility of his nervous system, which made his emotions intense, made also the impressions of his external senses deep and clear: and agreeably to the law of association by which, as already remarked, the strongest impressions are those which associate themselves the most easily and strongly, these vivid sensations were readily recalled to mind by all objects or thoughts which had coexisted with them, and by all feelings which in any degree resembled them. Never did a fancy so teem with sensuous imagery as Shelley's. Wordsworth economizes an image, and detains it until he has distilled all the poetry out of it, and it will not yield a drop more: Shelley lavishes his with a profusion which is unconscious because it is inexhaustible.

If, then, the maxim *Nascitur poëta* [a poet is born not bred], mean, either that the power of producing poetical compositions is a peculiar faculty which the poet brings into the world with him, which grows with his growth like any of his bodily powers, and is as independent of culture as his height, and his complexion; or that any natural peculiarity whatever is implied in producing poetry, real poetry, and in any quantity — such poetry too, as, to the majority of educated and intelligent readers, shall appear quite as good as, or even better than, any other; in either sense the doctrine is false. And nevertheless, there *is* poetry which could not emanate but from a mental and physical constitution peculiar, not in the kind, but in the degree of its susceptibility: a constitution which makes its possessor capable of greater happiness than mankind in general, and also of greater unhappiness; and because greater, so also more various. And such poetry, to all who know enough of nature to own it as being in nature, is much more poetry, is poetry in a far higher sense, than any other; since the common element of all poetry, that which constitutes poetry, human feeling, enters far more largely into this than into the poetry of culture. Not only because the natures which we have called poetical, really feel more, and consequently have more feeling to express; but because, the capacity of feeling being so great, feeling, when excited and not voluntarily resisted, seizes the helm of their thoughts, and the succession of ideas and images becomes the mere utterance of an emotion; not, as in other natures, the emotion a mere ornamental colouring of the thought.

Ordinary education and the ordinary course of life are constantly at work counteracting this quality of mind, and substituting habits more suitable to their own ends: if instead of substituting, they were content to superadd, there would be nothing to complain of. But when will education consist, not in repressing any mental faculty of power, from the uncontrolled action of which danger is apprehended, but in training up to its proper strength the corrective and antagonist power?

In whomsoever the quality we have described exists, and is not stifled, that person is a poet. Doubtless he is a greater poet in proportion as the fineness of his perceptions, whether of sense or of internal consciousness, furnishes him with an ampler supply of lovely images — the vigour and richness of his intellect with a greater abundance of moving thoughts. For it is through these thoughts and images that the feeling speaks, and through their impressiveness that it impresses itself, and finds response in other hearts; and from these media of transmitting it (contrary to the laws of physical nature) increase of intensity is reflected back upon the feeling itself. But all these it is possible to have, and not be a poet; they are mere materials, which the poet shares in common with other people. What constitutes the poet is not the imagery nor the thoughts, nor even the feelings, but the law according to which they are called up. He is a poet, not because he has ideas of any particular kind, but because the succession of his ideas is subordinate to the course of his emotions.

Passage 1.4

(from *Alexander Smith, 'The Philosophy of Poetry',* in Blackwood's Magazine, *1835. This article is discussed at length by M.H.* Abrams in The Mirror and the Lamp: Romantic Theory and the Critical Tradition, *1953, pp. 149-54. On the use of the term 'picturesque', taken from Burke's essay, 'On the Sublime and the Beautiful', 1757, compare Smith's comments with those of A.H. Hallam in his well-known article on the distinction between the poetry of 'reflection' and the 'poetry of sensation' in relation to Tennyson's early work published in the* Englishman's Magazine, *1831, and reprinted in Isobel Armstrong,* Victorian Scrutinies: Reviews of Poetry 1830 to 1870, *1972, pp. 84-101)*

To illustrate the distinction between poetry and prose, we may remark, that words of precisely the same grammatical and verbal import, nay, the *same words,* may be either prose or poetry, according as they are pronounced without, or with *feeling*; according as they are uttered, merely to inform or to express and communicate emotion. 'The sun is set', merely taken as stating a fact, and uttered with the enunciation, and the tone in which we communicate a fact, is just as truly prose, as 'it is a quarter past nine o'clock'. 'The sun is set', uttered as an expression of the emotion which the contemplation of that event excites in a mind of sensibility, is poetry; and, simple as are the words, would, with exceptional propriety, find place in a poetical composition. 'My son Absalom' is an expression of precisely similar import to 'my brother Dick', or 'my uncle Toby', not a whit more poetical than either of these, in which there is assuredly no poetry. It would be difficult to say that 'oh! Absalom, my son, my son' [2 Samuel 18:33] is not poetry; yet the grammatical and verbal import of words is exactly the same in both cases. The interjection 'oh' and the repetition of the words 'my son', add nothing whatever to the meaning; but they have the effect of making words which are otherwise but the intimation of a fact, the expression of an *emotion* of exceeding depth and interest, and thus render them eminently poetical. [See an instance of a singular effect produced by the passionate repetition of a name in the ballad of 'Oriana' (1832), by Alfred Tennyson.]

The poem 'Unimore', published some time ago by Professor Wilson in *Blackwood's Magazine*, commences with these words:

Morven, and morn, and spring, and solitude.

Suppose these to be the explanatory words at the beginning of a dramatic piece, and stated thus: 'Scene, Morven, a solitary tract in the Highlands — season, spring — time, the morning', it would be absurd to say that the import conveyed is not precisely the same. Why is the second mode of expression prose? Simply because it informs. Why is the first poetry? (and who, in entering on the perusal of the composition, the commencement of which it forms, would deny it to be poetry?) because it conveys not information, but emotion; or at least what information it contains is not offered as such, being only an indirect intimation of the objects in regard to which the emotion is felt. The words, pronounced in a certain rhythm and tone, are those of a person placed in the situation described, and in the state of feeling which that situation would excite, the feeling, namely, of *sublimity*, inspired by solitude and mountainous or romantic scenery; of *beauty* [The philosophical reader will sufficiently understand what I mean by the *feelings* of sublimity and beauty, taken as distinct from certain *qualities* in outward objects supposed to be the cause of those feelings; to which qualities, however, and not the feelings, the terms *sublimity* and *beauty* are, in common discourse, more exclusively applied. The word *heat* either means something in the fire, or something in the sentient body affected by the fire. It is in a sense resembling the latter, that I here use sublimity and beauty], by the brilliant hues of the morning sky, the splendour of the rising sun, and the bright green of the new leaves yet sparkling with dew; the feeling of *tenderness*, which we experience in regard to the infancy, not less of the vegetable, than of the animal world; the feeling, lastly, of complacent delight with which we compare the now passed desolation and coldness of winter, with the warmth and animation of the present and the approaching period. These are the feelings, joined perhaps with various legendary associations connected with the scene, that would be conveyed by the words we are considering. Pronouncing these words in the tone and manner which disposes to sympathize with the feelings with which they were uttered, and exerting our imagination to promote that sympathy, we experience a peculiar delight which no words, conveying mere information, could create; we attribute that delight to the poetical character of composition.

So much for what may be called the soul of poetry. Let us next consider the peculiarities of its bodily form, and outward appearance.

It is well known that emotions express themselves in different *tones* and *inflections* of voice from those that are used to communicate mere processes of thought, properly so called; and also that, in the former case, the words of the speaker fall into more smooth and rhythmical combinations than in the latter. Our feelings are conveyed in a melodious succession of tones, and in a measured flow of words; our thoughts (and in a greater degree the less they are accompanied with feeling) are conveyed in irregular periods, and at harsh intervals of tone. Blank verse and rhyme are *but more artificial dispositions of the natural expressions of feeling.* They are adapted to the expression of feeling, *ie* suitable for poetry — but not necessary to it. They do not constitute poetry when they do not express feeling. The propositions of Euclid, the laws of Justinian, the narratives of Hume, might be thrown into as elaborate verse as ever Pope or [Erasmus] Darwin composed; but they would never, even in that shape, be taken for poetry, unless so far as a certain structure of words is a natural indication of *feeling.* Indeed, when there is a possibility, from the nature of the subject, that feeling may be excited, the use of a measured structure of words, and a harmonious inflection of tones, implies that the speaker is in a *state of feeling*; and hence what he utters we should denominate poetry.

And in this behold the true reason why verse and poetry pass in common discourse for synonymous terms — verse, especially when recited in the modulations of voice requisite to give it its proper effect, possessing *necessarily* the peculiar qualities which distinguish an *expression of feeling.* Hence it may perhaps be truly said that, that though all poetry is not verse, all serious verse is poetry — poetry in its kind, at least, if not of the degree of excellence to which we may choose to limit the designation. I say, all *serious* verse — because a great part of the amusement we find in humorous and burlesque poetry, arises from the incongruity observed between the language — that of feeling — and the subject, which may not only have no tendency to excite such feeling, but to excite a feeling of an opposite kind. But that — although verse, generally speaking, is poetry — poetry may exist without verse (although never without rhythmical language) is evident from a reference, for example, to the composition ascribed to Ossian,[5] which none would deny to be poetry.

These considerations explain how that which, in its original language, is poetry, becomes, in a translation, however exactly and properly conveying the meaning, the merest prose. The following translation of Horace, by Smart, conveys the exact meaning of the original. Why, then, is it not poetry? (For who would ever take it for poetry?) Simply, because it is not formed into the rhythmical periods, and thence does not suggest the melodious inflections in which we convey emotion. And it is yet in our power, by speaking it in a feeling manner, to give it the character of poetry:

> The royal edifices will, in a short time, leave but a few acres for the plough. Ponds of wider extent than the Lucrine lake, will be every where to be seen; and the barren plane-tree will supplant the elms. Then banks of violet, and myrtle groves, and all the tribe of nosegays, shall diffuse their odours in the olive plantations, which were fruitful to their preceding master. Then the dense boughs of the laurel shall exclude the burning beams. It was not so prescribed by the institutes of Romulus, and the unshaven Cato, and ancient custom. Their private revenue was contracted, while that of the community was great. No private men were then possessed of ten-foot galleries, which collected the shady northern breezes; nor did the laws permit them to reject the casual turf for their own huts, though at the same time they obliged them to ornament, in the most sumptuous manner, with new stone, the buildings of the public, and the temples of the gods, at a common expense.[6]

[I have said that no one would take this for poetry, which is true generally; yet there is as much even here as would indicate it to be a translation from poetry. Thus the second and third sentences — the epithet, 'unshaven' — the expression, 'reject the casual turf'. These parts are distinguished from the rest (which might be taken to convey mere information) as intimating that the speaker is affected or moved by the subject of this statement.] But although verse, however highly adapted to poetry, is not essential to it, it is found very materially to heighten the intrinsic charms of poetical composition. There is a pleasure derived from the reading of harmonious [It may not be superfluous to observe, that such words as *melodious, harmonious*, or *musical*, applied to verse, are purely figurative, possessing nothing whatever of the kind to which these terms are applied in music. The only thing that verse and music possess in common, is rhythmical measure. The musical qualities applied to verse have regard to mere articulations of sound, not to intervals or combinations of it. In the audible reading of verse, however, and even of poetical prose, there is room for the introduction of musical intervals; and, so far as my own observation goes, the inflections of a good speaker are not, as is usually stated, performed by chromatic or imperceptible slides, but by real diatonic intervals, and these generally of the larger kinds, such as fifths, sixths, and octaves — bearing a considerable resemblance, in fact, to the movements of a fundamental bass — the difference, if I mistake not, being mostly in the nature of the rhythm and the cadences. So intimate is the connection between a musical sound and its concords (3rd, 5th, and 8th), so natural and easy the transition, that any but a practised ear is apt to take for an imperceptible slide what is in reality a *large* interval] verse, whether blank or rhymed, altogether distinct from any that is conveyed by the mere sense or meaning of a composition, and which indeed is capable of being excited by the verse of an unknown language. Of the cause of this pleasure we can (so far as I am aware) give no other account than that such is our constitution; although there is no doubt that our perception of contrivance and ingenuity — of difficulty overcome (and apparently no slight difficulty) — enters largely into the delight we feel; a delight too which admits of receiving great increase from the infinite varieties of form and combination which verses and rhymes are capable of assuming. The same observation holds with regard to music; the pleasure derived from the different varieties of musical rhythm being distinct from — but eminently auxiliary to — that excited by melody and harmony. Music, however, is far more dependent for its full effect upon rhythmical division, than poetry is upon verse. In the former, as well as the latter, the observation of contrivance adds very materially to the gratification. Hence, the use of musical fugues, canons, &c. And I would observe, by the way, that a censure frequently passed in regard to musical compositions of a more elaborate cast, by persons whose ear is not sufficiently exercised to discern the merits of such — namely, that a taste for such composition is an unnatural and false taste — is by no means a reasonable one; or at least it is no more reasonable than a similar censure would be on our permitting ourselves to be gratified by the varieties of verse and rhyme in poetry. I am not sure, indeed, but there have been persons of so etherealized a taste, as even to profess a squeamishness in regard to the use of rhyme.

Nor is verse merely adapted, in a general way, to the

expression of emotion. The infinite variety of particular measures and rhymes — some swift and lively, some slow and melancholy — are available by the poet for the purpose of heightening every expression of sentiment. Hence, while he ministers to the physical delight of the ear, and gratifies by the perception of the art displayed in his easy and correct versification, he humours the character or the caprices of his subject by causing his verses sometimes to dash away with a noisy and startling vehemence.

But farther — the language of *emotion* is generally *figurative* or *imaginative* language. It is of the nature of emotion to express itself in the most forcible manner — in the manner most adapted to justify itself, and light up a kindred flame in the breast of the auditor. Hence the poet flies from the use of literal phraseology as unfit for his purpose; and the eye of his fancy darts hither and thither, until it lights on the figures or images that will most vividly and rapidly convey the sentiment that fills his soul. The mind, anxious to convey not the truth or fact with regard to the object of its contemplation, but its own feelings as excited by the object, pours forth the stream of its associations as they rise from their source. The feelings, which such objects excite are dim, fluctuating, general. Our language is correspondent in each case. Hence many expressions highly poetical, that is, eminently fitted for conveying a *feeling* from one mind to another, would be, if taken in reference to the object, and considered in their grammatical meaning, absolutely nonsensical. Washington Irving speaks of the 'dusty splendour' of Westminster Abbey[7] — an expression deservedly admired for the vividness of the impression it conveys. Taken as conveying a specific matter of information, it is absolute nonsense. *Splendour* is not a subject of which *dusty* could be an attribute; a space or a body might be dusty; but the splendour of an object might, in the strict propriety of language, as well be spoken of as long, or loud, or square. So in the line,

> The starry Galileo and his woes
>   [Byron, 'Childe Harold's Pilgrimage', 1812 (4.485)][8]

the literal inapplicability of the epithet 'starry' to an astronomer is obvious. The expression is one, not of a truth that is *perceived*, but of an association that is *felt*. No epithet, signifying the mere addiction of Galileo to astronomical pursuits, could have struck us like that which thus suggests the visible glories that belong to the field of his speculations. From the consideration now illustrated, it results also, that the imagery, having often no essential connexion with the object, but merely an accidental connexion in the mind of the poet, strikes one class of readers in the most forcible manner, and fails of all effect with others. The expression of Milton — 'smoothing the raven plume of darkness till it smiled',[9] is greatly admired, or at least often quoted. I must confess, that, to my mind, it is like a parcel of words set down at random. I may observe, indeed, that many persons of an imaginative frame of mind, and who, in consequence, take a great delight in the mere exercise of imagination (and who at the same time possess a delicate ear for verse), find any poetry exquisite, however destitute of meaning, which merely suggests ideas or images that may serve as the germs of fancy in their own minds. There are many passages in Byron — Wordsworth — Young — and these enthusiastically admired, which, I must confess, are to me utterly unintelligible; or at least, the understanding of which (where that is possible) I find to require as great an exercise of thought as would be required by so much of Butler's *Analogy* [*of Religion* (1736)], or Euclid's demonstrations.

Lastly — as regards the peculiar character of the *language* of poetry — it is important to observe, that a principal cause of the boldness and variety that may be remarked to belong to poetical expression, is one which would, at first sight, seem to produce an effect directly the reverse; this is — *the fetters imposed by the verse.* The expression which would be the most obvious, and even the most exact (if exactitude were what was most required), is often not the one that will suit the verse. The consequence is, that a new one must be coined for the purpose; and I believe every poet would admit that some of his happiest epithets and most adorned expressions have been lighted upon in the course of a search for terms of a certain *metrical dimension.* The necessity of obeying the laws of verse leads also to a peculiar latitude in the application of terms; and as the impression of this necessity is also present to the mind of the reader, he readily grants the poetical license to the composer, and admits of verbal combinations, which, in prose, would seem far-fetched and affected. Thus the verse, then, instead of contracting, extends the choice of expression. The aptitude of a term or an epithet to fill the verse, becomes part of its aptitude in general; and what is first tolerated from its necessity, is next applauded for its novelty.

Behold now the whole character of poetry. It is *essentially the expression of emotion*; but the expression of emotion *takes place* by measured language (it may be verse, it may not) — harmonious tones — and figurative phraseology. And it will, I think, invariably be found, that wherever a passage, line, or phrase of poetical composition is censured as being of a *prosaic* character, it is from its conveying some matter of mere *information*, not subsidiary to the prevailing emotion, and breaking the continuity of that emotion.

Passage 1.5.

(from George Henry Lewes, 'Hegel's Aesthetics', British and Foreign Review, *1842, reprinted as 'The Inner Life of Art' in* The Principles of Success in Literature, *1865. A helpful analysis of Lewes' response to German aesthetics is to be found in Rosemary Ashton,* The German Idea: Four English Writers and the Reception of German Thought, 1800-1860, *Cambridge, 1980, pp. 105-46)*

The definite meaning of the word 'aesthetics' it may not be superfluous to explain. The mere word is vague and poor enough; it was invented by Baumgarten [in *Aesthetics*, 1750] many years ago to express 'the doctrine of emotions' (αб αἰσθάνομαι), because Art addresses the *feelings* rather than the intellect. But this, as all abstract terms, requires elucidation; and this elucidation can only be completely gained by a study of the living *thing*, to which after a few remarks we shall address ourselves.

Aesthetics then is the *philosophy of art*. It is not criticism, neither is it technical knowledge, but the theory of the inner life and essence of Art. It is not purely *empirical*, like criticism, which is the knowledge of peculiar facts or laws, derived from observation of works; but the theory of art generally — the development of the fundamental Idea through its particular forms and manifestations, thus deducing all secondary laws, all critical canons, from the one primary law. Such is aesthetics as a science — the *a priori* theory of Art — the absolute statement of the conditions, means and end of art, rigorously deduced from philosophical principles. Criticism of course, if it would be philosophical, must grow out of an aesthetical foundation, as the practical and applied form of its philosophy, and so in common conversation or writing, aesthetics and criticism are often confounded. Nor is there much harm in this, if the empirical and philosophical natures of the two be always distinguished. When an incident, character, or sentiment, is said to be not aesthetical, it is meant that such is *a violation of the feeling which it is the end of art to produce*. Prosaic passages are therefore nonaesthetical, as also are contradictions of known laws of pleasurable emotion. Criticism is to aesthetics what the practice of medicine is to physiology — the application to particular cases of the fundamental knowledge of the constitution and organization of man, aided by a mass of particular observations. Aesthetics is the *physiology of art*, and as all Art has a philosophical foundation, so it necessarily demands a philosophical elucidation. The necessity for a philosophical *fundus*, not only to criticism, but to all forms of speculation, cannot, one would think, for an instant be doubted, and certainly not by those imbued with German literature, where the existence of such a stratum lying underneath the whole of practical thought is the one thing prominent and distinctive.

But the deplorable condition in which criticism is tossing restlessly about on the great ocean of uncertainty, on all points deeper than mere technic, may be best ascertained by a consideration of the want of definiteness, the want of unanimity on the first question of all — on the question which must be clearly comprehended and solved before one single step can be taken, containing as it does the *germ* of all Art — we mean the oft-mooted question — *What is poetry?* Have there not been innumerable essays, disquisitions, discussions, definitions and prefaces on this subject, are we nearer the mark? Alas, no! The only cheering sign in the whole matter is the restlessness, which, not satisfied with these vague generalities, ever prompts man to fresh attempts. This is an old question, and one which, from its very simplicity and our familiarity with its subject, is not easily analysed. Hence the vagueness and inapplicability of all definitions. Men do not look steadily and patiently *at* the thing, but follow its shifting lights, dancing now here, now there, and give us but a sense of their own uneasiness for result. Thus when [A.W.] Schlegel calls it [in *Athenaüm Fragments*, 1798] 'the mirror of ideas eternally true', he is not only wrong (as we shall see), but extremely vague — what application can be made of such a definition? Schiller does not advance the matter by calling it 'the representation of the supersensuous'. Aristotle's celebrated dictum of poetry being 'imitative art', does not distinguish it from the other arts, and is moreover false. To say poetry is an imitative art is saying nothing if true, but it is not true. An image is defined by Quatremère de Quincey [*On Imitation in the Fine Arts*, 1837] to

53

be 'morally speaking the same as its model, though physically it is some other', and imitation is 'to produce the resemblance of a thing which becomes the image of it'. This is the best possible explanation for Aristotle, and yet it does not render his definition correct. Poetry is *substitutive* and suggestive, not imitative; *words*, not *images*, are employed; nor let it be supposed, as it too generally is, that words raise the images in our minds — they seldom, if ever, raise an *image* of the *thing*, often no images at all, as some of the finest passages will evidence. Compare Aeschylus, Milton, or Shakespeare on this point. 'It is one thing to make an idea clear, and another to make it *affecting* to the imagination' [Burke, *On the Sublime and the Beautiful*, 1757]. What *images* does Milton's description of Death call up?

> The other shape
> If shape it might be call'd that shape had none
> Distinguishable in member, joint or limb;
> Or substance might be called that shadow seemed
> For each seemed either; black he stood as Night;
> Fierce as ten Furies — terrible as Hell.
>
> [*Paradise Lost*, 1674, 2.666-71]

If poetry is an imitative art — imitative of what? of external reality? images of what? of things seen or felt? Of what is the above passage imitative? 'Whoever attentively considers the best passages of poetry will find that it does not in general produce its end by raising the images of things, but by *exciting a passion similar to that which real objects will excite by other means.*' This is profoundly true, and goes to the root of the matter. Even in description, when imitation would naturally be more close, the poet does *not* present images of the thing described.

Descriptive poetry consists, no doubt in description, but in description of things as they *appear*, not as they *are*; and it paints them, not in their bare natural lineaments, but arrayed in the colours and seen through the medium of the imagination set in action by the feelings. If a poet is to describe a lion, he will not set about it as a naturalist would, intent on stating the truth, but by suggesting the most striking likenesses and contrasts *which might occur to a mind contemplating the lion* in the state of awe, wonder, terror, which the spectacle naturally excites' [see Passage 1.3a, John Stuart Mill, 'Thoughts on Poetry and Its Varieties'].

The error we are uprooting is deeply seated and far-spread; its traces are constantly visible in criticism; and it was so firmly believed in by Dr Darwin, that he made it the groundwork of his poetry. A single instance of his misapprehension occurs in the 'Botanic Garden', where he thus criticises Pope: 'Mr Pope has written a bad verse in the Windsor Forest,

The Kennet swift, for silver eels *renown'd*
['Windsor Forest', 1713 (341)]

The word 'renown'd' *does not present the idea of a visible object to the mind*, and thence is prosaic. But change the line thus,

And Kennet swift, where silver graylings *play*

it becomes poetry, *because the scenery is then brought before the eye*' [Erasmus Darwin, *Botanic Garden*, 1789, 1791]. If this were once admitted it would sweep away the finest poetry, and substitute *an animated catalogue of things*. This error is, as indeed is all error, an incomplete truth. It is true in part, and only false when applied to the *whole*. An image that is addressed to the *eye* should of course be clear and defined, or it is useless. Images in poetry are used to intensify, or render intelligible that which would otherwise not be so clear, and therefore a *visual* object may be brought to illustrate one that is not visual — but when thus selected it should be correct. So far Darwin's theory is admissible; but he makes the grand mistake of supposing *all* images in poetry must be addressed to the eye; forgetting that the other senses, physical and moral (so to speak), are also addressed. Poetry is not then imitative art, in any sense which may be legitimately given to imitation; nor can we think, with the Marquis de Santillana, that it is an invention of 'useful things', which, being enveloped in a beautiful veil, are arranged, exposed and concealed according to a certain calculation, measurement and weight. '*E que poesia, que en nuestra vulgar llamamos gaya sciencia, sino un fingimento de cosas utiles, e veledas con una hermosa cobertura, compuestas, distinguidas, escondidas porcierto cuento, peso e medida?*'[10] Our English critics talk elaborately about it being derived from ποιέω, and meaning *creation* — whereupon many rhetorical flourishes, and the thing is done!

Done certainly, and to the complete satisfaction of the doer, but unhappily to the complete satisfaction of no other mortal, since the only possible value of a definition is, not the mere utterance of rhetoric, but the being able to use a searching, definite expression as a safety-lamp to guide us through the perplexed labyrinth of philosophy; and that no man *can* grasp any lamp hitherto proffered, arises from the fact of its being, like Macbeth's dagger, a mere phantom 'proceeding from the heat-oppressed brain' [II.i.39] of the definer — a delusive Will-o'-the-wisp leading the confiding traveller through the muddiest bogs of error. The old scientific writers used to comfort their ignorance by saying that 'nature abhors a vacuum', and so most men think poetry abhors a definition. We, on the contrary, think she abhors nothing, but eminently invites inspection; and 'let us therefore', to use the words of a philosophical critic, 'attempt in the way of modest inquiry, not to coerce and confine nature within the bounds of an arbitrary definition, but rather to find the boundaries she herself has set, and erect a barrier around them; not calling mankind to account for having misapplied the word poetry, but attempting to clear up to them the conception which they already attach to it, and to bring before their minds as a distinct *principle* that which as a vague *feeling* has really guided them in the actual employment of the term' [cf. passage 1.3b].

We think poetry demands two separate definitions, each the complement to the other.

1 Its *abstract* nature, *ie* Art as Art — the 'spirit which informs' architecture, sculpture, painting, music, and poetry, considered in its abstract existence.

2 Its *concrete* nature, *ie* poetry as an individual art, and as such distinguished from the others, and from all forms of thought whatever. These definitions we offer as

1 *Poetry is the beautiful phasis of a religious Idea.*

2 *Poetry is the metrical utterance of emotion.* (This either expressive of emotion in itself, or calculated to raise emotion in the minds of others.) These two definitions, united into one general definition, may therefore stand thus: — the metrical utterance of emotion, having beauty for its result, and pervaded by a religious Idea which it thereby symbolizes.

The wording of these definitions may be questionable, and they require elucidation: the first may be called *the religious Idea*

incarnate in the beautiful; but any formula must needs be eluci-
dated: and this we proceed to attempt — till after which we beg
the reader to suspend his judgement. The second we must
consider first. Poetry must be emotive, it must be metrical —
these are its conditions.

The domain of Art is not the intellect, but the emotions — not
thought, but feeling; it occupies itself with thoughts only as they
are associated with feelings; as Bettina profoundly says [in Goethe's
Correspondence with a Child, 1837), 'art is the intuition of spirit into the
senses. *What you feel becomes thought, and what you strive to invent
becomes sensual feeling*'; and thus, as Coleridge and Wordsworth
have long taught, the true antithesis to poetry is not prose, but
science. 'Poetry is the breath and finer spirit of all knowledge; it is
the impassioned expression which is in the countenance of
science' [Preface to *Lyrical Ballads*, 1802]. Thoughts do and must
abound in all good poetry, but they are there not for their *own
sake*, but for the *sake of a feeling*; a thought is sometimes the *root*, of
which the feeling is the *flower*, and sometimes the *flower*, of which
feeling is the *root*. Thought for thought's sake is science —
thought for feeling's sake, and feeling for feeling's sake are poetry.

And therefore must poetry be emotive. Take as an illustration
Shakespeare's description of morning —

But look, the morn, in russet mantle clad,
Walks o'er the dew of yon high eastern hill.

[Hamlet, I.i.166-7]

Every one recognizes this as poetry; yet change the *emotive expression* of it into a *statement* and it ceases to be poetry, or even change
it into figurative prose, and by thus altering its emotive expression, which the 'lo!' so well commences, the poetry is gone. Thus,
'The morning now arises clothed in his mantle of russet, and
walks over the dew on the high hill lying yonder in the east' —
this is ornate prose. But perhaps the intense figurativeness of the
language obscures our meaning; so take a line from [Byron's]
'Childe Harold' —

The moon is up — but yet it is not night! [4.235]

These are two *statements*, which if put as *facts* in conversation are
as prosaic as the statement of the weather, or the time of day; yet
here the speaker himself is in a state of emotion — he utters it in

awe, in mystery, in meditation — he does not announce it as a fact, and his emotion communicates itself to us. So Shakespeare's most religious saying, that there is a soul of goodness in things evil, is *it itself* no more than a philosophical opinion addressed to the understanding; but as such it would be thought for thought's sake (*ie* science): here the *emotive expression* of it shows it to be for the sake of feeling —

> God Almighty
> There is some soul of goodness in things evil,
> Would men observingly distill it out.
>
> [*Henry V*, IV.i.3-5]

Pity that the solemn and fitting adjuration, 'God Almighty', should always be omitted when the passage is quoted!

But although *not always expressing* emotion, poetry must *always by some art excite it*, and never let its necessary statements or prosaic passages be prosaic in effect. Wordsworth often offends in this way by descriptions which are nothing more than *catalogues*; as take the following, which is, except a word here and there, ten-feet prose: —

> 'tis nothing more
> Than the rude embryo of a little Dome
> Or Pleasure-house, one destined to be built
> Among the birch trees of this rocky isle.
> But as it chanced, Sir William having learned
> That from the shore a full-grown man might wade,
> And make himself a freeman of this spot
> At any hour he chose, the Knight forthwith
> Desisted, and the quarry and the mound
> Are monuments of this unfinished task.
>
> [Wordsworth, 'Lines Written with a Slate-Pencil
> Upon a Stone', 1800 (4-13)]

If there were not so many hundred similar prosaic passages in Wordsworth, one would wonder that he could have let this pass; it is certainly antagonistic to the spirit of poetry, and is felt to be so, all critical canons apart. 'These are the axioms of poetry', says Solger [in his *Aesthetics*, 1829]. 'Everything must be action or emotion. Hence a purely *descriptive* poetry is impossible, if it confine itself to its subject without action or emotion; on which point Lessing has some admirable remarks in the "Laocoon". In Homer you never see a particular subject merely *described*, but the description is always contained in some action. So the clothing of Agamemnon, or the shield of Achilles, where the subjects represented appear themselves as living and in action'; and the reason of this is given by Hegel when he says, 'not *things* and their practical existence, but pictures and imaginative symbols are the materials of poetry.'

Passage 1.6

(from *Ralph Waldo Emerson, 'The Poet', 1840*)

The poet is the sayer, the namer, and represents beauty. He is a sovereign, and stands on the centre. For the world is not painted, or adorned, but is from the beginning beautiful; and God has not made some beautiful things, but Beauty is the creator of the universe. Therefore the poet is not any permissive potentate, but is emperor in his own right. Criticism is infested with a cant of materialism, which assumes that manual skill and activity is the first merit of all men, and disparages such as say and do not, overlooking the fact, that some men, namely poets, are natural sayers, sent into the world to the end of expression, and confounds them with those whose province is action, but who quit it to imitate the sayers. But Homer's words are as costly and admirable to Homer, as Agamemnon's victories are to Agamemnon. The poet does not wait for the hero or the sage, but, as they act and think primarily, so he writes primarily what will and must be spoken, reckoning the others, though primaries also, yet, in respect to him, secondaries and servants; as sitters or models in the studio of a painter, or as assistants who bring materials to the architect.

For poetry was all written before time was, and whenever we are so finely organized that we can penetrate into that region where the air is music, we hear the primal warblings, and attempt to write them down, but we lose ever and anon a word, or a verse, and substitute something of our own, and thus miswrite the poem. The men of more delicate ear write down the cadences more faithfully, and these transcipts, though imperfect, become the songs of the nations. For nature is as truly beautiful as it is good, or as it is reasonable, and must as much appear, as it must be done, or be known. Words and deeds are quite indifferent modes of the divine energy. Words are also actions, and actions are a kind of words.

The sign and credentials of the poet are, that he announces that which no man foretold. He is the true and only doctor; he knows and tells; he is the only teller of news, for he was present and privy to the appearance which he describes. He is a beholder of ideas, and an utterer of the necessary and casual. For we do not speak now of men of poetical talents, or of industry and skill in metre, but of the true poet. I took part in a conversation the other day, concerning a recent writer of lyrics, a man of subtle mind, whose head appeared to be a music-box of delicate tunes and rhythms, and command of language, we could not sufficiently praise. But when the question arose, whether he was not only a lyrist, but a poet, we were obliged to confess that he is plainly a contemporary, not an eternal man. He does not stand out of our low limitations, like a chimborazo under the line, running up from the torrid base through all the climates of the globe, with belts of the herbage of every latitude on its high and mottled sides; but this genius is the landscape-garden of a modern house, adorned with fountains and statues, with well-bred men and women standing and sitting in the walks and terraces. We hear, through all the varied music, the ground-tone of conventional life. Our poets are men of talents who sing, and not the children of music. The argument is secondary, the finish of the verses is primary.

For it is not metres, but a metre-making argument, that makes a poem — a thought so passionate and alive, that, like the spirit of a plant or an animal, it has an architecture of its own, and adorns nature with a new thing. The thought and the form are equal in the order of time, but in the order of genesis the thought is prior to the form. The poet has a new thought; he will tell us how it was with him, and all men will be the richer in his fortune. For, the experience of each new age requires a new confession, and the world seems always waiting for its poet. I remember, when I was young, how much I was moved one morning by the tidings that genius had appeared in a youth who sat near me at table. He had left his work, and gone rambling none knew whither, and had written hundreds of lines, but could not tell whether that which was in him was therein told: he could tell nothing but that all was changed, — man, beast, heaven, earth, and sea. How

gladly we listened! how credulous! Society seemed to be com-
promised. We sat in the aurora of a sunrise which was to put out
all the stars. Boston seemed to be at twice the distance it had the
night before, or was much farther than that. Rome, — and what
was Rome? Plutarch and Shakespeare were in the yellow leaf,
and Homer no more should be heard of. It is much to know that
poetry has been written this very day, under this very roof, by
your side. What! that wonderful spirit has not expired! these
stony moments are still sparkling and animated! I had fancied
that the oracles were all silent, and nature had spent her fires,
and behold! all night, from every pore, these fine auroras have
been streaming. Every one has some interest in the advent of the
poet, and no one knows how much it may concern him. We
know that the secret of the world is profound, but who or what
shall be our interpreter, we know not. A mountain ramble, a new
style of face, a new person, may put the key into our hands. Of
course, the value of genius to us is in the veracity of its report.
Talent may frolic and juggle; genius realizes and adds. Mankind,
in good earnest, have arrived so far in understanding themselves
and their work, that the foremost watchman on the peak
announces his news. It is the truest word ever spoken, and the
phrase will be the fittest, most musical, and the unerring voice of
the world for that time.

All that we call sacred history attests that the birth of a poet is
a principal event in chronology. Man, never so often deceived,
still watches for the arrival of a brother who can hold him steady
to a truth, until he has made it his own. With what joy I begin to
read a poem, which I confide in as an inspiration! And now my
chains are to be broken: I shall mount above these clouds and
opaque airs in which I live, — opaque, though they seem trans-
parent, — and from the heaven of truth I shall see and comprehend my relations. That will reconcile me to life, and renovate
nature, to see trifles animated by a tendency, and to know what I
am doing. Life will no more be a noise; now I shall see men and
women, and know the signs by which they may be discerned
from fools and satans. This day shall be better than my birthday:
then I became an animal: now I am invited into the science of the
real. Such is the hope, but the fruition is postponed. Oftener it
falls, that this winged man, who will carry me into the heaven,
whirls me into mists, then leaps and frisks about with me as it
were from cloud to cloud, still affirming that he is bound
heavenward; and I, being myself a novice, am slow in perceiving

that he does not know the way into the heavens, and is merely bent that I should admire his skill to rise, like a fowl or flying fish, a little way from the ground or the water; but the all-piercing, all-feeding, and ocular air of heaven, that man shall never inhabit. I tumble down again as soon into my old nooks, and lead the life of exaggerations as before, and have lost some faith in the possibility of any guide who can lead me thither where I would be.

But leaving these victims of vanity, let us, with new hope, observe how nature, by worthier impulses, has ensured the poet's fidelity to his office of announcement and affirming, namely, by the beauty of things, which becomes a new, and higher beauty, when expressed. Nature offers all her creatures to him as a picture-language. Being used as a type, a second wonderful value appears in the object, far better than its old value, as the carpenter's stretched cord, if you hold it to the ear close enough, is musical in the breeze. 'Things more excellent than every image', says Jamblicus, 'are expressed through images.'[11] Things admit of being used as symbols, because nature is a symbol, in the whole, and in every part. Every line we can draw in the sand, has expression; and there is no body without its spirit or genius. All form is an effect of character; all condition, of the quality of life; all harmony, of health; (and, for this reason, a perception of beauty should be sympathetic, or proper only to the good). The beautiful rests on the foundations of the necessary. The soul makes the body, as the wise Spenser teaches: —

So every spirit, as it is most pure.
And hath in it the more of heavenly light,
So it the fairer body doth procure
To habit it, and it more fairly dight,
With cheerful grace and amiable sight.
For, of the soul, the body form doth take,
For soul is form, and doth the body make.
['A Hymn in Honour of Beauty', 1596 (127-33)]

Here we find ourselves, suddenly, not in a critical speculation, but in a holy place, and should go very warily and reverently. We stand before the secret of the world, there where Being passes into Appearance, and Unity into Variety.

The Universe is the externalization of the soul. Wherever the life is, that bursts into appearance around it. Our science is sensual, and therefore superficial. The earth, and the heavenly bodies, physics, chemistry, we sensually treat, as if they were self-existent; but these are the retinue of that Being we have. 'The mighty heaven', said Proclus [in *Commentaries on Plato's Timaeus*], 'exhibits, in its transfigurations, clearer images of the splendour of intellectual perceptions; being moved in conjunction with the unapparent periods of intellectual natures.' Therefore, science always goes abreast with the just elevation of the man, keeping step with religion and metaphysics; or, the state of science is an index of our self-knowledge. Since everything in nature answers to a moral power, if any phenomenon remains brute and dark, it is because the corresponding faculty in the observer is not yet active.

No wonder, then, if these waters be so deep, that we hover over them with a religious regard. The beauty of the fable proves the importance of the sense; to the poet, and to all others; or, if you please, every man is so far a poet as to be susceptible of these enchantments of nature: for all men have the thoughts of which the universe is a celebration. I find that the fascination resides in the symbol. Who loves nature? Who does not? Is it only poets, and men of leisure and cultivation, who live with her? No; but also hunters, farmers, grooms, and butchers, though they express their affection in their choice of life, and not in their choice of words. The writer wonders what the coachman or the hunter values in riding, in horses, and dogs. It is not superficial qualities. When you talk with him, he holds these at as slight a rate as you. His worship is sympathetic; he has no definitions, but he is commanded in nature, by the living-power which he feels to be there present. No imitation, or playing of these things, would content him; he loves the earnest of the north wind, of rain, of stone, and wood, and iron. A beauty not inexplicable, is dearer than a beauty which we can see to the end of. It is nature the symbol, nature certifying the supernatural, body overflowed by life, which he worships, with coarse, but sincere rites.

The inwardness, and mystery, of this attachment, drive men of every class to the use of emblems. The schools of poets, and philosophers, are not more intoxicated with their symbols, than the populace with theirs. In our political parties, compute the power of badges and emblems. See the huge wooden ball rolled by ardent crowds from Baltimore to Bunker Hill! In the political procession, Lowell goes in a loom, and Lynn in a shoe, and Salem in a ship.[12] Witness the cider-barrel, the log-cabin, the hickory-stick, the palmetto, and all the cognizances of party. See the power of national emblems. Some stars, lilies, leopards, a crescent, a lion, an eagle, or other figure, which came into credit God know how, on an old rag of bunting, blowing in the wind, on a fort, or the most conventional exterior. The people fancy they hate poetry, and they are all poets and mystics!

Passage 1.7

(from *Thomas Carlyle, 'The Hero as Poet: Dante, Shakespeare' in* On Heroes, Hero-Worship, and the Heroic in History, *1840. One of the best accounts of Carlyle's poetics is to be found in Peter Allen Dale,* The Victorian Critic and the Idea of History: Carlyle, Arnold, Pater, *Cambridge, Mass., 1978, pp. 15-88*)

The Hero as Divinity, the Hero and Prophet, are productions of old ages; not to be repeated in the new. They presuppose a certain rudeness of conception, which the progress of mere scientific knowledge puts an end to. There needs to be as it were, a world vacant, a world almost of scientific forms, if men in their loving wonder are to fancy their fellow-men either a god or one speaking with the voice of a God. We are now to see our hero in the less ambitious, but also less questionable, character of a Poet; a character which does not pass. The Poet is a heroic figure belonging to all ages; whom all ages possess, which once he is produced, whom the newest age as the oldest may produce: — and will produce, always when Nature pleases. Let Nature send a Hero-soul; in no age is it other than possible that he may be shaped into a Poet.

Hero, Prophet, Poet, — many different names, in different times and places, do we give to great Men; according to varieties we note in them, according to the sphere in which they have displayed themselves! We might give them many more names, on this same principle. I will remark again, however, as a fact not unimportant to be understood, that the different *sphere* constitutes the grand origin of such distinction; that the Hero can be Poet, Prophet, King, Priest or what you will, according to the kind of world he finds himself born into. I confess, I have no notion of a truly great man that could not be *all* sorts of men. The Poet who could merely sit on a chair, and compose stanzas, would never make a stanza worth much. He could not sing the Heroic warrior, unless he himself were at least a Heroic warrior too. I fancy there is in him the Politician, the Thinker, the Legislator, Philosopher; — in one or the other degree, he could have been, he is all these. So too I cannot understand how a Mirabeau,[13] with that great glowing heart, with the fire that was in it, with the bursting tears that were in it, could not have written verses, tragedies, poems, touched all hearts in that way, had his course of life and education led him thitherward. The grand fundamental character is that of a Great Man; that the man be great. Napoleon has words in him which are like Austerlitz Battles. Louis Fourteenth's Marshals are a kind of poetical men withal; the things Turenne says are full of sagacity and geniality, like sayings of Samuel Johnson. The great heart, the clear, deep-seeing eye: there it lies; no man whatever, in what province soever, can prosper at all without these. Petrarch and Boccaccio did diplomatic messages, it seems, quite well: one can easily believe it; they had done things a little harder than these! Burns, a gifted songwriter, might have made a still better Mirabeau. Shakespeare, — one knows not what *he* could not have made, in the supreme degree.

True, there are the aptitudes of Nature too. Nature does not make all great men, more than all other men, in the self-same mould. Varieties of aptitude doubtless; but infinitely more of circumstance; and far oftenest it is the *latter* only that are looked to. But it is as with common men in the learning of trades. You take any man, as yet a vague capability of a man, who could be any kind of craftsman; and make him into a smith, a carpenter, a mason: he is then and thenceforth that and nothing else. And if, as Addison complains, you sometimes see a street-porter staggering under his load of spindle-shanks, and near at hand a tailor with the frame of a Samson handling a bit of cloth and small Whitechapel needle, — it cannot be considered the aptitude of Nature has been consulted here either! — The Great Man also, to what shall he be bound apprentice? Given your Hero, is he to become Conqueror, King, Philosopher, Poet? It is an inexplicably complex controversial-calculation between the world and him! He will read the world and its laws; the world with its laws will be there to be read. What the world, on *this* matter, shall permit and bid is, as we said, the most important fact about the world. —

Poet and Prophet differ greatly in our loose modern sense of them. In some old languages, again, the titles are synonymous: *Vates* means both Prophet and Poet: and indeed at all times,

Prophet and Poet, well understood, have had much kindred of meaning. Fundamentally, indeed they are still the same; in this most important respect especially, That they have penetrated both of them into the sacred mystery of the Universe: what Goethe calls the 'open secret'.'Which is the great secret?' asks one. — 'The *open* secret' — open to all, seen by almost none! That divine mystery, which lies everywhere in all Beings, 'the Divine Idea of the World, that which lies at the bottom of Appearance', as Fichte styles it; of which all Appearance, from the starry sky to the grass of the field, but especially the Appearance of Man and his work, is but the *vesture,* the embodiment that renders it visible. This divine mystery *is* in all times and in all places; veritably is.[14] In most times and places it is greatly overlooked; and the Universe, definable always in one or the other dialect, as the realised Thought of God, is considered a trivial, inert, commonplace matter, as if, says the Satirist, it were a dead thing, which some unholsterer had put together! It could do no good, at present, to *speak* much about this; but it is a pity for every one of us if we do not know it, live ever in the knowledge of it. Really a most mournful pity: — a failure to live at all, if we live otherwise!

But now, I say, who ever may forget this divine mystery, the *Vates,* whether Prophet or Poet, has penetrated into it; is a man sent hither to make it more impressively known to us. That always is his message; he is to reveal that to us, — that sacred mystery which he more than others lives ever present with. While others forget it, he knows it: — I might say, he has been driven to know it; without consent asked of *him,* he finds himself living in it, bound to live in it. Once more, here is no Hearsay, but a direct Insight and Belief; this man too could not help being a sincere man! Whosoever may live in the shows of things, it is for him a necessity of nature to live in the very fact of things. A man once more, in earnest with the Universe, though all others were but toying with it. He is a *Vates,* first of all, in virtue of being sincere. So far Poet and Prophet, participators in the 'open secret' are one.

With respect to their distinction again: The *Vates* Prophet, we might say, has seized that sacred mystery rather on the moral side, as Good and Evil, Duty and Prohibition; the *Vates* Poet on what the Germans call the aesthetic side, as Beautiful and the like. The one we may call a revealer of what we are to do, the other of what we are to love. But indeed these two provinces run into one another, and cannot be disjoined. The Prophet too has his eye on what we are to love: how else shall he know what it is we are to do? The highest voice ever heard on this earth said withal, 'Consider the lilies of the field; they toil not, neither do they spin: yet Solomon in all his glory was not arrayed like one of these' [Matthew 28]. A glance, that, into the deepest deep of Beauty. The 'lilies of the field', — dressed finer than earthly princes, springing-up there in the humble furrow-field; a beautiful *eye* looking-out on you, from the great inner sea of Beauty! How could the rude Earth make these, if her Essence, rugged as she looks and is, were not inwardly Beauty? In this point of view, too, a saying of Goethe's, which has staggered several, may have meaning: 'The Beautiful', he intimates, 'is higher than the Good: the Beautiful includes in it the Good.' The *true* Beautiful; which however, I have said somewhere, 'differs from the *false* as Heaven does from Vauxhall!' So much for the distinction and identity of Poet and Prophet. —

In ancient and also in modern periods we find a few Poets who are accounted perfect; whom it were a kind of treason to find fault with. This is noteworthly; this is right: yet in strictness it is only an illusion. At bottom, clearly enough, there is no perfect Poet! A vein of poetry exists in the hearts of all men; no man is made altogether of poetry. We are all poets when we *read* a poem well. The 'imagination that shudders at the hell of Dante', is not that the same faculty, weaker in degree, as Dante's own? No one but Shakespeare can embody, out of *Saxo Grammaticus*, the story of *Hamlet* as Shakespeare did: but every one models some kind of story out of it; every one embodies better or worse. We need not spend time in defining. Where there is no specific difference, as between round and square, all definition must be more or less arbitrary. A man that has *so* much more the poetic element developed in him as to have become noticeable, will be called Poet by his neighbours. World-Poets too, those whom we are to take for perfect Poets, are settled by critics in the same way. One who rises *so* far above the general level of Poets will, to such and such critics, seem a Universal Poet; as he ought to. And yet it is, and must be, an arbitrary distinction. All Poets, all men, have some touches of the Universal; no man is wholly made of that. Most Poets are very soon forgotten; but not the noblest Shakespeare or Homer of them can be remembered *for ever* — a day comes when he too is not !

Nevertheless, you will say, there must be a difference between true Poetry and true Speech not poetical: what is the difference? On this point many things have been written, especially by late German Critics, some of which are not very intelligible at first. They say, for example, that the Poet has an *infinitude* in him; communicates an *Unendlichkeit* [unendingness], a certain character of 'infinitude', to whatsoever he delineates. This, though not very precise, yet on so vague a matter is worth remembering: if well meditated, some meaning will gradually be found in it. For my own part, I find considerable meaning in the old vulgar distinction of Poetry being *metrical,* having music in it, being a Song. Truly, if pressed to give a definition, one might say this as soon as anything else: If your delineation be authentically *musical,* musical, not in word only, but in heart and substance, in all the thoughts and utterances of it, in the whole conception of it, then it will be poetical; if not,not. — Musical: how much lies in that! A *musical* thought is one spoken by a mind that has penetrated into the inmost heart of the thing; detected the inmost mystery of it, namely the *melody* that lies hidden in it; the inward harmony of coherence which is its soul, whereby it exists, and has a right to be, here in this world. All inward things, we may say, are melodious, naturally utter themselves in Song. The meaning of Song goes deep. Who is there that, in logical words, can express the effect music has on us? A kind of inarticulate unfathomable speech, which leads us to the edge of the Infinite, and lets us for moments gaze into that!

Nay, all speech, even the commonest speech, has something of song in it: not a parish in the world but has its parish-accent; — the rhythm or *tune* to which the people there *sing* what they have to say! Accent is a kind of chanting; all men have an accent of their own, — though they only *notice* that of others. Observe too how all passionate language does of itself become musical, — with a finer music than the mere accent; the speech of a man even in zealous anger becomes a chant, a song. All deep things are Song. It seems somehow the very central essence of us, Song; as if all the rest were but wrappages and hulls! The primal element of us; of us, and of all things. The Greeks fabled of Sphere-Harmonies; it was the feeling they had of the inner structure of Nature; that the soul of all her voices and utterances was perfect music. Poetry, therefore, we will call *musical Thought.* The Poet is he who *thinks* in that manner. At bottom, it turns still on power of intellect; it is a man's sincerity and depth of vision that makes him a Poet. See deep enough, and you see musically;

the heart of Nature *being* everywhere music, if you can only reach it.

The *Vates* Poet, with his melodious Apocalypse of Nature, seems to hold a poor rank among us, in comparison with the *Vates* Prophet; his function, and our esteem of him for his function, alike slight. The Hero taken as Divinity; the Hero taken as Prophet; then next the Hero taken only as Poet: does it not look as if our estimate of the Great Man, epoch after epoch, were continually diminishing? We take him first for a god, then for one god-inspired; and now in the next stage of it, his most miraculous word gains from us only the recognition that he is a Poet, beautiful verse-maker, man of genius, or such like! — It looks so; but I persuade myself that intrinsically it is not so. If we consider well, it will perhaps appear that in man still there is the *same* altogether peculiar admiration for the Heroic Gift, by what name soever called, that there at any time was.

I should say, if we do not now reckon a Great Man literally divine, it is that our notions of God, of the supreme unattainable Fountain of Splendour, Wisdom and Heroism, are ever rising *higher*; not altogether that our reverence for these qualities, as manifested in our like, is getting lower. This is worth taking thought of. Sceptical Dilettantism, the curse of these ages, a curse which will not last for ever, does indeed in this the highest province of human things, as in all provinces, make sad work; and our reverence for great men, all crippled, blinded, paralytic as it is, comes out in poor plight, hardly recognisable. Men worship the shows of great men; the most disbelieve that there is any reality of great men to worship. The dreariest, fatalest faith; believing which, one would literally despair of human things. Nevertheless look, for example, at Napoleon! A Corsican lieutenant of artillery; that is the show of *him*: yet is he not obeyed, *worshipped* after his sort, as all the Tiaraed and Diademed of the world put together could not be? High Duchesses, and ostlers of inns, gather round the Scottish rustic, Burns; — a strange feeling dwelling in each that they had never heard a man like this; that, on the whole, this is the man! In the secret heart of these people it still dimly reveals itself, though there is no accredited way of uttering it at present, that this rustic, with his black brows and flashing sun-eyes, and strange words moving laughter and tears, is of a dignity far beyond all others, incommensurable with all others. Do not we feel it so? But now, were Dilettantism, Scepticism, Triviality, and all that sorrowful brood, cast out of us, — as, by God's blessing, they shall one day be; were faith in the shows of things entirely swept out, replaced by clear faith in the *things*, so that a man acted on the impulse of that only, and counted the other non-extant; what a new livelier feeling towards this Burns were it!

Passage 1.8

(from *Matthew Arnold, 'Preface' to the first edition of* Poems, *1853*)

In two small volumes of Poems, one in 1849 [*The Strayed Reveller, and Other Poems*] and the other in 1852 [*Empedocles on Etna, and Other Poems*], many of the Poems which compose the present volume have already appeared. The rest are now published for the first time.

I have, in the present collection, omitted the poem from which the volume published in 1852 took its title. I have done so, not because the subject of it was a Sicilian Greek born between two and three thousand years ago, although many persons would think this a sufficient reason. Neither have I done so because I had, in my own opinion, failed in the delineation which I intended to effect. I intended to delineate the feelings of one of the last Greek religious philosophers, one of the family of Orpheus and Musaeus, having survived his fellows, living on into a time when the habits of Greek thought and feeling had begun fast to change, character to dwindle, the influence of the Sophists to prevail. Into the feelings of a man so situated there entered much that we are accustomed to consider as exclusively modern; how much, the fragments of Empedocles himself which remain to us are sufficient at least to indicate. What those who are familiar only with the great monuments of early Greek genius suppose to be its exclusive characteristics, have disappeared; the calm, the cheerfulness, the disinterested objectivity have disappeared; the dialogue of the mind with itself has commenced; modern problems have presented themselves; we have already the doubts, we witness the discouragement, of Hamlet and of Faust.

The representation of such a man's feelings must be interesting, if consistently drawn. We all naturally take pleasure, says Aristotle, in any imitation or representation whatever: this is the basis of our love of poetry; and we take pleasure in them, he adds, because all knowledge is naturally agreeable to us; not to the philosopher only, but to mankind at large. Every representation therefore which is consistently drawn may be supposed to be interesting, inasmuch as it gratifies this natural interest in knowledge of all kinds. What is *not* interesting, is that which does not add to our knowledge of any kind; that which is vaguely conceived and loosely drawn; a representation which is general, indeterminate, and faint, instead of being particular, precise, and firm.

Any accurate representation may therefore be expected to be interesting; but, if the presentation be a poetical one, more than this is demanded. It is demanded, not only that it shall interest, but also that it shall inspirit and rejoice the reader; that it shall convey a charm, and infuse delight. For the Muses, as Hesiod [*Theogony*, 53-55] says, were born that they might be a 'forgetfulness of evils, and a truce from cares': and it is not enough that the Poet should add to the knowledge of men, it is required of him also that he should add to their happiness. 'All art', says Schiller [in Preface to *Die Braut von Messina* (1803)], 'is dedicated to joy, and there is no higher and more serious problem, than how to make men happy. The right art is that alone, which creates the highest enjoyment.'

A poetical work, therefore, is not yet justified when it has been shown to be an accurate, and therefore interesting representation; it has to be shown also that it is a representation from which men can derive enjoyment. In presence of the most tragic circumstance, represented in a work of art, the feeling of enjoyment, as is well known, may still subsist; the representation of the most utter calamity, of the liveliest anguish, is not sufficient to destroy it; the more tragic the situation, the deeper becomes the enjoyment; and the situation is more tragic in proportions as it becomes more terrible.

What then are the situations, from the representation of which, though accurate, no poetical enjoyment can be derived? They are those in which suffering finds no vent in action; in which a continuous state of mental distress is prolonged, unrelieved by incident, hope, or resistance; in which there is everything to be endured, nothing to be done. In such situations there is inevitably something morbid, in the description of them something monotonous. When they occur in actual life, they are painful, not tragic; the representation of them in poetry is painful also.

To this class of situations, poetically faulty as it appears to me, that of Empedocles, as I have endeavoured to represent him, belongs; and I have therefore excluded the poem from the present collection.

And why, it may be asked, have I entered into this explanation respecting a matter so unimportant as the admission or exclusion of the poem in question? I have done so, because I was anxious to avow that the sole reason for its exclusion was that which has been stated above; and that it has not been excluded in deference to the opinion which many critics of the present day appear to entertain against subjects chosen from distant times and countries: against the choice, in short, of any subjects but modern ones.

'The poet', it is said, and by an intelligent critic [R.S. Rintoul] 'the poet who would really fix the public attention must leave the exhausted past, and draw his subjects from matters of present import, and *therefore* both of interest and novelty' [*Spectator*, 2 April 1853].

Now this view I believe to be completely false. It is worth examining, inasmuch as it is a fair sample of critical dicta everywhere current at the present day, having a philosophical form and air, but no real basis in fact; and which are calculated to vitiate the judgement of readers of poetry, while they exert, so far as they are adopted, a misleading influence on the practice of those who make it.

What are the eternal objects of poetry, among all nations and at all time? They are actions; human actions; possessing an inherent interest in themselves, and which are to be communicated in an interesting manner by the art of the poet. Vainly will the latter imagine that he has everything in his own power; that he can make an intrinsically inferior action delightful with a more excellent one by his treatment of it. He may indeed compel us to admire his skill, but his work will possess, within itself, an incurable defect.

The poet, then, has in the first place to select an excellent action; and what actions are the most excellent? Those, certainly, which most powerfully appeal to the great primary human affections: to those elementary feelings which subsist permanently in the race, and which are independent of time. These feelings are permanent and the same; that which interests them is permanent and the same also. The modernness or antiquity of an action, therefore, has nothing to do with its fitness for poetical representation; this depends upon its inherent qualities. To the elementary part of our nature, to our passions, that which is great and passionate is eternally interesting; and interesting solely in proportion to its greatness and to its passion. A great human action of a thousand years ago is more interesting to it than a smaller human action of to-day, even though upon the representation of this last the most consummate skill may have been expended, and though it has the advantage of appealing by its modern language, familiar manners, and contemporary allusions, to all our transient feelings and interests. These, however, have no right to demand of a poetical work that it shall satisfy them; their claims are to be directed elsewhere. Poetical works belong to the domain of our permanent passions; let them interest these, and the voice of all subordinate claims upon them is at once silenced.

Achilles, Prometheus, Clytemnestra, Dido — what modern poem presents personages as interesting, even to us as moderns, as these personages of an 'exhausted past'? We have the domestic epic dealing with the details of modern life which pass daily under our eyes; we have poems representing modern personages in contact with the problems of modern life, moral, intellectual, and social; these works have been produced by poets the most distinguished of their nation and time; yet I fearlessly assert that *Hermann and Dorothea* [Goethe, 1797], *Childe Harold* [Byron, 1812-28], *Jocelyn* [Lamartine, 1835], *The Excursion* [Wordsworth, 1814], leave the reader cold in comparison with the effect produced upon him by the later books of the *Iliad*, by the *Oresteia*, or by the episode of Dido. And why is this? Simply because in the three last-named cases the action is greater, the personages nobler, the situations more intense; and this is the true basis of the interest in a poetical work, and this alone.

It may be argued, however, that past actions may be interesting in themselves, but that they are not adopted by the modern poet, because it is impossible for him to have them clearly present to his own mind, and he cannot therefore feel them deeply, nor represent them forcibly. But this is not necessarily the case. The externals of a past action, indeed, he cannot know with the precision of a contemporary; but his business is with its essentials. The outward man of Oedipus or of Macbeth, the houses in which they lived, the ceremonies of their courts, he cannot accurately figure to himself; but neither do they essentially concern him. His business is with their inward man; with their feelings and behaviour in certain tragic situations, which engage their passions as men; these men have in them nothing local and casual; they are as accessible to the modern poet as to a contemporary.

The date of an action, then, signifies nothing: the action itself, its selection and construction, that is what is all-important. This the Greeks understood far more clearly than we do. The radical difference between their poetical theory and ours consists, as it appears to me, in this: that, with them, the poetical character of the action in itself, and the conduct of it, was the first consideration; with us, attention is fixed on the value of separate thoughts and images which occur in the treatment of an action. They regarded the whole; we regard the parts. With them, the action predominated over the expression of it; with us, the expression predominates over the action. Not that they failed in expression, or were inattentive to it; on the contrary, they are the highest models of expression, the unapproached masters of the *grand style*. But their expression is so excellent because it is so admirably kept in its right degree of prominence; because it is so simple and so well subordinated; because it draws its force directly from the pregnancy of the matter which it conveys. For what reason was the Greek tragic poet confined to so limited a range of subjects? Because there are so few actions which unite in themselves, in the highest degree, the conditions of excellence: and it was not thought that on any but an excellent subject could an excellent poem be constructed. A few actions, therefore, eminently adapted for tragedy, maintained almost exclusive possession of the Greek tragic stage. Their significance appeared inexhaustible; they were as permanent problems, perpetually offered to the genius of every fresh poet. This too is the reason of what appears to us moderns a certain baldness of expression in Greek tragedy; of the triviality with which we often reproach the remarks of the chorus, where it takes part in the dialogue: that the action itself, the situation of Orestes, or Merope, or Almaeon, was to stand the central point of interest, unforgotten, absorbing, principal; that no accessories were for a moment to distract the spectator's attention from this; that the tone of the parts was to be perpetually kept down, in order not to impair the grandiose effect of the whole. The terrible old mythic story on which the drama was founded stood, before he entered the theatre, traced in its bare outlines upon the spectator's mind; it stood in his memory, as a group of statuary, faintly seen, at the end of a long and dark vista. Then came the poet, embodying outlines, developing situations, not a word wasted, not a sentiment capriciously thrown in: stroke upon stroke, the drama proceeded; the light deepened upon the group; more and more it revealed itself to the riveted gaze of the spectator; until at last, when the final words were spoken, it stood before him in broad sunlight, a model of immortal beauty.

This was what a Greek critic demanded; this was what a Greek poet endeavoured to effect. It signified nothing to what time an action belonged. We do not find that the *Persae* occupied a particularly high rank among the dramas of Aeschylus, because it represented a matter of contemporary interest; this was not what a cultivated Athenian audience wanted. He required that the permanent elements of his nature should be moved; and dramas of which the action, though taken from a long-distant mythic time, yet was calculated to accomplish this in a higher degree than that of the *Persae*, stood higher in his estimate accordingly. The Greeks felt, no doubt, with their exquisite sagacity of taste, that an action of present times was too near them, too much mixed up with what was accidental and passing, to form a sufficiently grand, detached, and self-subsistent object for a tragic poem. Such objects belonged to the domain of the comic poet, and of the lighter kinds of poetry. For the more serious kinds, the *pragmatic* poetry, to use an excellent expression of Polybius, they were more difficult and severe in the range of subjects which they permitted. Their theory and practice alike, the admirable treatise of Aristotle [*Poetics*], and the unrivalled works of their poets, exclaim with a thousand tongues — 'All depends upon the subject: choose a fitting action, penetrate yourself with the feeling of its situations; this done, everything else will follow.'

But for all kinds of poetry alike there was one point on which they were rigidly exacting: the adaptability of the subject to the kind of poetry selected, and the careful construction of the poem.

How different a way of thinking from this is ours! We can hardly at the present day understand what Menander meant, when he told a man who inquired as to the progress of his comedy that he had finished it, not having written a single line, because he had constructed the action of it in his mind. A modern critic would have assured him that the merit of his piece depended on the brilliant things that arose under his pen as he went along. We have poems which seem to exist merely for the sake of single lines and passages; not for the sake of producing any total impression. We have critics who seem to direct their attention merely to detached expressions, to the language about the action, not to the action itself. I verily think that the majority of them do not in their hearts believe that there is such a thing as a total impression to be derived from a poem at all, or to be demanded from a poet; they think the term a commonplace of metaphysical criticism. They will permit the poet to select any action he pleases, and to suffer that action to go as it will, provided he gratifies them with occasional bursts of fine writing, and with a shower of isolated thoughts and images. That is, they permit him to leave their poetical sense ungratified, provided that he gratifies their rhetorical sense and their curiosity. Of his neglecting to gratify these, there is little danger. He needs rather to be warned against the danger of attempting to gratify these alone; he needs rather to be perpetually reminded to prefer his action to everything else; so to treat this, as to permit its inherent excellences to develop themselves, without interruption from the intrusion of personal peculiarities; most fortunate, when he most entirely succeeds in effacing himself, and in enabling a noble action to subsist as it did in nature.

But the modern critic not only permits a false practice; he absolutely prescribes false aims. 'A true allegory of the state of one's own mind in a representative history', the poet is told, 'is perhaps the highest thing that one can do in the way of poetry.'[15] And accordingly he attempts it. An allegory of the state of one's own mind, the highest problem of an art which attempts to imitate actions! No assuredly, it is not, it never can be so: no great poetical work has ever been produced with such an aim. *Faust* itself, in which something of the kind is attempted, wonderful passages as it contains, and in spite of the unsurpassed beauty of the scenes which relate to Margaret, *Faust* itself, judged as a whole, and judged strictly as a poetical work, is defective: the illustrious author, the greatest poet of modern times, the greatest critic of all times, would have been the first to acknowledge it; he only defended his work, indeed, by asserting it to be 'something incommensurable'.

The confusion of the present time is great, the multitude of voices counselling different things bewildering, the number of existing works capable of attracting a young writer's attention and of becoming his models, immense. What he wants is a hand to guide him through the confusion, a voice to prescribe to him the aim which he should keep in view, and to explain to him the value of the literary works which offer themselves to his attention is relative to their power of helping him forward on his road

towards this aim. Such a guide the English writer at the present
day will nowhere find. Failing this, all that can be looked for, all
indeed that can be desired, is, that his attention should be fixed
on excellent models; that he may reproduce, at any rate, something of their excellence, by penetrating himself with their works
and by catching their spirit, if he cannot be taught to produce
what is excellent independently.

Passage 1.9

(from *Sydney Dobell, 'Lecture on the "Nature of Poetry", 1857, in*
Thoughts on Art, Philosophy, and Religion, *1876. Dobell briefly
discusses Ruskin's essay on the 'pathetic fallacy': see Passage 1.11. Dobell
gained notoriety as one of the 'spasmodic' poets, lauded by George
Gilfillan, and calumniated by the editor of* Blackwood's, *W.E. Aytoun.
'Spasmodic' became a byword for experimental and highly discursive poetry
with Miltonic ambitions, such as the immensely popular* Festus, *1839, by
Philip James Bailey. On the 'spasmodic' controversy, which prevailed in
reviews of poetry during the 1850s, see Mark A. Weinstein,* William
Edmounstone Aytoun and the 'Spasmodic' School, *New Haven
and London, 1973*)

A single look often suffices to give the actor his bodily cue: a
word, a thought, a feeling may be sufficient for the mental transformation of the Poet. In this transformation the proportionate
activity of his various qualities is so much altered that the proportion of the inherent qualities themselves seems, for the time
being, changed: attributes that were large and notable become
insignificant, and those that were in comparative abeyance
during ordinary life arise into signal and masterful exercise. The
possession of this gift does not make a man a Poet, but I think no
imperfect Man can be a great Poet without possessing it. When
possessed by one otherwise fitted to be a Poet it has two principal
modes of manifestation. The one — and primary — is that at any
beautiful or sublime influence it transfigures the mind towards
Perfection — approaching the perfect state in proportion to its
own power in the given mind and the nature of the mental
materials on which it has to work: — in this state the Poem is
designed. The second is that in representing the human characters of the poem it transfigures the mind into those characters
for the time being — and by a succession of such states the

characterization of the Poem is executed. The amount of completeness in this second transfiguration makes one difference between the epic and the Drama.

The Epic being like some Dramatic story told by a great Tragedian wherein his successive but partial impersonations of the different characters meet in the permanent unity of himself, the one narrator; and the Drama the action of the same story enacted by him *en costume*, without the narrative, and with no central figure of himself in which the various dissimilar personifications might unite and cohere. A Poet has therefore a world — the world of imagined facts — of infinite possible variety, and an inexhaustible stock of men and women in the transmutable substance of his own character: and by the peculiarity of his nature the environments of this imaginary world affect him as actual circumstances affect ordinary men, and he lives, for a time, in these men and women as naturally as in his own personality. Out of the world and from these men and women he has to select and construct the Poem. The primary character of the individual Poet and the degree to which he possesses the transfiguring power will determine the character of the Poem and regulate its approach to perfection. Where Love predominates the Lyric will be as its expression in modes of predominating Beauty, and in the Epic the main subject will be the beautiful: where worship the Lyric will be reverent and sublime and the Epic will take a subject of awe and terror: and in proportion to the sense of truth and relation the materials of the Poem will be more or less perfect. In the highest type of Poet the Lyric will be the expression of combined Love and Reverence, and the subject chosen for the Epic will be at once Beautiful and Sublime.

Having thus come down from the heights of that perfect Ideal which we are not likely to see realized, to those regions of the possible which human poets may hope to climb, and to the topmost ledges of which they have now and then ascended, let us look, in the light of the general principle I have been endeavouring to set forth, more minutely at some of the peculiarities of all poetic expression. We have seen that as a poem is the expression of a Poet's mind, every portion of a Poem, from the Epic to the single passage, is the result of the same principles, almost as we see in the beautiful science of crystallography that the whole crystal is but a larger atom. Let us take one of the poetic atoms for analysis. We shall be met at the onset by the question 'how if the whole Poem be but an equivalent to the Poet's mind, can the single passage be an equivalent to the same characteristics?'

This is readily explained by an inward glance at the manner of our mental activities.

Take for instance our whole power to love.

We shall find the total love of which we are capable to be like the Ocean, which though it be one water yet by meeting and incalculably crossing forces — invariable sway of the rolling globe, variable beat of all manner of winds, Sun-stroke, and Moon-stroke, actions, reactions, and interactions, multiplied past mortal skill, of waves, tides, shores, promontories, reefs, and rivers, — is roused into innumerable apparitions of the same substance, each having the form of separation without the power thereof, each diverse as to its momentary manifestation but indifferent as to its permanent nature, and holding, for its own space and season, the same shapeless, motionless, colourless, general element in a special moving, figured, coloured individuality. Now these billows, ripples, flakes and drops of a great general feeling or other attribute have, when they can be expressed at all, each for itself correlatives in the external world, and by the serial expression of this temporary *personae* the great flood finds, as it were, its narrow way by the straits of successional utterance. And thus, though no single fact of the imagination may be able, in the words of our great Poet, to 'take up the whole of Love and utter it', the Poet, through his ordinating power, creates by the ordered assemblage of forms individually beautiful, an organized whole of Beauty sufficient for the Whole of Love, and corresponding in its parts to the vibration of its successional activity. What is true in the case of Love, has analogous truth in the activity of the other mental powers.

Let us therefore out of that organized imaginative Whole which the Poet has produced take any one of the complete facts of Imagination whereof it is made up, and examine its constituents. Under the simplest conditions of expression, the expressed fact must consist of itself and the words that express it. As we have seen that it must itself be either beautiful or sublime, it corresponds to the poet's love or worship. Proceeding outwards from the mind, you have therefore, first the fact, the equivalent of a feeling, and then the words, the equivalent of the fact.

And as the truth of the fact is the equivalent of the faculty to know, and the relationship of the fact to the feeling and the words to the fact, the equivalent of that sense of relation which is characteristic of the power to order, you have in the single expressed fact what you had in the great combination of such facts, the Poem, an equivalent for to feel, to know, and to order.

This is an instance of the simplest kind: proceed to one more difficult. Suppose the fact of the imagination is one that has no equivalent in words, or that from familiarity, popular misuse, or double meanings, its original verbal signs are no longer poetic equivalents. Suppose you have to express such a fact. You must find for that fact an equivalent in some other fact that has equivalent in words. An equivalent is, as we have seen, something which being presented to the quiet mind will produce there the thing of which it is the equivalent. You require therefore a fact that shall produce in the mind another fact; you require something more, a fact that shall produce a beautiful or sublime fact; and yet something more, a fact that shall produce such a fact in a mind whose primary characteristics are a sense of truth and a sense of relation. Your equivalent, therefore, must truly and essentially correspond to the beautiful or sublime fact for which it stands. That it does so makes it not only an equivalent for that fact but for your sense of truth and relationship. And as that first fact was an equivalent to certain feelings, this second fact not only stands for the first, but stands also for your characteristics of feeling, knowing, and ordering. Now a fact that thus stands for another is its metaphor — that every true metaphor is not only a metaphor of the thing for which it stands but of *the Poet who placed it*.

Time does not allow me to multiply the instances and to carry out the principle into still more minute detail, but I think, if at leisure you examine any variety of examples, you will find that this is the law of all poetic equivalents and that it explains those erroneous figures of speech which are so often mistaken for Poetry. What are critically called concetti, or conceits, and those misperceptions of Nature which arise from what an eminent writer [John Ruskin] has lately denominated 'the pathetic fallacy', and those substitutions or horrors for terrors and the carnal for the human which we call melodrama, are the equivalents of minds in whom, either constitutionally, or for the time being, there is something wrong in the kind or the balance of the powers to love, to worship, to know and to order.

Having formed our poetic passage in the imagination — having found for our feelings metaphors in facts and for our unspeakable facts metaphors in facts that have corresponding words, the remainder of the act of expression would not need examination if words were arbitrary signs. But, as we all know (however much philologers may differ about the precise primitive roots and their values), there can be no doubt that in the first origin of language all words were metaphors — that it had an essential relationship to the facts for which they stood. And since every word of our modern languages is the result of some modification, combination, and recombination of those primitives, something of the essential relationship must still exist. But since those modifications and combinations have often taken place under the control of very artificial conditions, and since in the lapse of ages the various conditioning forces have crossed and recrossed into a complexity not often to be unravelled, the consciousness of original relation is so far lost that the words of a modern language are neither algebraic signs nor metaphorical equivalents, but range between these extremes and frequently approach either. In such a language (since he must not create a new one) the Poet has to express himself. In it he must find an equivalent for his imagined facts. We have seen the laws of poetic equivalents. An arbitrary sign does not fulfil those laws. The Poet requires his equivalent to be not a sign but a metaphor, *and the whole action of his mind in language is therefore to elevate it from the sign towards the metaphor.* The first result of this action is to instinctively select from the mass of verbal signs those words that retain most of their old essential relation to the thing signified. The next is to impart to them what shall, as far as may be, be restored what is lost of that relation: to make them essentially akin to the facts they represent. Now one of the proofs that two apparently different things agree is the identity of their effects. If I strike you, successively, with a rod of iron, of silver, and of gold, it will seem at first sight indeed that one effect is produced by very different causes: but on closer enquiry we shall see that the pain produced was neither because the producing rod was iron, silver, or gold, but because it was hard, and that the iron, silver, and gold produced the same pain because they agreed in being *hard.* Identical effects are therefore evidence of a relationship in the causes, and when such effects occupy in such a mind as we are investigating identical effects are evidence of *essential* relationship. The Poet therefore adds to his selected works something which by having the same effect as the fact for which they stand shows itself to be essentially related to that fact. That 'something' is *rhythm.*

Words rhythmically combined affect the feelings of the poetic hearer or utterer in the same way as the fact they represent: and thus by a reflex action the fact is reproduced in the imagination. By instinctive selection and rhythmic combination the verbal utterance is thus elevated from a sign to or towards a metaphor, and becomes, like other metaphors, not only a metaphor of the proximate fact *but of the characteristics of the Poet.*

We saw a little while ago that the law of the whole Epic, that it is one subject with its congruous accessories, must apply to every passage of which the Epic is made up. We have now seen by an analysis of one such passage that the other law of the whole Epic, that it should be a metaphor of the Poet's characteristics, is not only fulfilled in every passage, but in every cardinal portion of a passage: in every complete act of expression and in the sub-acts of which it is composed. Carrying out the homology of the wholes and the parts, let us now, reasoning from the less to the greater, by one or more examination of the passage explain a difficulty in the Epic. Select a complete expression and pull it to pieces. I will take a well-known saying of Shakespeare because it not only illustrates what I am going to say, but also happens to be exemplary of a truth I have just now been bringing before you. Othello, bending over Desdemona and prefiguring what he is going to do, says not, 'when I have killed thee', but 'when I have plucked thy rose' [V.ii.13].

Here you have an instance in which the fact of the imagination had no equivalent in words, and had to be expressed by another act for which an equivalent existed. That somewhat by which the living differed from the dead, — that wonder of vital form and colour, that visible presence of thought and passion, that fragrant atmosphere of sweet influences, that spiritual mystery of an incarnate soul by which she was not a corpse but *Desdemona*, had not — and never will have — a name or phrase among men. But in the language of God there was a fact essentially akin to it for which we had a human sign; the Poet instinctively turned to that equivalent, and the ineffable became effable in a Rose. But I quote this sentence 'when I have plucked thy rose' that having perceived its surpassing beauty as a whole you may take it in pieces and so, to use its own metaphor, 'pluck the rose' of it. For that somewhat by which the whole sentence lives, and the parts live while forming a whole, is like the living Desdemona, something not to be defined. 'When I have plucked thy rose', separate those words altogether from the general idea and restrict them to their several utterly independent meanings. You will find that they have all expired a something with which they before were warm, and that some of them, 'when' and 'have' for instance, are almost without any life or significance at all. Look out 'when' and the auxiliary verb 'to have' in the dictionary and see how empty and effete they are. Now reunite the sentence, and behold the same 'when' and the same 'have' full, and brimming over, with the life, colour, and beauty of the whole.

Now this circulation of vitality and beauty from the whole into its parts which you have seen in the single sentence, takes place also in the total Epic and explains how some members of a great Poem — as it were the prepositions and conjunctions of that mighty syntax — which taken separately do not seem to express either the Love or Worship of the Poet are, nevertheless, by their essential union with wholes of which they are perceived by his peculiar gifts to be necessary parts, and of whose essence they are therefore partakers, as truly the fulfilment of the great primary Poetic Law as the most dazzling centres of the Beautiful or the Sublime.

We have now in endeavouring to find the principles of Perfect poetry investigated a perfect Poem in its origin, its wholes, and its parts. We have enquired into the principles of the producing Mind, into the Principles of the total thing produced, and all the members which compose it, and we have discovered the human means by which its production becomes impossible to imperfect humanity. We have found a Poem to be from first to last, in things and in words, *the manifold metaphor of a human mind,* and to approach perfection within and without, in spirit and in matter, in design and execution, in the ratio wherein the mind of whose activity it is the equivalent is *at the time of its production* perfect.

To elaborate these general truths into all their completeness would require a whole season of Lectures, but I would remind you, in passing, that whereas we have been compelled to confine ourselves this evening to a mere sketch of the main characteristics of the Poet and of his work, the perfect Poem should really be the equivalent of his whole nature, the expression of every quality by which he is truly, though ideally, human.

Passage 1.10

(from *John Ruskin, 'Of The Pathetic Fallacy' in* Modern Painters III, *1856. Compare passage 1.12 by Roden Noel for a Victorian response to Ruskin's dicta on the 'pathetic fallacy'. See also Passage 1.9 by Sydney Dobell. Robert Browning demonstrates one Victorian usage of the terms — taken from Schiller — 'subjective' and 'objective': Passage 1.11)*

German dullness, and English affectation, have of late much multiplied among us the use of two of the most objectionable words that were ever coined by the troublesomeness of metaphysicians, — namely, 'Objective', and 'Subjective'.

No words can be more exquisitely, and in all points, useless; and I merely speak of them that I may, at once and for ever, get them out of my way, and out of my reader's. But to get that done, they must be explained.

The word 'Blue', say certain philosophers, means the sensation of colour which the human eye receives in looking at the open sky, or at a bell gentian.

Now, they say farther, as this sensation can only be felt when the eye is turned to the object, and as, therefore, no such sensation is produced by the object when nobody looks at it, therefore the thing, when it is not looked at, is not blue; and thus (say they) there are many qualities of things which depend as much on something else as on themselves. To be sweet, a thing must have a taster; it is only sweet while it is being tasted, and if the tongue had not the capacity of taste, then the sugar would not have the quality of sweetness.

And then they agree that the qualities of things which thus depend upon our perception of them, and upon our human nature as affected by them, shall be called Subjective; and the qualities of things which they always have, irrespective of any other nature, as roundness or squareness, shall be called Objective.

From these ingenious views the step is very easy to a farther opinion, that it does not much matter what things are in themselves, but only what they are to us; and that the only real truth of them is their appearance to, or effect upon, us. From which position, with a hearty desire for mystification, and much egotism, selfishness, shallowness, and impertinence, a philosopher may easily go so far as to believe, and say, that everything in the world depends upon his seeing and thinking of it, and that nothing, therefore, exists, but what he sees or thinks of.

Now, to get rid of all these ambiguities and troublesome words at once, be it observed that the word 'Blue' does *not* mean the *sensation* caused by a gentian on the human eye; but it means the *power* of producing that sensation; and this power is always there, in the thing, whether we are there to experience it or not, and would remain there, though there were not left a man on the face of the earth. Precisely in the same way gunpowder has a power of so exploding, and is therefore called an explosive compound, which it very positively and assuredly is, whatever philosophy may say to the contrary.

In like manner, a gentian does not produce the sensation of blueness, if you don't look at it. But it has always the power of doing so; its particles being everlastingly so arranged by its Maker. And, therefore, the gentian and the sky are always verily blue, whatever philosophy may say to the contrary; and if you do not see them blue when you look at them, it is not their fault, but yours. [It is quite true, that in all qualities involving sensation, there may be a doubt whether different people receive the same sensation from the same thing; but though this makes such facts not distinctly explicable, it does not alter the facts themselves. I derive a certain sensation, which I call sweetness, from sugar. That is a fact. Another person feels a sensation, which *he* also calls sweetness, from sugar. That is also a fact. The sugar's power to produce these two sensations, which we suppose to be, and which are, in all probability, very nearly the same in both of us, and, on the whole, in the human race, is its sweetness.]

Hence I would say to these philosophers: If, instead of using the sonorous phrase, 'It is objectively so', you will say, in plain old English, 'It does so', or 'It seems so to me', you will, on the whole, be more intelligible to your fellow-creatures; and besides, if you find that a thing which generally 'does so' to other people (as a gentian looks blue to most men), does *not* do so to you, on any particular occasion, you will not fall into the impertinence of saying, that the thing is not so, or did not so, but you will say simply (what you will be all the better for speedily finding out), that something is the matter with you. If you find you cannot explode the gunpowder, you will not declare that all gunpowder is subjective, and all explosion imaginary, but you will simply suspect and declare yourself to be an ill-made match. Which, on the whole, though there may be a distant chance of a mistake about it, is, nevertheless, the wisest conclusion you can come to until further experiment. [In fact (for I may as well, for once, meet our German friends in their own style), all that has been objected to us on the subject seems subject to this great objection; that the subjection of all things (subject to no exceptions) to senses which are, in us, both subject and object, and objects of perpetual contempt, cannot but make it our ultimate object to subject *ourselves* to the senses, and to remove whatever objections existed to such subjection. So that, finally, that which is the subject of examination or object of attention, uniting thus in itself the characters of subness and obness (so that, that which has no obness in it should be called sub-subjective, or a sub-subject, and that which has no subness in it should be called upper or ober-objective, or an ob-object); and we also, who suppose ourselves the objects of every arrangement, and are certainly the subjects of every sensual impression, thus uniting in ourselves, in an obverse or adverse manner, the characters of obness and subness, must both become metaphysically dejected or rejected, nothing meaning in *us* objective, but subjectivity, and the very objectivity of the object being lost in the abyss of this subjectivity of the Human.

There is, however, some meaning in the above sentence, if the reader cares to make it out; but in a pure German sentence of the highest style there is often none whatever.]

Now, therefore, putting these tiresome and absurd words quite out of our way, we may go on at our ease to examine the point in question, — namely, the difference between the ordinary, proper, and true appearances of things to us; and the extra-ordinary, or false appearances, when we are under the influence of emotion, or contemplative fancy; false appearances, I say, as being entirely unconnected with any real power or character in the object, and only imputed to it by us.

For instance: —

The spendthrift crocus, bursting through the mould
Naked and shivering with his cup of gold.
        [O.W. Holmes, 'Astraea', 1850, cited in Miss Mitford's
                Recollections of a Literary Life, 1852]

This is very beautiful, and yet very untrue. The crocus is not a spendthrift, but a hardy plant; its yellow is not gold, but saffron. How is it that we enjoy so much having it put into our heads that it is anything else than a plain crocus?

It is an important question. For, throughout our past reason-ings about art, we have always found that nothing could be good or useful, or ultimately pleasurable, which was untrue. But here is something pleasurable in written poetry which is nevertheless *un*true. And what is more, if we think over our favourite poetry, we shall find it full of this kind of fallacy, and that we like it all the more for being so.

It will appear also, on consideration of the matter, that this fallacy is of two principal kinds. Either, as in this case the crocus, is the fallacy of wilful fancy, which involves no real expectation that it will be believed; or else it is a fallacy caused by an excited state of the feelings, making us, for the time, more or less irrational. Of the cheating of the fancy we shall have to speak presently; but, in this chapter, I want to examine the nature of the other error, that which the mind admits when affected strongly by emotion. Thus, for instance, in [Charles Kingsley's] *Alton Locke* [1850] —

They rowed her in across the rolling foam —
The cruel, crawling foam.

The foam is not cruel, neither does it crawl. The state of mind which attributes to it these characters of a living creature is one in which the reason is unhinged by grief. All violent feelings have the same effect. They produce in us a falseness in all our impressions of external things, which I would generally characterize as the 'pathetic fallacy'.

Now we are in the habit of considering this fallacy as eminently a character of poetical description, and the temper of mind in which we allow it, as one eminently poetical, because passionate. But I believe, if we look well into the matter, that we shall find the greatest poets do not often admit this kind of falseness, — that it is only the second order of poets who much delight in it. [I admit two orders of poets, but no third; and by these two orders I mean the creative (Shakespeare, Homer, Dante), and Reflective or Perceptive (Wordsworth, Keats, Tennyson). But both of these must be *first*-rate in their range, though their range is different; and with poetry second-rate in *quality* no one ought to be allowed to trouble mankind. There is quite enough of the best, — much more than we can ever read and enjoy in the length of a life; and it is a literal wrong or sin in any person to encumber us with inferior work. I have no patience with apologies made by young pseudo-poets, 'that they believe there is *some* good in what they have written: that they hope to do better in time', etc. *Some* good! If there is not *all* good, there is no good. If they ever hope to do better, why do they trouble us now? Let them rather courageously burn all they have done, and wait for the better days. There are few men, ordinarily educated, who in moments of strong feeling could not strike out a poetical thought, and afterwards polish it so as to be presentable. But men of sense know better than so to waste their time; and those who sincerely love poetry, know the touch of the master's hand on the chords too well to fumble among them after him. Nay, more than this, all inferior poetry is an injury to the good, inasmuch as it takes away the freshness of rhymes, blunders upon and gives a wretched commonalty to good thoughts; and, in general, adds to the weight of human weariness in a most woeful and culpable manner. There are few thoughts likely to come across ordinary men in the best possible way; and it is a wiser, more generous, more noble thing to remember and point out the perfect words, than to invent poorer ones, wherewith to encumber temporarily the world.]

Thus, when Dante describes the spirits falling from the back of Acheron 'as dead leaves flutter from a bough' ['Inferno' (3.112)], he gives the most perfect image possible of their utter lightness, feebleness, passiveness, and scattering irony of despair, without, however, for an instant losing his own clear perception that *these* are souls, and *those* are leaves; he makes no confusion of one leaf with the other. But when Coleridge speaks of

> The one red leaf, that last of its clan,
> That dances often as dance it can
>
> ['Christabel', 1797 (49-50)]

he has a morbid, that is to say, a so far false, idea about the leaf; he fancies a life in it, and will, which there are not; confuses its powerlessness with choice, its fading death with merriment, and the wind that shakes it with music. Here, however, there is some beauty, even in the morbid passage; but take an instance in Homer and Pope. Without the knowledge of Ulysses, Elpenor, his youngest follower, has fallen from an upper chamber in the Circean palace, and has been left dead, unmissed by his leader or companions, in the haste of their departure. They cross the sea to the Cimmerian land; and Ulysses summons the shades from Tartarus. The first which appears is that of the lost Elpenor. Ulysses, amazed, and in exactly the spirit of bitter and terrified lightness which is seen in Hamlet ['Well said, old mole can'st work i' the ground so fast?' (I.v.162)], addresses the spirit with the simple, startled words:—

Elpenor? How camest thou under the shadowy darkness?
Hast thou come faster
on foot than I in my black ship?

[*Odyssey* (9.56)])

Which Pope renders thus:—

O, say, what angry power *Elpenor* led
To glide in shades, and wander with the dead?
How could thy soul, by realms and seas disjoined,
Out-fly the nimble sail, and leave the lagging wind?

[*Odyssey* (9.71-74)]

I sincerely hope the reader finds no pleasure here, either in the nimbleness of the sail, or the laziness of the wind! And yet how is it that these conceits are so painful now, when they have been pleasant to us in the other instances?

For a very simple reason. They are not a *pathetic* fallacy at all, for they are put into the mouth of the wrong passion — a passion which never could possibly have spoken them — agonized curiosity. Ulysses wants to know the facts of the matter; and the very last thing his mind could do at the moment would be to pause, or suggest in anywise that was *not* a fact. The delay in the last three lines, and conceit in the last, jar upon us instantly like the most frightful discord in music. No poet of true imaginative power could possibly have written the passage. [It is worthwhile comparing the way a similar question is put with exquisite sincerity by Keats:—

he wept, and his bright tears
Went trickling down the golden bow he held.
Thus, with half-shut suffused eyes he stood;
While from beneath some cumbrous boughs hard by
With solemn step an awful Goddess came,
And there was purport in her looks for him,
Which he with eager guess began to read
Perplexed, the while melodiously he said,
'*How camest thou over the unfooted sea?*']

[*Hyperion*, 1820 (3.42-50); Ruskin's italics]

Therefore we see that the spirit of the truth must guide us in some sort, even in our enjoyment of fallacy. Coleridge's fallacy has no discord in it, but Pope's has our teeth set on edge. Without farther questioning, I will endeavour to state the main bearings of this matter.

The temperament which admits the pathetic fallacy, is, as I said above, that of a mind and body of some sort too weak to deal fully with what is before them or upon them; borne away, or over-clouded, or over-dazzled by emotion; and it is a more or less noble state, according to the force of the emotion which has induced it. For it is no credit to a man that he is not morbid or inaccurate in his perceptions, when he has no strength of feeling to warp them; and it is in general a sign of higher capacity and stand in the ranks of being, that the emotions should be strong enough to vanquish, partly, the intellect, and make it believe what they choose. But it is still a grander condition when the intellect also rises, until it is strong enough to assert its rule against, or together with, the utmost efforts of the passions; and the whole man stands in an iron glow, white hot, perhaps, but still strong, and in nowise evaporating; even if he melts, losing none of his weight.

So, then, we have the three ranks: the man who perceives rightly, because he does not feel, and to whom the primrose is very accurately the primrose, because he does not love it. Then, secondly, the man who perceives wrongly, because he feels, and to whom the primrose is anything else than a primrose: a start, or a sun, or a fairy's shield, or a forsaken maiden. And then, lastly, there is the man who perceives rightly in spite of his feelings, and to whom the primrose is for ever nothing else than itself — a little flower apprehended in the very plain and leafy fact of it, whatever and how many soever the associations and passions may be, that crowd around it. And, in general, these three classes may be rated in comparative order, as the men who are not poets at all, and the poets of the second order, and the poets of the first; only however great a man may be, there are always some subjects which *ought* to throw him off his balance; some, by which his poor human capacity of thought should be conquered, and brought into the inaccurate and vague state of perception, so that the language of the highest inspiration becomes broken, obscure, and wild in metaphor, resembling that of the weaker man, overborne by weaker things.

And thus, in full, there are four classes: the men who feel nothing, and therefore see truly; the men who feel strongly, think weakly, and see untruly (second order of poets); the men who feel strong, think strongly, and see truly (first order of poets); and the men who, strong as human creatures can be, are yet submitted to influences stronger than they, and see in a sort untruly, because what they see is inconceivably above them. This last is the usual condition of prophetic inspiration.

I separate these classes, in order that their character may be clearly understood; but of course they are united each to the other by imperceptible transitions, and the same mind, according to the influences to which it is subjected, passes at different times into the various states. Still, the difference between the great and less man is, on the whole, chiefly on this point of *alterability*. That is to say, the one knows too much, and perceives and feels too much of the past and future, and of all things beside and around that which immediately affects him, to be in anywise shaken by it. His mind is made up; his thoughts have an accustomed current; his ways are steadfast; it is not this or that new sight which will at once unbalance him. He is tender to impression at the surface, like moss with deep moss upon it; but there is too much mass of him to be moved. The smaller man, with the same degree of sensibility, is at once carried off his feet; he wants to do something he did not want to do before; he views all the universe in a new light through his tears; he is gay or enthusiastic, melancholy or passionate, as things come and go to him. Therefore the high creative poet might even be thought, to a great extent, impassive (as shallow people think Dante stern), receiving indeed all feelings to the full, but having a great centre of reflection and knowledge in which he stands serene, and watches the feeling, as it were, from far off.

Dante, in his most intense moods, has entire command of himself, and can look around calmly, at all moments, for the image or the word that will best tell what he sees to the lower or upper world. But Keats and Tennyson, and the poets of the second order, are generally themselves subdued by the feelings under which they write, or, at least, write as choosing to be so; and therefore admit certain expressions and modes of thought which are in some sort diseased or false.

Now so long as we see that the *feeling* is true, we pardon, or are even pleased by, the confessed fallacy of sight which it induces: we are pleased, for instance, with those lines of **Kingsley's**, above quoted, not because they fallaciously describe foam, but because they faithfully describe sorrow. But the moment the mind of the speaker becomes cold, that moment every such expression becomes untrue, as being for ever untrue in the external facts. And there is no greater baseness in literature than the habit of using these metaphorical expressions in cold blood. An inspired writer, in full impetuosity of passion, may speak wisely and truly of 'paging waves', 'remorseless floods', 'ravenous billows', etc; and it is one the signs of the highest power in a writer to check all such habits of thought, and to keep his eyes fixed firmly on the *pure fact*, out of which if any feeling comes to him or his reader, he knows it must be a true one.

To keep to the waves, I forget who it is who represents a man in despair desiring that his body may be cast into the sea,

> *Whose changing mound, and foam that passed away,*
> Might mock the eyes that questioned where I lay.[16]

Observe, there is not here a single false, or even overcharged expression. 'Mound' of the sea wave is perfectly simple and true: 'changing' is as familiar as may be; 'foam that passed away', strictly literal; and the whole line descriptive of the reality with a degree of accuracy which I know not any other verse, in the range of poetry, that altogether equals. For most people have not a distinct idea of the clumsiness and massiveness of a large wave. The word 'wave' is used too generally of ripples and breakers, and bendings in light drapery or grass; it does not by itself convey a perfect image. But the word 'mound' is heavy, large, dark, definite; there is no mistaking the kind of wave meant, nor missing the sight of it. Then the term 'changing' has a peculiar force also. Most people think of waves as rising and falling. But if they look at the sea carefully, they will perceive that the waves do not rise and fall. They change. Change both place and form, but they do not fall; one wave goes on, and on, and still on; now lower, now higher, now tossing its mane like a horse, now building itself together like a wall, now shaking, now steady, but still the same wave, till at last it seems struck by something, and changes, one knows not how, — becomes another wave.

The close of the line insists on this image, and paints it still more perfectly, — 'foam that passed away'. Not merely melting, disappearing, but passing on, out of sight, on the career of the wave. Then, having put the absolute ocean fact as far as he may before our eyes, the poet leaves us to feel about it as we may, and to trace for ourselves the opposite fact, — the image of the green mounds that do not change, and the white and written stones that do not pass away; and thence to follow out also the associated images of the calm life with the quiet grave, and the despairing life with the fading foam: —

Let no man move his bones [2 Kings 23.18]
As for Samaria, her king is cut off like the foam upon the water [Hosea 10.7]

But nothing of this is actually told or pointed out, and the expressions, as they stand, are perfectly severe and accurate, utterly uninfluenced by the firmly governed emotion of the writer. Even the word 'mock' is hardly an exception, as it may stand merely for 'deceive' or 'defeat', without implying any impersonation of the waves.

Passage 1.11

(from *Robert Browning, 'Introductory Essay [Essay on Shelley]', 1852. Published in 1852 as an introduction to an edition entitled* Letters of Percy Bysshe Shelley, *the 'Essay on Shelley', as it is popularly known, had the misfortune of prefacing a book whose contents turned out to be forgeries and were quickly withdrawn from sale. The 'Essay', however, stands as one of the most significant critical accounts of poetry by a Victorian poet, and is especially important for understanding Browning's Romantic inheritance. If, after his Shelleyan pastiche,* Pauline *(1833), Browning turned away from imitating Shelley's language, developing to a large extent what Walter Bagehot (in 1864) called the 'grotesque' style, Browning none the less modified to his religious needs a radical tradition of sceptical thought that promoted the idea of human perfectibility. It is curious to observe how Browning uses this notion of perfectibility to suggest that the atheistical Shelley, had he lived beyond his twenty-nine years, would have become a Christian. The trajectory of Browning's poetry is towards a perfect understanding of the infinite power that creates finite man. Infinitude, for Browning, is apprehended but never wholly known because the gap between God and man can never be broached; it can only be negotiated endlessly. Browning's human soul cannot (but always strives to) be perfect.*

On Browning's use of the terms 'objective' and 'subjective', as categories for defining types of poet, see M.H. Abrams, The Mirror and the Lamp: Romantic Theory and the Critical Tradition, *1953, pp. 235-44, which traces the translation of these terms from German aesthetics*

— notably Schiller's distinction between naïve and sentimental poetry — into English criticism in the early nineteenth century. For a humorous Victorian treatment of these categories, see Ruskin, 'Of The Pathetic Fallacy', Passage 1.10)

Doubtless we accept gladly the biography of an objective poet, as the phrase now goes; one whose endeavour has been to reproduce things external (whether the phenomena of the scenic universe, or the manifested action of the human heart and brain) with an immediate reference, in every case, to the common eye and apprehension of his fellow men, assumed capable of receiving and profiting by this reproduction. It has been obtained through the poet's double faculty of seeing external objects more clearly, widely, and deeply, than is possible to the average mind, at the same time that he is so acquainted and in sympathy with its narrower comprehension as to be careful to supply it with no other materials than it can combine into an intelligible whole. The auditory of such a poet will include, not only the intelligences which, save for such assistance, would have missed the deeper meaning and enjoyment of the original objects, but also the spirits of a like endowment with his own, who, by means of his abstract, can forthwith pass to the reality it was made from, and either corroborate their impressions of things known already, or supply themselves with new from whatever shows in the inexhaustible variety of existence may have hitherto escaped their knowledge. Such a poet is properly the ποιητής, the fashioner; and the thing fashioned, will of necessity be substantive, projected from himself and distinct. We are ignorant what the inventor of 'Othello' conceived of that fact as he beheld it in completeness, how he accounted for it, under what known law he registered its nature, or to what unknown law he traced its coincidence. We learn only what he intended we should learn by that particular exercise of his power, — the fact itself, — which, in its infinite significances, each of us receives for the first time as a creation, and is hereafter left to deal with, as, in proportion to his own intelligence, he best may. We are ignorant, and would fain be other wise.

Doubtless, with respect to such a poet, we covet his biography. We desire to look back upon the process of gathering together in a lifetime, the materials of the work we behold entire; of elaborating, perhaps under difficulty and with hindrance, all that is familiar to our admiration in the apparent facility of success. And the inner impulse of this effort and operation, what induced it? Does a soul's delight in its own extended sphere of vision set it, for the gratification of an insurpressible power, on labour, as other men are set on rest? Or did a sense of duty or of love lead it to communicate its own sensations to mankind? Did an irresistible sympathy with men compel to bring down and suit its own provision of knowledge and beauty to their narrow scope? Did the personality of such a one stand like an open watch-tower in the midst of the territory it is erected to gaze on, and were the storms and calms, the stars and meteors, its watchman was wont to report of, the habitual variegation of its everyday life, as they glanced across its open roof or lay reflected on its four-square parapet? Or did some sunken and darkened chamber of imagery witness, in the artificial illumination of every storied compart-ment we are permitted to contemplate, how rare and precious were the outlooks through here and there an embrasure upon a world beyond, and how blankly would have pressed on the artificer the boundary of his daily life, except for the amorous diligence with which he had rendered permanent by art whatever came to diversify the gloom? Still, fraught with instruction and interest as such details undoubtedly are, we can, if needs be, dispense with them. The man passes, the work remains. The work speaks for itself, as we say: and the biography of the worker is no more necessary to an understanding or enjoyment of it, than is a model or anatomy of some tropical tree, to the right tasting of the fruit we are familiar with on the market-stall, — or a geologist's map and stratification, to the prompt recognition of the hill-top, our landmark of every day.

We turn with stronger needs to the genius of the opposite tendency — the subjective poet of modern classification. He, gifted like the objective poet with the fuller perception of nature and man, is impelled to embody the thing he perceives, not so much with reference to many below as to the one above him, the supreme Intelligence which apprehends all things in their absolute truth, — an ultimate view ever aspired to, if but partially attained, by the poet's own soul. Not what man sees, but what God sees — the *Ideas* of Plato, seeds of creation lying burningly on the Divine Hand — it is toward these that he struggles. Not with the combination of humanity in action, but with the primal elements of humanity he has to do, and he digs where he stands — preferring to seek them in his own soul as the nearest reflex of that absolute Mind, according to the intuitions of which he desires to perceive and speak. Such a poet does not deal habitually with the picturesque groupings and tempestuous tossings of the forest-trees, but with their roots and fibres naked to the chalk and stone. He does not paint pictures nor hang them on the walls, but rather carries them on the retina of his own eyes: we must look deep into his human eyes, to see those pictures on them. He is accordingly, rather a seer, than a fashioner, and what he produces will be less a work than an effluence. That effluence cannot be considered easily in abstraction from his personality, — being indeed the very radiance and aroma of his personality, projected from it but not separated. Therefore, in our approach to the poetry, we necessarily approach the personality of the poet; in apprehending it we apprehend him, and certainly we cannot love it without loving him. But for love's and for understanding's sake we desire to know him, and as readers of his poetry must be readers of his biography also.

I shall observe, in passing, that it seems not so much from any essential distinction in the faculty of the two poets or in the nature of the objects contemplated by either, as in the more immediate adaptability of these objects to the distinct purpose of each, that the objective poet, in his appeal to the aggregate human mind, chooses to deal with the doings of men, (the result of which dealing, in its pure form, when even description, as suggesting a describer, is dispensed with, is what we call dramatic poetry), while the subjective poet, whose study has been himself, appealing through himself to the absolute Divine mind, prefers to dwell upon those external scenic appearances which strike out most abundantly and uninterruptedly his inner light and power, selects that silence of the earth and sea in which he can best hear the beating of his individual heart, and leaves the noisy, complex, yet imperfect exhibitions of nature in the manifold experience of man around him, which serve only to distract and suppress the working of his brain. These opposite tendencies of genius will be more readily described in their artistic effect than in their moral spring and cause. Pushed to an extreme and manifested as a deformity, they will be seen plainest in all in the fault of either artist, when subsidiarily to the human interest of his work his occasional illustrations from scenic nature are introduced as in the earlier works of the originative painters — men and women filling the foreground with consummate mastery, while mountain, grove and rivulet show like an anticipatory revenge on that succeeding race of landscape-painters whose 'figures' disturb the perfection of their earth and sky. It would be idle to inquire, of these two kinds of poetic faculty in operation, which is the higher or even rarer endowment. If the subjective might seem to be the ultimate requirement of every age, the objective, in the strictest state, must still retain its original value. For it is with this world, as starting point and basis alike, that we shall always have to concern ourselves; the world is not to be learned and thrown aside, but reverted to and relearned. The spiritual comprehension may be infinitely subtilized, but the raw material it operates upon, must remain. There may be no end of poets who communicate to us what they see in an object with reference to their own individuality; what it was before they saw it, in reference to the aggregate human mind, will be desirable to know as ever. Nor is there any reason why these two modes of poetic faculty may not issue hereafter from the same poet in successive perfect works, examples of which, according to what are now considered the exigencies of art, we have hitherto possessed in distinct individuals only. A mere running-in of the one faculty upon the other, is, of course, the ordinary circumstance. Far more rarely it happens that either is found so decidedly prominent and superior, as to be pronounced comparatively pure; while of the perfect shield, with the gold and the silver side set up for all comers to challenge, there has yet been no instance. Either faculty in its eminent state is doubtless conceded by Providence as a best gift to men, according to their especial want. There is a time when the general eye has, so to speak, absorbed its fill of the phenomena around it, whether spiritual or material, and desires rather to learn the exacted significance of what it possesses, than to receive any augmentation of what is possessed. Then is the opportunity for the poet of loftier vision, to lift his fellows, with their half-apprehensions, up to his own sphere, by intensifying the import of details and rounding the universal meaning. A tribe of successors (Homerides) working more or less in the same spirit, dwell on his discoveries and reinforce his doctrine, till, at unawares, the world is found to be subsisting on the shadow of a reality, on sentiments diluted from passions, on the tradition of a fact, the convention of a moral, the straw of last year's harvest. Then is the imperative call for the appearance of another sort of poet, who shall at once replace this intellectual rumination of food swallowed long ago, by a supply of the fresh and living swathe; getting at new substance by breaking up the assumed wholes into parts of independent and unclassed value, careless of the unknown laws for re-combining them (it will be the business of another poet to suggest those hereafter), prodigal of objects of men's outer and not inner sight, shaping for their uses a new and different creation from the last, which it displaces by the right of life over death, — to endure until, in the inevitable process, its very sufficiency to itself shall require, at length, an exposition of its affinity to something higher, — when the positive yet conflicting facts shall again precipitate them themselves under a harmonizing law, and one more degree will be apparent for a poet to climb in that mighty ladder, of which, however cloud-involved and undefined may glimmer the topmost step, the world dares no longer doubt that its gradations ascend.

Such being the two kinds of artists, it is naturally, as I have shown, with the biography of the subjective poet that we have the deeper concern. Apart from his recorded life altogether, we might fail to determine with satisfactory precision to what class his productions belong, and what amount of praise is assignable to the producer. Certainly, in the face of any conspicuous achievement of genius, philosophy, no less than sympathetic instinct, warrants our belief in a great moral purpose having mainly inspired even where it does not visibly look out of the same. Greatness in a work suggests an adequate instrumentality; and none of the lower incitements, however they may avail to initiate or even effect many considerable displays of power, simulating the nobler inspiration to which they are mistakenly referred, have been foundable, under the ordinary conditions of humanity, to task themselves to the end of so exacting a performance as a poet's complete work. As soon will the galvanism that provokes to violent action the muscles of a corpse, induce it to cross the chamber steadily: sooner. The love of displaying power for the display's sake, the love of riches, of distinction, of notoriety, — the desire of a triumph over rivals, and the vanity in the applause of friends, — each and all of such whetted appetites grow intenser by exercise and increasingly sagacious as to the best and readiest means of self-appeasement, — while for any of their ends, whether the money or the pointed finger of the crowd, or the flattery and hate to heart's content, there are cheaper prices to pay, they will all find soon enough, than the bestowment of a life upon a labour, hard, slow, and not sure. Also, assuming the proper moral aim to have produced a work, there are many and various states of an aim: it may be more intense than clear-sighted, or too easily satisfied with a lower field of activity than a steadier aspiration would reach. All the bad poetry in the world (accounted poetry, that is, by its affinities) will be found to result from some of the infinite degrees of discrepancy between the attributes of the poet's soul, occasioning a want of correspondency between his work and the verities of nature, — issuing in poetry, false under whatever form, which shows a thing not as it is to mankind generally, nor as it is to the particular describer, but as it is supposed to be for some unreal neutral mood, midway between both and of value to neither, and living its brief minute simply through the indolence of who accepts it or his incapacity to denounce a cheat. Although of such depths of failure there can be question here in every case we must betake ourselves to the review of a poet's life ere we determine some of the nicer questions concerning his poetry, — more especially in the performance we seek to estimate the poetry aright, has been obstructed and cut short of completion by circumstances, — a disastrous youth or a premature death. We may learn from the biography whether his spirit invariably saw and spoke from the last height to which it had attained. An absolute vision is not for this world, but we are permitted a continual approximation to it, every degree of which in the individual, provided it exceed the attainment of the masses, must procure him a clear advantage. Did the poet ever attain to a higher platform than where he rested and exhibited a result? Did he know more than he spoke of?

I concede however, in respect to the subject of our study as well as some few other illustrious examples, that the unmistakable quality of the verse would be evidence enough, under usual circumstances, not only of the kind and degree of the intellectual but of the moral constitution of Shelley: the whole personality of the poet shining forward from the poems, without much need of going further to seek it. The 'Remains' — produced within a period of ten years, and at a season of life when other men of at all comparable genius have hardly done more than prepare the eye for future sight and the tongue for speech — present with the complete enginery of a poet, as signal in the excellence of its several aptitudes as transcendent in the combination of effects, — examples, in fact, of the whole poet's function of beholding with an understanding keenness the universe, nature and man, in their actual state of perfection in imperfection, — of the whole poet's virtue of being untempted by the manifold partial developments of beauty and good on every side, into leaving them the

ultimates he found them, — induced by the facility of the gratification of his own sense of these qualities, or by the pleasure of
acquiescence in the shortcomings in his predecessors in art, and
the pain of disturbing their conventionalisms, — the whole poet's
virtue, I repeat, of looking higher than any manifestation yet
made of both beauty and good, in order to suggest from the
utmost actual realization of the one a corresponding capability in
the other, and out of the calm, purity and energy of nature, to
reconstitute and store up for the forthcoming stage of man's
being, a gift in repayment of that former gift, in which man's own
thought and passion had been lavished by the poet on the else-
incompleted magnificence of the sunrise, the else-uninterpreted
mystery of the lake, — so drawing out, lifting up, and assimil-
ating this ideal of a future man, thus descried as possible, to the
present reality of the poet's soul already arrived at a higher state
of development, and still aspirant to elevate and extend itself in
conformity with its still-improving perceptions of, no longer the
eventual Human, but the actual Divine. In conjunction with
which noble and rare powers, came the subordinate power of
delivering these attained results to the world in an embodiment
of verse more closely answering to and indicative of the process of
the informing spirit, (failing as it occasionally does, in art, only to
succeed in highest art), — with a diction more adequate to the
task its natural and acquired richness, its material colour and
spiritual transparency, — the whole being moved by and suffused
with a music at once of the soul and the sense, expressive both of
an external might of sincere passion and an internal fitness and
consonancy, — than can be attributed to any other writer whose
record is among us. Such was the spheric poetical faculty of
Shelley, as its own self-sufficing central light, radiating equally
through immaturity and accomplishment, through many fragments and occasional completion, reveals it to a competent
judgement.

But the acceptance of this truth by the public, has been
retarded by certain objections which cast us back on the evidence
of biography, even with Shelley's poetry in our hands. Except for
the particular character of these objections, indeed, the non-
appreciation of his contemporaries would simply class, now that
it is over, with a series of experiences which have necessarily
happened and needlessly been wondered at, ever since the world
began, and concerning which any present anger may well be
moderated, no less in justice to our forerunners than in policy to

ourselves. For the misapprehensiveness of his age is exactly what a poet is sent to remedy; and the interval between his operation and the generally perceptible effect of it, is no greater, less indeed, than in many other departments of the great human effort. The 'E pur si muove' ['Nevertheless, it moves!'] of the astronomer [Galileo] was as bitter a word as any uttered before or since by a poet over his rejected living work, in that depth of conviction which is so like despair.

But in this respect was the experience of Shelley peculiarly unfortunate — that the disbelief in him as a man, even preceded the disbelief in him as a writer, the misconstruction of his moral nature preparing the way for the misappreciation of his intellectual labours. There existed from the beginning, — simultaneous with, indeed anterior to his earliest noticeable works, and not brought forward to counteract any impression they had succeeded in making, — certain charges against his private character and life, which, if substantiated in their whole breadth, would materially disturb, I do not attempt to deny, our reception and enjoyment of his works, however wonderful the artistic qualities of these. For we are not sufficiently supplied with instances of genius of his order, to be able to pronounce certainly how many of its constituent parts have been tasked and strained to the production of a given lie, and how high and pure a mood of the creative mind may be dramatically simulated as the poet's habitual and exclusive one. The doubts, therefore, arising from such a question, required to be set at rest, as they were effectually, by those early authentic notices of Shelley's career and the corroborative accompaniment of his letters, in which not only the main tenor and principal result of his life, but the purity and beauty of many of the processes which had conduced to them, were made apparent enough for the general reader's purpose; — whoever lightly condemned Shelley first, on the evidence of reviews and gossip, as lightly acquitting him now, on that of memoirs and correspondence. Still, it is advisable to lose no opportunity of strengthening and completing the chain of biographical testimony; much more, of course, for the sake of the poet's original lovers, whose volunteered sacrifice of particular principle in favour of absorbing sympathy we might desire to dispense with, than for the sake of his foolish haters, who have long since diverted upon other objects their obtuseness or malignancy. A full life of Shelley should be written at once, when the materials for it continue in reach; not to minister to the curiosity of the public, but to obliterate the last stain of that false life which was forced on the public's attention before it had any curiosity on the matter, — a biography, composed in harmony with the present general disposition to have faith in him, yet not shrinking from a candid statement of all ambiguous passages, through a reasonable confidence that the most doubtful of them will be found consistent with a belief in the eventual perfection of his character, according to the poor limits of our humanity. Nor will men persist in confounding, any more than God confounds, with genuine infidelity and an atheism of the heart, those passionate, impatient struggles of a boy towards distant truth and love, made in the dark, and ended by one sweep of the natural seas before the full moral sunrise could shine on him. Crude convictions of boyhood, conveyed in imperfect and inapt forms of speech, — for such things all boys have been pardoned. There are growing-pains, accompanied by temporary distortion, of the soul also. And it would be hard indeed upon this young Titan of genius, murmuring in divine music his human ignorances, through his very thirst for knowledge, and his rebellion, in mere aspiration to law, if the melody itself substantiated the error, and the tragic cutting short of life perpetuated into sins, such faults as, under happier circumstances, would have been left behind by the consent of the most arrogant moralist, forgotten on the lowest steps of youth.

Passage 1.12

(from *Roden Noel, 'On the Use of Metaphor and "Pathetic fallacy" in Poetry',* Fortnightly Review, *1866. Noel's essay is a detailed response to Ruskin's 'Of The Pathetic Fallacy', Passage 1.12*)

There is an important question connected with the principles of poetic art which the high authority of Mr Ruskin has been chiefly instrumental in deciding; but notwithstanding my profound sense of the value of Mr Ruskin's teaching on aesthetic matters, I venture to think that in this instance his decision has been too hastily accepted as final. I refer to the question of the use of metaphor, and what Mr Ruskin has termed 'pathetic fallacy' in poetry.

Now if there be a great fundamental principle, the slow recognition of which by modern art we owe to Mr Ruskin, it is this, that 'nothing can be good or useful or ultimately pleasurable which is untrue'. Yet here, he proceeds, in metaphor and pathetic fallacy, 'is something pleasurable in poetry which is nevertheless untrue'. For, according to him, these forms of thought result from the 'extraordinary or false appearance of things to us, when we are under the influence of emotion or contemplative fancy — false appearance being, as being entirely unconnected with any real power or character in the object, are only imputed to it by us'. Mr Ruskin further adds, that 'the greatest poets do not often admit this kind of falseness — that it is only the second order of poets who much delight in it'. Yet he admits that 'if we think that over our favourite poetry we shall find it full of this kind of fallacy, and that we like it all the more for being so'. Now there is here a contradiction which is well worthy of attentive examination. This attribution by metaphor of spiritual qualities to material objects is eminently characteristic of modern poetry — notably of Tennyson's — and has been a ground of serious objection to it, as fatal as to any claim it might put forward to be accounted first-rate, by more than one critic following in the wake of Mr Ruskin. And so far as such criticism has been a protest against the undiscriminating admiration for mere pretty disconnected freaks of fancy, which at one time threatened to break up our poetry into so many foam-wreaths of loose luxuriant images, the effect of it has been beneficial. There is danger, on the other hand, that this criticism may beget a blind dogmatism, very injurious to the natural and healthy develop-ment of the poetic art which may be proper to our own present age. For the intellectual and aesthetic development of each different race and age will have a characteristic individuality of their own. And criticism ought to point us to the great models of the past, not that we may become their cold and servile imitators, but that we may nourish on them our own creative genius. The classification of artists as first, second, and third rate, must always be somewhat arbitrary; but the criticism which disposes of a quality that is essential to such poety as Tennyson's, by calling it a weakness and a 'note' of inferiority, may itself be suspected of shallowness.

Let us first take for brief examination some instances of alleged fallacy in the use of metaphorical expressions. The following Mr Ruskin takes from Keats: —

Down whose green-back the short-lived foam, all hoar,

Bursts gradual with a *wayward indolence*.
[*Endymion*, 1820 (2.349-50)]¹⁷

Now salt water cannot be either wayward or indolent; on this
plain fact the charge of falsehood in the metaphor is grounded.
Yet this expression is precisely the most exquisite bit in the
picture. Can plain falsehood then be truly poetic and beautiful?
Many people will reply, 'certainly', believing that poetry is essentially pleasing by the number of pretty falsehoods told or
suggested. We believe with Mr Ruskin that poetry is only good in
proportion to its truth. Now, we must first enquire what the poet
is here intending to describe. If a scientific man were to explain to
us the nature of foam by telling us it is a wayward and indolent
thing, this would clearly be a falsehood. But does the poet profess
to explain with what the man of science would profess to explain,
or something else? What are the physical laws according to which
water becomes foam, and foam falls along the back of a wave —
that is one question; and what impression does this condition of
things produce on a mind that observes closely, and feels with
exquisite delicacy of sense the beauty in the movement of the
foam, and its subtle relations to other material things, as well as
to certain analogues in the sphere of the spirit, to functions and
states of the human spirit — this is a totally different question.
Now I submit that the office of the poet in this connection is to
answer the latter question, and that of the scientific man to
answer the former. But observe that this is not granting license of
scientific ignorance or wanton inaccuracy to the poet which some
critics are disposed to grant. For if the poet ignorantly and
wantonly contradicts such results of scientific inquiry as are
generally familiar to cultivated minds of his age, he puts himself
out of harmony with them, and does not announce truth, which
can command itself to them as such. But the poetic aspects of a
circumstance do not disappear when the circumstance is
regarded according to the fresh light scientific inquiry has thrown
upon it. Such poetic aspects are increased as knowledge
increases. Keats, in this instance, contradicts no legitimate
scientific conclusion. The poet who does so wantonly, shows little
of the true poet's reverence for nature. The poet undertakes to
teach what the man of science does not undertake to teach; their
provinces are different, but if they contradict one another, they
are so far bunglers in their respective trades.

Let us here at once, as briefly as may be, dispose of an

erroneous popular assumption which simply results from inaccurate thought. It may be conceded that we have shown how the metaphor of Keats correctly describes the effect of foam breaking up along the back of a wave on a poetic mind sensitive to its beauty; but it will probably be urged that while the scientific man investigates the nature of things in themselves, the poet, after all, only describes things as they appear to us. This is a complete mistake. The water, the foam, and the laws of their existence, which it is the object of science to investigate, are *phenomena*; that is, products of something external to us and of our perceiving faculty in reciprocal action. Out of deference to the constitutional objection of Englishmen to careful thought, Mr Ruskin, while giving us some metaphysics of his own on this topic, humorously denounces the 'troublesomeness of metaphysicians' who do not agree with him. It is plain matter-of-fact, however, that blueness and saltness and fluidity are effects of things on our senses and perceiving faculties, — are the appearances of things to us. The scientific man, therefore, in describing these phenomena, the fixed order of the co-existence and succession, describes certain other features of their appearance to us, and the poet equally chooses certain other features of their appearance to us. The analogies of natural things to spiritual, and the beauty of these which the poet discerns, are as much facts as the more obvious facts that sea-water is salt and green, and that foam is white or grey. True indeed it is that nearly every one can see and acknowledge the latter facts to be facts, and that much fewer persons can see the wayward indolence of the foam on the back of the green wave; but colour-blind people cannot see the greenness of the wave; and to those who know nothing of science, many undoubted facts the man of science can tell will seem unintelligible. There are many truths we unhesitatingly receive as such, although some persons of less perfect and cultured faculty cannot receive them. Now, whether the faculty whereby we attain to truth be called judgement, reasoning, imagination, or fancy, can be of little consequence. One source of error in this matter is, that in the popular use of words, we 'fancy' and 'imagine' what is not the fact.

But we can here only afford room to refer the reader on this point to Mr Ruskin's own fine dissertations on the respective functions of true imagination and fancy — one of his definitions of imagination being that it is the faculty of seeing things falsely. The question is, does the metaphor of Keats express the poetic truth forcibly to kindred imaginative minds, or does it not? If, as is the case with so many fine-sounding metaphorical expressions, this expression when examined should prove inaccurate, far-fetched, affected, disturbing, and degrading, not intensifying and ennobling to the pictorial effect of that which the poet intended to represent, then is the metaphor false, and because false, therefore bad as art. Indolence and foam may be interesting separately, but they may be so remotely suggestive of one another that the association of them can serve no purpose but to prove the nimbleness of the poet's fancy. But we submit that the shredding forceless drift of the old foam on the wave's back cannot be painted more accurately than by this metaphor of Keats. It is verily analogous to — that is, partially identical with — the aimless drift of indolent thought, and I find that I know each phenomenon better by thus identifying them in conception. It may be strange that so it should be; it may even be repugnant to some pseudo-philosophical scheme which has found a lodging in our minds we do not know why or how, implying the absolute contrariety of mind and matter; but yet, if it be a fact that so it is, ought not we who reverence facts to receive it? And why should a poet be a teller of pleasant lies for pointing the fact out of us? It may indeed be urged that that Keats does not merely assert the mental and material phenomena to be *like*, but asserts the foam *to be* indolent and wayward, which it is not. Let it be remembered, however, that if the poet had introduced here an elaborate comparison, he would have diverted our sight and thought from the water itself to a distinct human sphere, with all its new and foreign associations, which would have been injurious to the harmonious progress of his poem, his object being merely to touch in the wave and its foam, as he passed onward, with as few and as telling touches as possible. Besides, in employing a metaphorical expression, you do not intend to make, and no one understands you to make, a literal assertion; you are making it metaphorically, and this because you feel that you can best express the character of one thing by ascribing it to the character of something analogous. You might multiply the epithets for ever, and not hit it off — not transfix the core of the thing's individuality — as you can do by a single happy metaphor. There are correspondences between spirit and matter, and it is in seizing these that we find each analogue in spirit and matter becoming suddenly luminous, intelligible, real. It would not, as is assumed, be *more accurate* to say, 'the foam falls gradually'. These terms are too abstract: other things also fall gradually; and therefore they do not give the individuality of the phenomenon in question. There is indeed some error involved in the use of Keats' metaphor; but this error is allowed for, and it is the most accurate expression possible of the fact; for the error of poverty and vagueness which the more abstract epithets would involve is a far more radical error; so that they are erroneously supposed to be more scientific and exact. The commonest term in use for expressing mental and moral qualities are derived from conditions and qualities of matter, that is, are used metaphorically, and yet we do not call them 'fallacies'. We talk of an 'upright man' in the moral sense as readily as we talk of an upright man in the bodily. Our most graphic and vigorous prose must share the fate of our best poetry if metaphor be simply falsehood. How are you to avoid speaking of a tortuous, crooked policy? The splendid vigour of Mr Ruskin's own prose-poetry is largely due to his felicitous use of metaphor.

Mr Ruskin, indeed, remarks justly that Homer 'would never have written, never have thought of such a metaphor as this of Keats'. He will call the waves 'over-roofed', 'full-charged', 'monstrous', 'compact-black', 'wine-coloured', and so on. These terms are as accurate, incisive, as terms can be, but they never show the slightest feeling of anything animated in the ocean. Now this faculty of seeing and giving the external appearance of a thing precisely is eminently Homeric, and is one without which a man can hardly be a poet at all. The ideal of which poetasters pique themselves means but a feeble, insecure grasp of reality; they do not know that to find the ideal they must first hold fast and see into the common external thing which they deem so despicable. But the fellowship of the external thing with certain spiritual things is an additional though latent quality in it, the perception of which may result from a keen gaze into the external appearance. Does Keats then see more than Homer? Mr Ruskin replies that Homer had a faith in the animation of the sea much stronger than Keats. But 'all this sense of something living in it he separates in his mind into a great abstract image of a sea power. He never says the waves rage or are idle. But he says there is somewhat in, and greater than, the waves which rages and is idle, and that he calls a god.'

We must remark upon this that the early poets of a people have seldom displayed so great a care for the beauties of external nature in general as their later poets have done. Compare Homer and Theocritus, Chaucer and Tennyson. The earlier poetry will deal chiefly with the outward active life of man — his wars, hunting, his passion for women and other excitements, with all the intrigues and adventures to which this may give rise; and the noblest songs have been sung about these simple, universally interesting themes. But the criticism which insists on the poetry of a later age being squared on the model of that of an earlier age may surely be reminded that the earlier poetry is so great and good precisely because it is spontaneous, the perfect expression of the age in which it was produced. As men come to lead more artificial quiet lives, they reflect more on themselves and on the nature around them, they stand in new relationships to external things, they acquire new habits of feeling, thinking and external nature becomes the mirror of their own more highly organised existence, so that the earlier poet cannot see these subtle meanings in the face of nature which the later poet sees. If the external features of nature remain the same, the spirit of men in relation with them changes ever. But even if we admitted with Mr Ruskin that Homer was as sensitively alive to the delicate play of expression on the mobile countenance of nature as Keats was, only that he ascribed it to some god and that Keats did not, we should be constrained to ask, does Mr Ruskin mean that Homer's was a more correct mode of embodying that animation that was the metaphorical mode of Keats? Are we to believe in the Pagan nature-divinities? Because if not, and if yet Mr Ruskin admits the animation in question, it is hard to see why he praises Homer and deems the metaphor of Keats a pleasant falsehood and a characteristic of the vicious modern manner. Surely we owe the restoration of our faith in the glorious animation of nature very largely to Mr Ruskin's own teaching, which makes his inconsistent doctrine of this subject of metaphor the more to be regretted. What makes the language of our poets often incorrect, confused, affected, is that while they cannot help feeling that there is a life and a spirit in nature, they are instructed by our teachers of authority that this feeling is but a pretty superstition, allowable, indeed, in poetry, yet not to be mistaken for a true belief. Poetry, therefore, becomes as 'elegant as time', by no means the expression of our deepest and most earnest insight. The result last century was that in our poetry 'mountains nodded drowsy heads', and 'flowers sweated beneath the night dew'. For if images of this kind be delusions, with no basis in truth, the elegance of them resolves itself into a mere matter of taste. And people at that time thought those ideas very lovely and poetic indeed. Even now many of our most intelligent minds believe:

> Earth goes by chemic forces; Heaven's
> A Méchanique Céleste!
> And heart and mind of human kind
> A watch-work at the rest!
> [Arthur Hugh Clough, 'The New Sinai', 1849 (55-8)]

Others of us believe that there is a deity indeed, but one who, having made all this, only watches it go, and occasionally inter- feres with the border of it to prove to us that it did not make itself, and to remind us of his own existence. But of the God of St Paul, 'in whom we (and all other things) live, move, and have our being', we hear very little. If, however, it were permitted in so enlightened an age as the present to broach so old-world an idea, we might believe with Homer that there is a great sea-power, a Divinity in the sea as well as a great deal of sea-water; then we might still believe with the great modern poet, with whom it was no pretty lie but a profound faith, that —

> And I have felt,
> A presence that disturbs us with the joy
> Of elevated thoughts, a sense sublime
> Of something far more deeply interfused,
> Whose dwelling is the light of setting suns,
> And the round ocean, and the living air,
> And the blue sky, and in the mind of man
> A motion and a spirit that impels
> All thinking things, all objects of all thought,
> And rolls through all things.
> [Wordsworth, 'Tintern Abbey', 1798 (93-102)]

I think it specially important to examine the position which Mr Ruskin has taken in this question in his third volume of 'Modern Painters' [1856] because it tends to neutralise the noble teaching of the second volume, to which our art owes incalculable benefit. We have only to turn the chapter on 'Imagination Pene- trative' to be assured of the inconsistency of his doctrine on this subject. As an instance of what he means by Imagination penetrative, he quotes from Milton —

Bring the rathe primrose that forsaken dies [...]
With cowslips wan that hang the pensive head,
And every flower that sad embroidery wears.

['Lycidas', 1637 (142, 147-8)]

How can a primrose be forsaken, or cowslips hang *pensive* heads?
According to the chapter on 'Pathetic Fallacy', only a poet of the
secondary order would indulge in such pretty fallacies. He goes
on, however, to quote Shakespeare's image of 'pale primroses
dying unmarried, before they can behold bright Phoebus in his
strength' [*The Winter's Tale*, IV.iv.142]; yet what is his comment
here? 'Observe how the imagination goes into the very inmost
soul of "every flower"' and 'never stops on their spots or bodily
shape', which last remark implies a half-censure of Milton for
describing 'the pansy freaked with jet', that being merely a touch
of inferior fancy, that mixes with and mars the work of imagination. Again, 'the imagination sees the heart and inner nature,
and makes them felt, but is often obscure, mysterious, and inter-
rupted in its giving of outer detail'. Even in the case of elaborate
imaginative structures such as those of Dante and Milton, the
poet's work, we would contend, is the product of sheer insight,
whose keen, long, ardent gaze into the eyes of nature, human and
material, has drawn the very soul out of her. From that central
point to which the seer has pierced, all parts are seen in their own
relative proportion, harmony, hidden meaning, and purpose;
and the several parts that are chosen and united in his work form
a perfect organic structure, because they are conjoined, not
according to the accidental juxtaposition in which the vulgar eye
may chance to behold them at the surface, but according to the
eternal affinities they have in nature for one another. The parts of
such a work are not pieced arbitrarily together; they have
chemical affinity for one another and they grow up into an
organic whole in the creative mind of the poet, which process is
just a reproduction in small of the grand evolution of the
universe. We see things in isolated broken pieces; but the poet,
with unerring instinct as by a spirit magnetism, brings together
the fragments that indeed belong to one another, and so forms for
us living models of the universal cosmos. In this manner great
artists have positively created new individualities — or at least
gone to the verge of creating them. If the idea of an imaginary
living creature were perfectly sufficient and self-consistent, it
would actually live. But if in the course of ages mind ever came to

evolve creations in the same sense as mind itself seems now to be evolved from material organisation, such creatures would probably transcend the minds we know as such as these minds transcend the bodily organisation. Meanwhile great imaginations approach such a goal. There is the Dragon of Turner in the Jason of his Liber Studorium [1810]; the terrible Lombard Griffin, so intensely portrayed by Ruskin [in *Modern Painters III*, 1856]; the Satan of Milton; the Caliban of Shakespeare. That creature may have actually breathed or may actually breathe some day, he seems so real, so possible. This doctrine that all real poetry tells the most fundamental truth about things, instead of being merely a play of pretty or pathetic fallacies, an elegant relaxation for another dinner, as modern critics seem to conceive, I venture to propound as having the sanction of no mean critic — Aristotle. For Aristotle, while defining poetry 'viewed generally' as μιμήσις, yet explains that he does not mean such imitation as modern photography might represent. 'Poetry', he explains, 'represents actions less ordinary and interchanged, and endows them with more rareness', than is found in nature. The poet's business is not to tell events as they have actually happened, but as they might possibly happen. 'Poetry is more sublime and more philosophical than history.' We contend then for Aristotle's definition of poetry as μιμήσις, the imitative art, as on the whole the best and most helpful. And I have merely wished here in passing to strengthen my argument by showing that the principles I apply to defend the use of metaphor are of universal application in all departments of poetry. Thus I might proceed to show that there is more essential truth in the few lines embodying Spenser's symbolic impersonations of the vices (envy, gluttony, jealousy, &c), than could be expressed in as many pages of abstact dissertation.

It is unfortunate that Wordsworth, in the course of those few discussions of his on the principles of Poetry which are worth their weight in gold (considering how little scientific standard criticism of our language can boast in comparison with the portentous amount of smart, conceited, futile Babel-utterances with which the weekly press teems to our bewilderment) — it is unfortunate that Wordsworth himself should have used some unguarded language relative to the question we are here discussing. He says that imagination 'confers additional properties on an object, or abstracts from it some of those which it actually possesses' [Preface to the 1815 edition of *Poetical Works*]. He gives several instances of this, which it may be well for us to examine. First from Milton —

> As when far off at sea a fleet descried
> Hangs in the clouds
>
> [*Paradise Lost*, 1674 (2.636-7)]

No fleet hangs in the clouds. But the poet, professing to describe the appearance of a fleet far out at sea, describes it exactly by these terms, and adds nothing to the picture that does not belong to the actual appearance. Wordsworth next quotes from his own perfect descriptive poetry, 'Over his own sweet voice the stock-dove broods' ['Resolution and Independence', 1807 (5)]. The word 'broods', Wordsworth himself remarks, conveys the manner in which the bird reiterates and prolongs the soft note, as if participating in a still and quiet satisfaction like that which may be supposed inseparable from the continuous process of incubation. Now it is probably true, scientifically as well as poetically, that the bird delights in, and broods over its own note, while his mate is sitting near upon their eggs. Again —

> O cuckoo! shall I call thee Bird,
> Or but a wandering Voice?
>
> ['To the Cuckoo', 1807 (3-4)]

If the poet, looking up at the grey cuckoo in the tree, were to address it as a voice rather than a bird, the thought would not be pleasing, but absurd, because untrue and affected. But we may conceive him wandering meditatively about Rydal, as was his wont, lying upon the fresh green grass, and listening to that beloved voice of the spring, with all its old, sweet, sad associations. Has not that cuckoo-voice become part of ourselves, a link of our hearts to some long and lovely past? Has not that happy quiet voice, falling into the hearts of lovers, beating very close to one another, thrilled them into a yet dearer fusion? And when such lovers have been parted, has not this gentle voice united them in spirit again as they listened? Is not the cuckoo voice indeed all this, the very spirit of our English spring, quite as much, nay, how very much more, than it is the love-call of one individual male cuckoo? The poet has told us one truth, and the naturalist may tell us another; the one 'lies' and 'alters nature' quite as little as the other. Wordsworth's genius steals like moonlight, silent and unaware, into many a hidden nook that seemed barren and formless before, but now teems with shy and rare loveliness as of herb and flower; yet the moonlight only reveals what is already latent there. Creative, indeed, are these isolated images and metaphors, having a vital truth and coherence of their own, quite as real as that of the vaster completed works of high art; and while in the highest work these subordinate features will have their meaning in strict subordination to the whole, yet criticism is wrong to ignore and decry beauty of detail, which, if genuine, is itself the offspring of the same quickening, creative spark, fusing diverse elements into one. Though Keats was no weakling of the Kirke White stamp,[18] to be 'snuffed out by an article', one pain more might have been less malignant, and intelligent enough to comprehend that if unity of plan be all in all, and the character of the details of no importance, then a symmetrical periwig, or a smart review, would be nobler than Endymion, — which is absurd.

We now come to pass to some instance of what Mr Ruskin terms 'pathetic fallacy' proper. Mr Ruskin takes one from Mr Kingsley's ballad, 'Sands of Dee'. Of Mary, who was drowned in calling the cattle home, across the sands of Dee, he sings —

They rowed her in across the rolling foam,
The cruel crawling foam.

Now, how can foam be cruel? Mr Ruskin admits there is a dramatic propriety in the expression; I mean, that the feeling with which a spectator would regard the foam in these circumstances is correctly expressed; but he contends that the reason in this condition is unhinged by grief: foam is not cruel, whether we fancy it so or not. He admits that a person feeling it so will probably be higher in nature than one who should feel nothing of the kind, but contends that there is a third order of natures higher than either — natures which control such fallacious feelings by the force of their intellects. Such men know and feel too much of past and future, and all things beside and around that which immediately affects them, to be shaken by it. Thus the high creative poet might be thought impressive (shallow people think Dante stern) because he has a great centre of reflection and knowledge in which he stands serene, and watches the feeling, as it were, from far off. We must admit that there is much truth in this fine criticism; yet we must remark upon it that it is one thing to be washed away from our anchorage of reason — which, however, as Mr Ruskin admits, there are circumstances wherein we should not think it a proof of men's nobleness not to be — and another to be tossed up and down on the strong billows of feelings, holding yet fast to the anchor of reason. I meant that the influence of feeling on our intellects need not necessarily be a distorting influence; feeling may teach us what we could not learn without it. Love, eg, may often blind us to the defects of a beloved person, and so far confuse our judgement; yet since love puts us *en rapport*, in sympathy with, that person, it imparts insight, and gives wider and more essential data for the exercise of the understanding. The man to whom a primrose is 'a yellow primrose and nothing more', by no means knows it correctly because he does not feel any love for it or interest in it. He knows nothing at all about it except the name. A dispassionate judgement means too often a blind indiscriminating judgement formed by men who want those fine inner organs of sensibility without which the data for a true judgement are necessarily wanting; and the stupid judgement of a cynic is infinitely more mischievous than that of a warm partisan, because it has the credit of exceptional impartiality and freedom from 'prejudice'.

Let us examine this special instance of pathetic fallacy from Kingsley. What and whence is this impression of cruelty in the foam? Is it not the appropriate expression of a sense that comes over us in such-like terrible circumstances that there is on the outside of our weak wills and impotent understandings some myterious destiny manifesting itself especially in that fixed and iron-bound order of Nature so pitiless towards us when, in our often innocent ignorance, we happen to be caught into the blind whirl of its relentless machinery? For then it whirls on and crushes not only the living flesh and blood itself has wrought so cunningly, but too often, alas! as it seems, our very human reason — the tenderest and holiest of human sensibilities. In the coolest blood regarding such a spectacle, I ask how shall we express the facts of it? The ancients had their cruel gods and their blind fate. Our faith, on the other hand, if faith we have at all, is in a Supreme Being whose nature we can best conceive by naming Him Love. And yet he who does not feel the weary burden and the mystery of all this unintelligible world — he who does not confess with a feeble glimmer in all our boasted light — that he is an infant crying in the dark, and with no language but a cry [Tennyson, *In Memoriam*, 1850 (54:20)] — he has not had the data upon which to form a real philosophy. What, then, is it worth? As men, as wise men, we must feel these terrible realities in the core of our beings. If we still retain our faith, after this, well and good. But how shall we express the bewildered anguish of the spirit in such seasons of calamity? To me it seems inevitable, and therefore as proper as it is natural, that we should upbraid the instrument — the second cause — the cruel crawling sea-foam that swallowed up the innocent one we loved. Let the philosopher at least furnish us with correcter formulae for the expression of the feeling due from us as human beings on such occasions as this.

Notes

1. Torquato Tasso, *Jerusalem Delivered*, Canto 1, 3 (7-8).
2. Ebenezer Elliott makes this comment in his Preface to *Corn-Law Rhymes*, 1831. On truth and emotion in poetry, compare Alexander Smith, 'The Philosophy of Poetry', passage 1.4.
3. Quotation unidentified, but very probably by 'Christopher North' (John Wilson), who contributed numerous articles on poetry (and on many other topics) to that journal. Lewes (passage 1.5) attributes this quotation to Wilson.
4. Mill was well acquainted with associationist philosophy, which decrees that the mind organizes its sense-data according to regulative laws. This philosophy has its roots in the work of John Hartley, *Observations on Man, his Frame, his Duty, and his Expectations* (1749), and is expounded by Samuel Taylor Coleridge in *Biographia Literaria* (1817) (Chapters 5, 6 and 7). Mill's father, James Mill, extends this tradition in his *Analysis of the Phenomena of the Human Mind* (1829).
5. Ossian is the Gaelic warrior, Oisin, whose supposed works were translated by James Macpherson (1736-96) in *Fragments of Ancient Poetry, Collected in the Highlands of Scotland* (1760) and *Fingal, An Ancient Epic Poem in Six Books* (1762). Macpherson is said to have drawn on original sources while supplementing these with much of his own material.
6. Smart translated Horace in 1767. Smith's remarks count among a great many made during the early Victorian period about the differences between poetry and prose. Compare William Henry Smith, 'A Prosing Upon Poetry', *Blackwood's Magazine*, vol. 46 (1839), pp. 194-202.
7. 'Westminster Abbey', *The Sketch Book of Geoffrey Crayon, Gent* (London, 1820).
8. G.H. Lewes, whose article on 'Hegel's Aesthetics' (passage 1.5) draws heavily on earlier Victorian essays on poetry, cites this line but wrongly attributes it to Milton. It is more than likely that Lewes was aware of Smith's article.
9. The line, if Miltonic in its 'grand style', does not belong to Milton but it resembles *In Memoriam* (1.10): 'Let darkness keep her raven gloss'.

10. The preceding sentence is a translation of this quotation from *Prohemio e carta que el Marques de Santillana envio al codestable de Portugal* (1449).

11. Emerson's editors have not been able to trace this source. See *The Collected Works of Ralph Waldo Emerson*, vol. 3, *Essays: Second Series*, eds Joseph Slater, Alfred R. Ferguson and Jean Ferguson Carr (Cambridge, Mass., Harvard University Press, 1983).

12. These emblems were prominent during Harrison's electoral campaign against Van Buren in 1840. For a detailed reference, see Emerson, *Works*, III, p. 174.

13. Comte de Mirabeau (1749-91) was a leader of the French Revolution.

14. Carlyle is repeating verbatim sentences from his earlier essay, 'The State of German Literature' (1827) in *Critical and Miscellaneous Essays* (5 vols, Chapman and Hall, 1896), I.

15. David Masson, 'Theories of Poetry and a New Poet', *North British Review*, vol. 19 (1853), p. 338.

16. Quotation unidentified.

17. Ruskin refers to this quotation in 'Of Classical Landscape', *Modern Painters III* (1856).

18. [Henry] Kirke White (1785-1806) was a poet whose verse published in 1803 attracted the attention of Robert Southey. Today Kirke White is remembered for his hymns, notably 'Oft in Danger, Oft in Woe'.

2

'The Poetry of the Period'

Passage 2.1

(from *Alfred Austin, 'Summary'* in The Poetry of the Period, *1870. See also Passage 3.6 by Austin*)

The reader who has been good enough to peruse the critical essays in which I have attempted to appraise the writings of Mr Tennyson, Mr Browning, Mr Swinburne, Mr Arnold, Mr Morris, and others, cannot have failed already to perceive that it was not without good reason (or, at any rate, without serious design) that I comprehended the works of them all under the appellation of 'The Poetry of the Period'. He will then have noticed that I have completely overlooked any mere faults of detail with which their verse may be infected — have abstained from all inquiry into what may be called their literary peculiarities and individual and intellectual deficiencies — have never for one moment separated them from the age in which they write; but that, whilst refusing to them, one and all, the faintest claim to be regarded as great poets, I have rather intimated my astonishment that, under the circumstances, their productions should be as good as they are. Of course it is possible that I form an exaggerated estimate of their worth, since none of us can help having some sympathy with the productions of the period in which we 'live, move, and have our being', and that posterity, necessarily still more impartial, will think less of them even than I do. It is quite certain, however, it will not think more of them. I desire in this summary to make that important point more definitely clear.

For it is one of the most common but most superficial of errors, and one whose predominance in a scientific age is singularly unpardonable, to suppose that poetry, and indeed all art, is exclusively an affair partly of individual inclination, and partly of public patronage. The notion is radically false in both particulars. As far as individuals are concerned, it is highly and antecedently probable that the number is pretty constant through successive generations. That it is variable can never by any possibility be proved. On the other hand, what the world can do for the poet in any particular age is just as much beyond its control as his own genius is beyond his — every age having a decided bent, just as absolutely as every individual. Very little reflection suffices to show that, if such be the case, the perseverance of the latter will be of little avail, supposing the disposition of the former to be opposed to it. It is the nature of an apple-tree to grow apples, and to shed its leaves; but take it to Ceylon, it becomes undeciduous, and bears no more fruit. The tree cannot help itself, neither can the people of Ceylon. The conditions under which apples are produced having been removed, naturally enough apples likewise disappear. The person who does not see that his own species — or any variation of it, *eg* poets — will equally, though, of course, not so obviously, suffer modification by a complete shifting of the conditions, is not much indebted to his epoch for the only thing, save material comfort, it has got to give him particularly worth having — viz an appreciation of the universality and permanence of law. If he be an ordinarily intelligent person, he can have no difficulty in understanding that the individual, whether poet, painter, statesman, or philosopher, must be largely indebted for what of excellent or defective there is in him, to the age, people, and intellects by which he is surrounded. They are his atmosphere — his soil, sun, and sky — in a word, his climate. In speaking of Mr Tennyson, I remarked that, could we imagine him transplanted to the Elizabethan era, he would have been a much smaller poet than he is now, and probably the mere writer of a few courtly masques; whereas, if we could imagine Shakespeare transplanted into ours, he would very likely not have worked as a poet at all — or, if he had persisted in the following of his bent, have been considerably inferior, in work done, to the actual Mr Tennyson with whom we are acquainted. The explanation, of course, is that the climate of the Elizabethan age was so fine and bracing — so favourable, in fact, to the growth and development of the one predisposed to be a really great poet — that Mr Tennyson would have been nipped to the ground, and where he now daintily clambers would have been compelled to crawl; whilst the climate of the Victorian era, on the contrary, is so relaxing, that where Mr Tennyson thrives and luxuriates to the full extent of his natural capacity, Shakespeare, like the tree transplanted to the equator, would have apparently changed his whole nature, and ceased altogether to bear poetical fruit.

This, then, is the real truth of the matter — that great poetry is, like everything else, an affair indispensably of external conditions, since the existence of the internal conditions may be presumed, and can never be proved absent. But the presence or absence of the requisite external conditions for the production of great poetry, or great art of any sort, can doubt, not only that they are absent in the present age, but that actively hostile conditions are ruling in their stead. What publishers call a 'demand' for poetry on the part of the reading public, and what severe critics would call an itch for versifying on the part of innumerable gentlemen and ladies, have nothing on earth to do with the production of great or even fairly good poetry. The versifying mania has raged in all known epochs with about equal severity — thus fortifying the presumption that mere individual proclivities are pretty constant generation after generation — and certainly there is no abatement of the disease just at present. The words of Garin d'Apchier are just as applicable now as they were in the days of the Troubadours: 'Les jongleurs se sont multipliés au point qu'il y en a autant que lapins dans une garenne: on en est inondé' [These minstrels have multiplied themselves to the point that there are as many of them as rabbits in a warren: we are overwhelmed by them]. How little their quantity contributes to improve their quality, let any impartial person decide. Just as little is its quality affected by the 'demand' for it, which during the last five or six years, at any rate, has been very remarkable. For art is not like dry-goods, whatever some people may think or indolently assume to the contrary. The law of demand and supply breaks down once you pass the limits of craft, and invade the region of art. Though the material and labour requisite for the production of art must be paid for somehow, all the money in the world cannot produce one stroke of art, any more than it can produce the notes of a nightingale. The proper conditions alone can produce that, and demand is not one of them, much less all of them. Financial patronage — whether it be the patronage of wealthy, cultured dilettanti, of a luxurious, getting-on, and aspiring public, or a centralized and tasteful State — is equally powerless to evoke manifestations of art if the social conditions are wanting to its development. Financial patronage may found academies, distribute prizes, instigate unbounded competition. But what then? Great art, whether it be poetry or any other of its branches, bears as much resemblance to birthday odes, or poems that run through innumerable editions, as a monarch of a forest does to a faultless park-paling, or a wind-stirred group of water-reeds to an exquisitely-finished cane-bottomed chair. Naturally this age, having plenty of money, and having procured with it an immense amount of desirable things — underground railways, ocean steamers, splendid carriages and horses, rare and long-kept vintages, enormous mirrors, miles of lace, new colours, exciting novels by eminent hands, newspapers without end, gorgeous spectacles, naked dancing-girls, deft cooks, and a mild religion — is desirous of having great art likewise, which it had always heard is a good thing, and which, moreover, it fancies that it has got. For why should it not have it? It is quite ready to pay for it. To pay what for it? That is the question. Ready money. Alas! ready money is not the price of great art. Great art is to be reached only through spontaneity, simplicity, faith, unconscious earnestness, and manly concentration. It is idle to inquire if the age would make a sacrifice of its artificiality, its self-consciousness, its feminine infirmities, its scepticism, its distracted aims, in order to obtain it, since it would argue a complete metamorphosis of the age into something quite different from what it is; and ages are just as powerless to change their character as leopards to change their skins. It can offer money, favourable criticisms, and the *entrée* to its most conspicuous drawing-rooms — for it has got these things to give. But the contemporary social atmosphere and climate are no more within its gift or control than is the direction of the winds, the stir of volcanoes, the tumult of the sea, or the electricity of the air. These are not the commodities of market overt, and the heavens have not yet been assailed by the law of demand and supply.

Here, then, we touch firm ground. We bring the poet *en rapport* with his age, and at best he can but say what he has got to say. The more his own disposition is in harmony with that of his time, the more complete, lucid, and satisfactory will be his poetry. If he clashes with it, the conflict will be evident in his verse — with discord, incompleteness, and obscurity as the result. It stands to reason that it must be so; for the resultant of two forces pushing in much the same direction is of necessity both simpler and stronger than that of the two forces pulling in different directions. Of this truth Mr Tennyson is a most remarkable example. He has never once, as I have previously remarked, betrayed the slightest symptom of possessing the highest of poetical gifts. There is not one sublime passage in the whole of his works; and, what is more, there is no attempt at one. Yet I repeat my opinion that he must be conceded the first place among our living poets, though some of them have occasionally aimed at higher flights than he has dreamed of. For whilst they are partly of the age, and partly at issue with it, he is of his age almost wholly and solely. Take, for instance, his idea of the poet; it will illustrate my meaning excellently well, particularly when we compare it with that entertained by poets of very different calibre.

> The poet in a golden clime was born,
>   With golden stars above,
>
> > [Tennyson, 'The Poet', 1830 (1-2)]

My Tennyson tells us; and he goes on to speak of his thoughts —

> Filling with light
>
> And vagrant melodies the winds which bore
>   Them earthward till they lit;
> Then, like the arrow-seeds of the field-flower,
>   The fruitful wit,
>
> Cleaving, took root, and springing forth anew
>   Where'er they fell, behold,
> Like to the mother-plant in semblance, grew
>   A flower all gold.
>
> Thus truth was multipied on truth, the world
>   Like one great garden showed,
> And through the wreaths of floating dark upcurled,
>   Rare sunrise flowed. (16-24, 33-6)

The poem, no doubt, is well known to my readers; and they will remember how Freedom is next invoked, with 'no blood upon her maiden robes' [41], and then Wisdom, of whom it is said that she was armed with only one poor poet's scroll, and that

> No sword
> Of wrath her right arm whirled. (53-4)

121

I have not quoted this as a specimen of Mr Tennyson's best manner — for, verily, it is artificial stuff — but as showing the tone of his mind on a cardinal point with which his own vocation and genius are indissolubly associated. In another short poem on the same subject, the view taken of the poet's ground and function is equally characteristic, and, if anything, still smaller: —

> Vex not thou the poet's mind
> . . . .
> Clear and bright it should be ever,
> Flowing like a crystal river.
> > [Tennyson, 'The Poet's Mind', 1830 (1, 6-7)]

The ground wherein he dwells is not to be invaded by the 'dark-brow'd sophist' [8]. Everything therein is holy water, spicy flowers, and laurel-shrubs; and it is thus finally described: —

> In the heart of the garden the merry bird chants.
> . . . .
> > In the middle leaps a fountain,
> > > Like sheet lightning
> > > Ever brightening
> > With a low melodious thunder;
> > All day and all night it is ever drawn
> > > From the brain of the purple mountain,
> > > Which stands in the distance yonder:
> > It springs on a level flowery lawn,
> > And the mountain draws it from Heaven above,
> > And it sings a song of undying love. (22, 24-33)

Did I exaggerate when I said that Mr Tennyson is the tenant of the garden? To be such is evidently his own *beau ideal.* To sing among laurel-shrubs, spicy flowers, sparkling fountains, flowery lawns — behold, according to his own confession, the 'holy ground' of the poet! There is a mountain in the distance yonder, but he does not go to it. Mountains are not for small birds. Hark to a different strain!
[Austin cites Byron, 'Childe Harold's Pilgrimage, 1812 (4.860-77, 895-913)]

That is not the Poetry of the Period. Not much holy water and laurel-shrubs there. It is not a matter of a purple mountain in the distance, but of black rattling crags, and the poet is a portion of them and their tumultuous glee. The mountains have found a tongue, and so has the poet, and yet not one that contents him. Mr Tennyson,

> Flowing like a crystal river,
> Bright as light, and clear as wind,

says without difficulty or deficiency what he has got to say; and no wonder. But the greater voice, when it has said immeasurably more, still feels that it has not said a millionth part enough. It will live and die unheard. The one feels that he ought to be hemmed 'in the heart of the garden', and accordingly is so. The other yearns 'to mingle with the universe', and cannot, altogether. The one is satisfied with a 'fountain, like sheet lightning, ever brightening'. The other is drawn instinctively to the surging, seductive, but for ever unsurrendering sea:—

> And I have loved thee, Ocean! and my joy
> Of youthful sports was on thy breast to be
> Borne, like thy bubbles, onward: from a boy
> I wantoned to thy breakers — they to me
> Were a delight; and if the freshening sea
> Made them a terror, 'twas a pleasing fear;
> For I was as it were a child of thee,
> And trusted to thy billows far and near,
> And laid my head upon thy mane — as I do here.
> ['Childe Harold's Pilgrimage' (4.1648-56)]

Nothing could more forcibly illustrate the abyss that lies between poetry that is beautiful, and poetry that is great, and between the periods which give birth to each respectively. The present age is set upon being proper, pious, peaceful, complete, and respectable. Not that it is necessarily any of the five; but they constitute its ideal. It thinks fighting highly undesirable, if not actually wrong. It hates rows. It regards a loudly avowed disbelief and discontent as disreputable, if not something worse. In reality it entertains doubts about everything, but it is a comfort-loving coward, and takes refuge in a more or less silent compromise. Fancy a poet saying nowadays, as Wordsworth said,

Carnage is God's eldest daughter!
['Carnage' (so Wordsworth tells you) 'is God's daughter'.
Byron, 'Don Juan' (8.70)]

On the contrary, there is now 'no blood upon the maiden robes' [Tennyson, 'The Poet' (4)] of Freedom. Not that, as a fact, there is not plenty of it; we are compelled to fight every now and then, but we do not like it, and we have not manliness enough to exult in it, when nothing but fighting is left. Even when we do fight, we openly profess to fight for our interests, not for right; sighing all the while for the return of peace, laurel-shrubs, fountains, and holy water.

All, as I have said, proves the feminine, timorous, narrow, domesticated temper of the times, and explains the feminine, narrow, domesticated, timorous Poetry of the Period. Take yet another sign, though it is only a fresh illustration of the same truth — a looking at the old fact in a new light. What is one of the chief marks of great poetry? Surely, action. Indeed, we may say of great poetry, what Demosthenes [the great Greek orator] said of great oratory, that the soul of it is — action, action, action. The 'Iliad' is all action. So, almost all, is the 'Aeneid'. Look at the action in 'Paradise Lost'! To name the poetry of Shakespeare is to name the poetry of action. What are the 'Lady of the Lake' [1810], 'Marmion' [1808], and 'Rokeby' [1813 — by Sir Walter Scott], but action — action? Byron's early tales bristle with movement; and in 'Childe Harold', the inanimate themselves, battlefields, ruins, mountains, sepulchres, the very air, are made to stir with vigorous and active pulses. Turn to see Mr Tennyson, and what do we see? Still life — almost uniform still life. There is a motion of a kind — but of what kind? You have the rustling of silks, the blowing of zephyrs, the caracoling of palfreys, the humming of bees, the sighing of lovers; you see leagues of grass washed by slow broad streams, languid pulses of the oar, Orion sloping slowly to the west, stately ships on placid waters, summers crisp with shining woods, all imbedded in exquisite verse, of which it may almost be said, as of the author's own 'Sleeping Beauty' [1830], that

> She sleeps, nor dreams, but ever dwells
> A perfect form in perfect rest. (23-4)

It wants shaking; but you would shake it in vain. Sound and fury, not always signifying nothing, would not come of it, for they are not there. Mr Tennyson can speak glibly and well of

> greaves and cuisses dash'd with drops
> By onset;
>
> ['Morte D'Arthur', 1842 (215-16)]

but he cannot take us into the onset, and show us how the drops come there, and all the glorious bloody thick of the fight. He can

> take Excalibur
> And fling him far into the middle mere;
>
> ['Morte D'Arthur' (36-7)]

but he cannot take him into the reek of battle, and make him strike and act. What could possibly be tamer than such lines as the following? —

> Then Enid waited pale and sorrowful,
> And down upon him bore the bandit three.
> And at the midmost charging, Prince Geraint
> Drave the long spear a cubit through his breast,
> And out beyond; and then against his brace
> Of comrades, each of whom had broken on him
> A lance that splintered like an icicle,
> Swung from his brand a windy buffet out,
> Once, twice, to right, to left, and stunned the twain,
> Or slew them.
>
> ['Geraint and Enid', 1870 (83-92)]

What could be poorer, again, than the description of wild Limours dashing against Geraint?

> Who closed with him, and bore
> Down by the length of lance or arm beyond
> The crupper, and so left him stunned or dead,
> And overthrew the next that followed him,
> And blindly rushed on all the rout behind.
>
> ['Geraint and Enid' (462-6)]

In plain English, all that is very miserable, and utterly unworthy of Mr Tennyson's powers, when exercised on a congenial subject. Many a schoolboy would have described it better. We feel, as we read either of these passages, that the man's heart was not in them. The description is accurate enough, and, in a sense, pictorial; but it smells ineffably of the studio and the lamp. There is no dust, and clang, and hot blood in it. In a word, it too is still life, where still life ought not to be; and nothing can be more certain than that whenever Mr Tennyson's admirers wish to cite examples of his real poetical powers — and the examples are endless — they will infallibly have to cite passages avowedly to still life belonging. It is surely needless to point out how an instinctive taste and preference for still life is not a masculine, but a feminine propensity; and equally so, that we have thus a fresh corroboration of the particular charge I have so strongly pressed against the age and its worthy Laureate.

Passage 2.2

(from *W.H. Mallock*, Every Man His Own Poet: Or, the Inspired Singer's Recipe Book By a Newdigate Prizeman, *1872. Mallock published a slightly enlarged edition of this pamphlet in 1877*)

On the nature of poetry

Poetry as practised by the latest masters, is the art of expressing what is too foolish, too profane, and too indecent to be expressed in any other way. And thus, just as a consummate cook will prepare a most delicate repast out of the most poor materials, so will the modern poet concoct us a most popular poem from the weakest emotions, and the most tiresome platitudes. The only difference is, that the cook would prefer good materials if he could get them, whilst the modern poet will take the bad from choice. As far, however, as the nature of materials goes, those which the two artists work with are the same — *viz*. animals, vegetables, and spirits. It was the practice of Shakespeare and other earlier masters to make us of all these together, mixing them in various proportions. But the moderns have found that it is better and far easier to empty each separately. Thus Mr Swinburne uses very little else but animal matter in the composition of his dishes, which it must be confessed are somewhat unwholesome in consequence, while the late Mr Wordsworth, on the contrary, confined himself almost exclusively to the confection of primrose pudding, and flint soup, flavoured with the lesser-celandine; and only now and then a beggar-boy boiled down in it to give it a colour. The robins are drowned lambs which he was wont to use, when an additional piquancy was needed, were employed so sparingly that they did not destroy in the least the general vegetable tone of his productions; and these form in consequence an unimpeachable lenten diet. It is difficult to know what to say to Mr Tennyson, as the milk and water which his books are composed chiefly, make it almost impossible to discover what was the original nature of the materials he has boiled down in it. Mr Shelley, too, is perhaps somewhat embarrassing to classify; as, though spirits are what he affected most, he made use of a large amount of vegetable matter also. We shall be probably not far wrong in describing his material as a kind of methylated spirits; or pure psychic alcohol, strongly tinctured with the barks of trees, and rendered below proof by a quantity of sea-water. In this division of the poets, however, into animalists, spiritualists, and vegetarians, we must not be discouraged by any such difficulties as these, but must bear in mind that in whatever manner we may neatly classify anything, the exceptions and special cases will always far outnumber those to which our rule applies.

But in fact, at present, mere theory may be set entirely aside: for although in the case of action, the making and adhering to a theory may be the surest guide to inconsistency and absurdity, in poetry these results can be obtained without such aid.

The following recipes, compiled by careful analysis of the best authors, will be found, we trust, efficient guides for the composition of genuine poems. But the tyro must bear always in mind that there is no royal road to anything, and that not even the most explicit directions will make a poet all at once of even the most fatuous, the most sentimental, or the most profane.

Recipes

The following are arranged somewhat in the order in which the student is recommended to begin his efforts. About the more elaborate ones, which come later, he may use his own discretion as to which he will try first; but he must previously have had some training in the simpler compositions, with which we deal before all others. These form as it were a kind of palaestra of folly, a very short training in which will suffice to break down that stiffness and self-respect in the soul, which is so incompatible with modern poetry. Taking, therefore, the silliest and common-est of all kinds of verse, and the one whose sentiments come most readily to hand in vulgar minds, we begin with directions.

HOW TO MAKE AN ORDINARY LOVE POEM

Take two large and tender human hearts, which match one another perfectly. Arrange these close together, but preserve them from actual contact by placing between them some cruel barrier. Wound them both in several places, and insert through the openings thus made a fine stuffing of wild yearnings, hopeless tenderness, and a general admiration for stars. Then completely cover up one heart with a sufficient quantity of chill church-yard mould, which may be garnished according to taste with dark waving weeds or tender violets; and promptly break over it the other heart.

HOW TO MAKE A PATHETIC MARINE POEM

This kind of poem has the advantage of being easily produced, yet being at the same time pleasing, and not unwholesome. As, too, it admits of no variety, the chance of going wrong in it is very small. Take one midnight storm, and one fisherman's family, which, if the poem is to be a real success, should be as large and as hungry as possible, and must contain at least one innocent infant. Place this last in a cradle, with the mother singing over it, being careful that the babe be dreaming of angels, or else smiling sweetly. Stir the father well up in the storm until he disappears. Then get ready immediately a quantity of cruel crawling foam, in which serve up the father directly on his re-appearance, which is sure to take place in an hour or two, in the dull red morning. This done, a charming saline effervescence will take place amongst the remainder of the family. Pile up the agony to suit the palate, and the poem will be ready for perusal.

HOW TO WRITE A POEM LIKE MR TENNYSON

(The following, apart from its intrinsic utility, forms in itself a great literary curiosity, being the original directions from which the Poet Laureate composed the Arthurian idylls)

To compose an epic, some writers instruct us first to catch our hero. As, however, Mr Carlyle is the only person on record who has ever performed this feat, it will be best for the rest of mankind to be content with the nearest approach to a hero available, namely a prig. These animals are very plentiful, and easy to catch, as they delight in being run after. These are however many different kinds, not all equally fit for the present purpose, and amongst which it is very necessary to select the right one. Thus, for instance, there is the scientific and atheistical prig, who may be frequently observed eluding notice between the covers of the 'Westminster Review'; the Anglican prig, who is often caught exposing himself in the 'Guardian'; the Ultramontane prig, who abounds in the 'Dublin Review'; the scholarly prig, who twitters among the leaves in the 'Academy'; and the Evangelical prig, who converts the heathen, and drinks port wine. None of these, and least of all the last, will serve for the central figure, in the present class of poem. The only one entirely suitable is the blameless variety. Take, then, one blameless prig. Set him upright in the middle of a round table, and place beside him a beautiful wife, who cannot abide prigs. Add to these, one married goodly man, and tie the three together in a bundle with a link or two of Destiny. Proceed, next, to surround this group with a large number of men and women of the nineteenth century, in fairy-ball costume, flavoured with a great many possible vices, and a few impossible virtues. Stir these briskly about for two volumes, to the great annoyance of the blameless prig, who is, however, to be kept carefully below swearing-point, for the whole time. If he once boils over into any natural action or exclamation, he is forthwith worthless, and you must get another. Next break the wife's reputation into small pieces, and dust them well over the blameless prig. Then take a few vials of tribulation, and wrath, and empty these generally over the whole ingredients of your poem, and, taking the sword of the heathen, cut into small pieces the greater part of your minor characters. Then wound slightly the head of the blameless prig, remove him suddenly from the table, and keep him in a cool barge for future use.

HOW TO WRITE A POEM LIKE
MR MATTHEW ARNOLD

Take one soulfull of involuntary unbelief, which has been previously well favoured with self-sufficient despair. Add to this one beautiful text of Scripture. Mix these well together, and as soon as ebullition commences grate in finely a few regretful alterations to the New Testament and the lake of Tiberias, one constellation of stars, half-a-dozen allusions to the nineteenth century, one to Goethe, one to Mont Blanc, or the Lake of Geneva, and one also, if possible, to some personal bereavement. Flavour the whole with a mouthful of 'faiths' and 'infinites', and a mixed mouthful of 'passions', 'finites', and 'yearnings'. This class .of poem is concluded usually with some question, about which we have to observe only that it shall be impossible to answer.

HOW TO WRITE A POEM LIKE MR BROWNING

Take a rather coarse view of things in general. In the midst of this, place a man and a woman, her and her ankles, tastefully arranged on a slice of Italy, or the country about Pornic. Cut an opening across the breast of each, until the soul becomes visible, but be very careful that none of the body be lost during the operation. Pour into each breast as much as it will hold of the new strong wine of love; and, for fear they should take cold by exposure, cover them quickly up with a quantity of obscure quotations, a few familiar allusions to an unknown period of history, and a half-destroyed fresco by an early master, varied every now and then with a reference to the tongues and toccatas of a quite-forgotten composer.

If the poem be still intelligible, take a pen and remove carefully all the necessary particles.

HOW TO WRITE A MODERN PRE-RAPHAELITE POEM

Take a packet of fine selected early English, containing no words but such as are obsolete and unintelligible. Pour this into about double the quantity of entirely new English, which must have never been used before, and which you must compose yourself, fresh as it is wanted. Mix these together thoroughly till they assume a colour quite different from any tongue that was ever spoken, and the materials will be ready for use.

Determine the number of stanzas of which your poem shall consist, and select a corresponding number of the most archaic and most peculiar vocabulary, allotting one of these to each stanza; and pour in the other words around them, until the entire poem is filled in.

This kind of composition is usually cast in shapes. These,

though not numerous — amounting in all in something under a dozen — it would take too long to describe minutely here; and a short visit to Mr ---------'s shop in King Street, where they are kept in stock, would explain the whole of them. A favourite one, however, is the following. Take three damozels, dressed in straight night-gowns. Pull out their hair-pins, and let their hair tumble all about their shoulders. A few stars may be sprinkled into this with advantage. Place an aureole about the head of each, and give each a lily in her hand, about half the size of herself. Bend their necks all different ways, and set them in a row before a stone wall, with an appletree between each and some larger flowers at their feet. Trees and flowers of the right sort are very plentiful in church windows. When you have arranged all these objects rightly, take a cast of them in the softest part of your brain, and pour in your word-composition as above described.

This kind of poem is much improved by what is called a burden. This consists of a few jingling words, generally to an archaic character, about which we have only to be careful that they have no reference to the subject of the poem they are to ornament. They are inserted without variation between the stanzas.

In conclusion we would remark to beginners that this sort of composition must be attempted only in a perfectly vacant atmosphere; so that no grains of common-sense may injure the work while in progress.

HOW TO WRITE A NARRATIVE POEM LIKE MR MORRIS

Take about sixty pages-full of the same word-mixture as that described in the preceding, and the dilute it with a double quantity of mild modern Anglo-Saxon. Pour this composition into two vessels of equal size, and into one of these empty a small mythological story. If this does not put your readers to sleep soon enough, add to it the rest of the language, in the remaining vessel.

HOW TO WRITE A SATANIC POEM, LIKE THE LATE LORD BYRON

(*This recipe is inserted for the benefit of those poets who desire to attain what is called originality. This is not only to be got by following some model of a past generation, which has ceased to be made use of by the public at large. We do not however recommend this course, feeling sure that writers in the end will derive far more real satisfaction from producing fashionable, than original verses; which two things it is impossible to do at one and the same time)*

Take a couple of fine deadly sins, and let them hang before your eyes until they become racy. Then take them down, dissect them, and stew them for some time in a solution of weak remorse; after which they are to be devilled with mock-despair.

HOW TO WRITE A PATRIOTIC POEM LIKE MR SWINBURNE

Take one blaspheming patriot, who has been hung [*sic*] or buried for some time, together with the oppressed country belonging to him. Soak these in a quantity of rotten sentiment, till they are completely sodden, and in the meanwhile get ready for an indefinite number of Christian kings and priests. Kick these until they are nearly dead, add copiously broken fragments of the Catholic Church, and mix all together thoroughly. Place them in a heap upon the oppressed country, season plentifully with very coarse expressions, and on the top carefully arrange your patriot, garnished with laurel or with parsley; surround with artificial hopes for the future, which are never meant to be tasted. This kind of poem is worked in verbiage, flavoured with Liberty, the taste of which is much heightened by the introduction of a few high gods, and the game of Fortune. The amount of verbiage which Liberty is capable of flavouring, is peculiarly infinite.

Conclusion

We regret to have to offer this work to the public in the present incomplete state, the whole of that part treating of the most recent section of poetry, *viz.* the blasphemous and the obscene, being entirely wanting. It was found necessary to issue this from an eminent publishing firm in Holywell Street, Strand, where by an unforeseen casualty, the whole of the first edition was seized by the police, and is at present in the hands of the Society for the suppression of Vice. We incline however to trust that this loss will have but little effect; as indecency and profanity are things in which, even to the dullest, external instruction is a luxury, rather than a necessity. Those of our readers, who, either from sense, self-respect, or other circumstances, are in need of special training in these subjects, will find excellent professors of them in any public-house, during the late hours of the evening; where the whole sum and substance of the fieriest school of modern poetry is delivered nightly; needing only a little dressing and flavouring with artificial English to turn it to very excellent verse.

3

Poetesses and Fleshly Poets

(from *M[ary]. A[nn]. Stodart*, Female Writers: Thoughts on Their Proper Sphere, and on Their Powers of Usefulness, *1842*)

The domain of poetry is wide; her power over the human heart immense. It is hers to describe, with truth and force, those objects which are too vast, and those which are too minute for ordinary ken; the former escaping common observation, from the inability of an ordinary eye to take the range of the whole at one view; and the latter, from the delicacy of observation required for their survey. It is hers to express in vigorous and powerful language the workings of the stronger passions of the human heart, when the whole man is convulsed, and when thought and feeling spurn the common words of calm, quiet, every-day life. And it is hers too to embody and give permanence to those delicate, evanescent emotions which pass over the mind like the blush over a maiden's brow, and which can no more be distinguished by the powers of an ordinary mind, than the blending and intermingling of the rainbow units. It is the province of poetry to arouse by her trumpet-call to vigorous action, and to melt by her plaintive warblings to gentle and tender emotion. Sometimes she is found amid scenes of horror and sublimity, hanging over the beetling precipice and listening to the roar of the torrent far, far beneath; at other times she delights to rove amid scenes of rural beauty, watching the sun-beams flickering on the fields, listening to the warbling of the birds, or rejoicing in even the simple little flowerets which spring up beneath her feet; but whether she is amid scenes of sublimity or scenes of beauty, still true to herself, she inspires feelings and sentiments and gives expressions to them. The 'thoughts that voluntary move harmonious numbers' are her gift. When religion takes poetry into her service, the province of the handmaid is yet farther extended, her power amazingly increased. Linked to eternal, immutable truth, how wide is her range, how sweet, how potent is her song! Secret springs of the human heart before untouched, because unknown, are now subject to her thrilling sway. And her sphere of vision is no longer bounded by an earthly horizon. Far, far away, 'beyond this dim spot which men call earth', she soars on the wings of faith and hope, till the harmonies of heaven fall upon her delighted ear, and the splendours of heaven beam upon her raptured eye.

The power of poetry is not confined to those who take rank and precedence as the poets of the land. That would be a cold and an inglorious doctrine.

> Many are poets, who have never penned
> Their inspiration, and perchance the best.[1]

Many unconsciously are poets; thoughts and feelings struggle within, and sometimes flash out in glowing, burning words, marking their path in a line of living light. Poetry is the forcible expression of truth. Far from us and ours to be debasing doctrine that its proper region is fiction. Poetry rejoices in the truth; there it can spread its wings with ease and freedom, unfettered and unimpeded. In the words of a living poet of great and heart-stirring power,

> Song is but the eloquence of truth.[2]

And a mighty, glorious eloquence it is. The monarch seated on his throne bends beneath its power, and the savage, roaming in his wild woods, acknowledges its sway.

Is the hand of poor weak women ever permitted to sweep the living lyre, and to elicit its thrilling tones? The notes are varied; it is a lyre of many strings, an instrument of wider range than any constructed by mortal hand; what tones, what notes vibrate most in unison with woman's heart, and will be most likely, when struck by her hand, to speak to the heart of others?

We cannot doubt the answer. All that is beautiful in form, delicate in sentiment, graceful in action, will form the peculiar province of the gentle powers of woman. O scorn us not! We may not, we cannot 'murmur tales of iron wars', follow the currents of a heady flight; portray with the vivid power of Homeric song, the horrid din of war, the rush of contending warriors, the prancing of the noble steed, the clang, the tumult, the stirring interest of the battle-field — no — but we can do what mightier man would perhaps disdain — we can follow one solitary soldier as he drags his wounded limbs beneath the sheltering hedge; and while we mark his glazing eye, we can read with woman's keenness, the thoughts of wife, children, and home, which are playing around his heart. We may not be able to sustain a strain of high and equal majesty like the bard of Martha,[3] but we can follow out the sorrows of the forsaken Dido, weep over the untimely fate of the warrior-friends, and sympathize with the feminine eagerness of Camilla, as, womanly even in her power, she forgets self-defence and a warrior's duties, in order to seize on the splendid ornaments of an officer in the opposing army [*Aeneid* 11.5.731]. We cannot range through heaven and hell with the fiery wing of our glorious poet Milton; we cannot ascend to the height of great argument, and justify the ways of God to man. No woman could have delineated the character of Satan, so evidently 'not less archangel ruined'; no woman could have tracked the flight of Satan across Chaos; or depicted that mysterious assemblage when the rebel angel stood before 'the anarch old'; but we can imagine that some wonderfully endowed woman *might* have pencilled out some of the light and graceful traits of that beautiful garden of Eden, and the happiness of our first parents, a picture which partakes so eminently of the beautiful as to afford a contrast to the sublimity of the other parts of our wonderful national poem. It is not within our province to dive into the deep recesses of the human heart with that myriad-minded man, our own Shakespeare, and to drag into the open day-light the hidden secrets of the soul. No! but there are light and delicate moments which a woman's pen may express, and which Shakespeare, though unrivalled amid poets for his knowledge of woman's heart, has not even guessed. We have struck on the point where lies the true poetic power of woman, it is in the heart — over the heart — and especially in the peculiarities of her own heart. We have but few remains of the earliest and best Greek poetesses; or her who earned the high title of the Lesbian muse; but those remains, 'more golden than gold' [the words of Sappho herelf, preserved by Demetrius Phalereus], are all breathings from the dearest affections of the heart. The exquisite fragment preserved by Longinus, and known to the English reader, through the translation of Phillips,[4] so praised in the Spectator, is of this class, and describes the strong but silent emotions of the heart, with delicate correctness of touch. A man could no more have written that ode, than he could touch the wing of a butterfly without striking off its plumage. And in the tender and affectionate hymn to Venus, how exquisitely beautiful is every touch! how graceful every line, every word! In perusing it, we cannot feel surprised that critics should hold up Sappho as an example of the beautiful in writing. And this thus illustrates another principle; if it is the part of every woman of cultivated life to admire what is beautiful, it is the part of the woman of genius to express it.

The domain of beauty is indeed peculiarly the sphere of the female poet. We can see the man of high poetic genius delighting in the wide-rolling ocean, as it leaves its yeasty waves, in dark restless might beneath a frowning sky; his soul is strengthened to hold high converse with the elements, and with the spirits which his magician-wand calls forth from the vasty deep. But the poetic power of woman will demand a greater scene; she will have to track the little streamlet, as like a thread of silver it winds along the peaceful vale; or she will watch the light smoke of the peaceful cottage as it gracefully curls above the surrounding trees, and her heart will ponder on what a true-hearted woman ever loves to portray, the kindly charities of home. We can see the poet watching with high exultation the bold and fearless eagle, as in steady grandeur, it rises from the earth and gazes unappalled on the splendours of the noon-tide sun; but woman, gentle woman, will sooner bend over the turtle-dove, admire its beautiful form, its delicate plumage, read the quick glances of its eye, and with responsive readiness give meaning to its tender cooing. The man of poetic genius will gaze perhaps on the old majestic oak, which has for ages, withstood the wintry winds as they careered wildly around; the woman in the meanwhile will stoop to gather the little 'Forget-me-not' that grows in the neighbouring hedge, and as she gazes on the blue-eyed flower, thoughts of meeting and parting, a theme of such potent influence over every human heart, and it may be, of especial interest to the female heart, will crowd over her mind, and perhaps fill her speaking with tears of deep feeling, of fond affection.

Passage 3.2

(from *Edmund Gosse, 'Christina Rossetti' in* Critical Kit-Kats, *1896. Gosse's essay dates from 1882*)

Woman, for some reason which seems to have escaped the philosopher, has never taken a very prominent position in the history of poetry. But she has rarely been absent altogether from any great revival of poetic literature. The example of her total absence which immediately flies to the recollection is the most curious of all. That Shakespeare should have had no female rival, that the age in which music burdened every bough, and in which poets made their appearance in hundreds, should have produced not a solitary authentic poetess, even of the fifth rank, this is curious indeed. But it is as rare as curious, for though women have not taken a very high position on Parnassus, they have seldom thus wholly absented themselves. Even in the iron age of Rome, where the Muse seemed to bring forth none but male children, we find, bound up with the savage verses of Juvenal and Persius, those seventy lines of pure and noble indignation against the brutality of Domitian which alone survive to testify to the genius of Sulpicia.[5]

If that distinguished lady had come down to us in seventy thousand verses instead of seventy lines, would her fame have been greatly augmented? Probably not. So far as we can observe, the strength of the great poet-women has been in their selection. Not a single poetess whose fame is old enough to base a theory upon has survived in copious and versatile numbers. Men like Dryden and Victor Hugo can strike every chord of the lyre, every essay mode and species of the art, and impress us by their bulk and volume. One very gifted and ambitious Englishwoman, Elizabethan Barrett Browning, essayed to do the same. But her success, it must be admitted, grows every day more dubious. Where she strove to be passionate she was often hysterical; a sort of scream spoils the effect of all her full tirades. She remains readable mainly where she is exquisite, and one small volume would suffice to contain her probable bequest to posterity.

It is no new theory that women, in order to succeed in poetry, must be brief, personal, and concentrated. This was recognised by the Greeks themselves. Into that delicious garland of the poets which was woven by Meleager to be hung outside the Gardens of the Hesperides he admits two woman from all the centuries of Hellenic song. Sappho is there, indeed, because 'though her flowers were few, they were all roses', and, almost unseen, a single virginal shoot of the crocus bears the name of Erinna.[6] That was all that womanhood gave of durable poetry to the literature of antiquity. A critic, writing five hundred years after her death, speaks of still hearing the swan-note of Erinna clear above the jangling clatter of the jays, and of still thinking those three hundred hexameter verses sung by a girl of nineteen as lovely as the loveliest of Homer's. Even at the time of the birth of Christ, Erinna's writings consisted of what could be printed on half a dozen pages of this volume. The whole of her extant work, and Sappho's too, could be pressed into a newspaper column. But their fame lives on, and of Sappho, at least, enough survives to prove beyond a shadow of a doubt the lofty inspiration of her genius. She is the type of the woman-poet who exists not by reason of the variety or volume of her work, but by virtues of its intensity, its individuality, its artistic perfection.

At no time was it more necessary to insist on this truth than it is today. The multiplication of books of verse, the hackneyed character of all obvious notation of life and feeling, should, one would fancy, tend to make our poets more exiguous, more concise, more trimly girt. There are few men now for whom the immense flood of writing can be endured without fatigue; few who can hold the trumpet to their lips for hours in the market-place without making a desert around them. Yet there never was a time when the pouring out of verse was less restrained within bounds. Everything that occurs to the poet seems, to-day, to be worth writing down and printing. The result is the neglect of really good and charming work, which misses all effect because it is drowned in stuff that is second- or third-rate. The women who write, in particular, pursued by that commercial fervour which is so curious a feature of our new literary life, and which sits so inelegantly on a female figure, are in a ceaseless hurry to work off and hurry away into oblivion those qualities of their style which might, if seriously and coyly guarded, attract a permanent attention.

Passage 3.3

(from *Robert Buchanan, 'The Fleshly School of Poetry'* in The Contemporary Review, *1871. Buchanan published this review of Dante Gabriel Rossetti's* Poems *(1871) under the pseudonym of Thomas*

Maitland. Buchanan produced an expanded version of this, with new passages referring to the work of Baudelaire, under the same title in 1872. For Rossetti's response, see Passage 3.4. These two documents created the 'Fleshly School' scandal, a complicated affair in which Swinburne's vituperative essay participates — see 'Notes on Poems and Reviews', Passage 3.5. For the circumstances surrounding this hot-tempered row, which, in its confusion, implicated Browning's recently published rewriting of the Don Juan myth, Fifine at the Fair (1872), see Christopher D. Murray, 'D.G. Rossetti, A.C. Swinburne and R.W. Buchanan: The Fleshly School Revisted', Parts 1 and 2, The Bulletin of the John Rylands Library, vol. 65, no. 1 (1982), pp. 206-34, and vol. 65, no. 2 (1983), pp. 176-207. For an altogether different approach to Rossetti's aesthetics, compare the review by Pater, Passage 3.7)

If, on the occasion of any public performance of Shakespeare's great tragedy, the actors who perform the parts of Rosencranz and Guildenstern were, by a preconcerted arrangement and by means of what is technically known as 'gagging', to make themselves fully as prominent as the leading character, and to indulge in soliloquies and business strictly belonging to Hamlet himself, the result would be, to say the least of it, astonishing; yet a very similar effect is produced on the unprejudiced mind when the 'walking gentlemen' of the fleshly school of poetry, who bear precisely the same relation to Tennyson as Rosencranz and Guildenstern do to the Prince of Denmark in the play, obtrude their lesser identities and parade their smaller idiosyncrasies in the front rank of leading performers. In their own place, the gentlemen are interesting and useful. Pursuing still the theatrical analogy, the present drama of poetry may be cast as follows: Mr Tennyson supporting the part of Hamlet, Mr Matthew Arnold that of Horatio, Mr [Philip James] Bailey that of Voltimand, Mr Buchanan that of Cornelius, Messrs Swinburne and Morris the parts of Rosencranz and Guildenstern, Mr Rossetti that of Osric, and Mr Robert Lytton that of 'A Gentleman'. It will be seen that we have left no place for Mr Browning, who may be said, however, to play the leading character in his own peculiar fashion on alternate nights.

This may seem a frivolous and inadequate way of opening our remarks on a school of verse-writers which some people regard as possessing merits; but in good truth, it is scarcely possible to discuss with any seriousness the pretensions with which foolish friends and small critics have surrounded the fleshly school,

which in spite of its spasmodic ramifications in the erotic directions, is merely one of the many sub-Tennysonian schools
expanded to supernatural dimensions, and endeavouring by
affectations of its own to overshadow its connection with the great
original. In the sweep of one single poem, the weird and doubtful
'Vivien' [1859], Mr Tennyson has concentrated all the epicene
force which, wearisomely expanded, constitutes the characteristic
of the writers at present under consideration; and if in 'Vivien' he
has indicated for them the bounds of sensualism in art, he has in
'Maud' [1855], in the dramatic person of the hero, afforded
distinct precedent for the hysteric tone and overloaded style
which is now so familiar to readers of Mr Swinburne. The fleshliness of 'Vivien' may indeed be described as the distinct quality
held in common by all the members of the last sub-Tennysonian
school, and it is a quality which becomes unwholesome when
there is no moral or intellectual quality to temper and control it.
Fully conscious of this themselves, the fleshly gentlemen have
bound themselves by solemn league and covenant to extol
fleshliness as the distinct and supreme end of poetic and pictorial
art; to aver that poetic expression is greater than poetic thought,
and by inference that the body is greater than the soul, and
sound superior to sense; and that the poet, properly to develop
his poetic faculty, must be an intellectual hermaphrodite, to
whom the very facts of day and night are lost in a whirl of
aesthetic terminology. After Mr Tennyson has probed the depths
of modern speculation in a series of commanding moods, all right
and interesting in him as the reigning personage, the walking
gentlemen, knowing that something of the sort is expected from
all leading performers, bare their roseate bosoms, and aver that
they are creedless; the only possible question here being, if any
disinherited person cares twopence whether Rosencranz,
Guildenstern, and Osric are creedless or not — their self-
revelation on that score being so perfectly gratuitous? But having
gone so far, it was and is too late to retreat. Rosencranz,
Guildenstern, and Osric finding it impossible to risk an
individual bid for the leading business, have arranged all to play
leading business together, and mutually to praise, extol, and
imitate each other; and although by these measures they have
fairly earned for themselves the title of the Mutual Admiration
School, they have in a great measure succeeded in their object —
to the general stupefaction of a British audience. It is time,
therefore, to ascertain whether any of these gentlemen has

actually in himself the making of a leading performer. When the *Athenaeum* — once more cautious in such matters — advertised nearly every week some interesting particular about Mr Swinburne's health, Mr Morris's holiday making, or Mr Rossetti's genealogy, varied with such startling statements as 'We are informed that Mr Swinburne dashed off his noble ode *at a sitting*', or 'Mr Swinburne's songs have already reached a second edition', or 'Good poetry seems to be in demand; the first edition of Mr [Arthur] O'Shaughnessy's poems is exhausted',[7] when the *Academy* informed us that 'During the past year or two Mr Swinburne has written several novels' (!), and that some review or other is to be praised for giving Mr Rossetti's poems 'the attentive study which they demand' — when we read these things we might or might not know pretty well how and where they originated; but to a provincial eye, perhaps, the whole thing really looked like a leading business. It would be scarcely worth while, however, to inquire into the pretensions of the writers on merely literary grounds, because sooner or later all literature finds its own level, whatever criticism may say or do in the matter; but it unfortunately happens in the present case that the fleshly school of verse-writers are, so to speak, public offenders, because they are diligently spreading the seeds of disease broadcast wherever they are read and understood. Their complaint too is catching, and carries off many young persons. What the complaint is, and how it works, may be seen on a very slight examination of the workds of Mr Dante Gabriel Rossetti, to whom we shall confine our attention in the present article.

Mr Rossetti has been known for many years as a painter of exceptional powers, who, for reasons best known to himself, has shrunk from publicly exhibiting his pictures, and from allowing anything like a popular estimate to be formed of their qualities. He belongs, or is said to belong, to the so-called Pre-Raphaelite school, a school which is generally considered to exhibit much genius for colour, and great indifference to perspective. It would be unfair to judge the painter by the glimpses we have had of his works, or by the photographs which are sold of the principal paintings. Judged by the photographs, he is an artist who conceives unpleasantly, and draws ill. Like Mr Simeon Solomon,[8] however, with whom he seems to have many points in common, he is distinctively a colourist, and of his capabilities in colour we cannot speak, though we should guess that they are great; for if there is any good quality by which his poems are specially marked, it is a great sensitiveness to hues and tints as conveyed in poetic epithet. These qualities, which impress the casual spectator of the photographs from his pictures, are to be found abundantly among his verses. There is the same thinness and transparence of design, the same combination of the simple and the grotesque, the same morbid deviation from unhealthy forms of life, the same sense of weary, wasting, yet exquisite sensuality; nothing virile, nothing tender, nothing completely sane; a superfluity of extreme sensibility, a delight in beautiful forms, hues, and tints, and a deep-seated indifference to all the agitating forces and agencies, all tumultuous griefs and sorrows, all the thunderous stress of life, and all the straining storm of speculation. Mr Morris is often pure, fresh, and wholesome as his own great model; Mr Swinburne startles us more than once by some fine flash of insight; but the mind of Mr Rossetti is like a glassy mere, broken only by the dive of some water-bird or the hum of winged insects, and brooded over by an atmosphere of insufferable closeness, with a light blue sky above it, sultry depths mirrored within it, and a surface so thickly sown with water-lilies that it retains its glassy smoothness even in the strongest wind. Judged relatively to his poetic associates, Mr Rossetti must be pronounced inferior to either. He cannot tell a pleasant story like Mr Morris, nor forge alliterative thunderbolts like Mr Swinburne. It must be conceded, nevertheless, that he is neither so glibly imitative as the one, nor so transcendently superficial as the other.

Although he has been known for many years as a poet as well as a painter — as a painter and poet idolized by his own family and personal associates — and although he has once or twice appeared in print as a contributor to magazines Mr Rossetti did not formally appeal to the public until rather more than a year ago, when he published a copious volume of poems, with the announcement that the book, although it contained pieces composed at intervals during a period of many years, 'included nothing which the author believes to be immature'. This work was inscribed to his brother, Mr William Rossetti, who, having written much both in poetry and criticism, will perhaps be known to bibliographers as the editor of the worst edition of Shelley which has yet seen the light. No sooner had the work appeared than the chorus of eulogy began. 'The book is satisfactory from end to end', wrote Mr Morris in the *Academy*; 'I think these lyrics, with all their other merits, the most complete of their time; nor do I know what lyrics of any time are to be called *great*, if we are to deny the title to these.' On the same subject, Mr Swinburne went into a hysteria of admiration: 'golden affluence', 'jewel-coloured words', 'chastity of form', 'harmonious nakedness', 'consummate fleshly sculpture', and so on in Mr Swinburne's well-known manner when reviewing his friends.[9] Other critics, with a singular similarity of phrase, followed suit. Strange to say, moreover, no one accused Mr Rossetti of naughtiness. What had been heinous in Mr Swinburne was majestic exquisiteness in Mr Rossetti. Yet we question if there is anything unfortunate in 'Poems and Ballads' quite so questionable on the score of thorough nastiness as many pieces in Mr Rossetti's collection. Mr Swinburne was wilder, more outrageous, more blasphemous, and his subjects were more atrocious in themselves; yet the hysterical tone slew the animalism, the furiousness of either lowered the sensation; and the first feeling of disgust in such themes as 'Laus Veneris' and 'Anactoria', faded away with comic amazement. It was only a little mad boy letting off squibs, not a great strong man, who might be really dangerous to society. 'I *will* be naughty!' screamed the little boy; but, after all, what did it matter? It is quite different, however, when a grown man with self-control and easy audacity of actual experience, comes forward to chronicle his amorous sensations, and, first proclaiming in a loud voice his literary maturity, and consequent responsibility, shamelessly prints and publishes a piece of writing as the sonnet on 'Nuptial Sleep' [1870]:

> *At length their long kiss severed, with sweet smart:*
> *And as the last slow sudden drops are shed*
> *From sparkling eaves when all the storm has fled,*
> *So singly flagged the pulses of each heart.*
> *Their bosoms sundered, with the opening start*
> *Of married flowers to either side outspread*
> *From the knit stem; yet still their mouths, burnt red,*
> *Fawned on each other where they lay apart.*

Sleep sank them lower than the tide of dreams,
    And their dreams watched them sink, and slid away.
Slowly their souls swam up again, through gleams
    Of watered light and dull drowned waifs of day;
Till from some wonder of new woods and streams
    He woke, and wondered more: for there she lay.

This, then, is 'the golden affluence of words, the firm outline, the justice and chastity of form'. Here is a full-grown man, presumably intelligent and cultivated, putting on record for other full-grown men to read, the most secret mysteries of sexual connection, and that with so sickening a desire to reproduce the sensual mood, as careful a choice of epithet to convey mere animal sensations, that we surely shudder at the shameless nakedness. We are no purists in such matters. We hold the sensual part of our nature to be as holy as the spiritual or intellectual part, and we believe that such things must find their equivalent in all; but it is neither poetic, nor manly, nor even human to obtrude such things as the themes of such poems. It is simply nasty. Nasty as it is, we are very mistaken if many readers do not think it nice. English society of one kind purchases the *Day's Doings*.[10] English society of another kind goes into ecstasy over Mr Solomon's pictures — pretty pieces of mortality, such as 'Love dying by the breath of Lust'. There is not much to choose between the two objects of admiration, except that painters like Mr Solomon lend actual genius to worthless subjects, and thereby produce veritable monsters — like the lovely devils that danced round St Anthony. Mr Rossetti owes his so-called success to the same causes. In poems like 'Nuptial Sleep', the man who is too sensitive to exhibit his pictures, and so modest that it takes him years to make up his mind to publish his poems, parades his private sensations before a coarse public, and is gratified by their applause.

Passage 3.4

(*Dante Gabriel Rossetti, 'The Stealthy School of Criticism', The* Athenaeum, *1871. This is a reply to Robert Buchanan's article, 'The Fleshly School of Poetry', Passage 3.3, published pseudonymously in the* Contemporary Review *in late 1870. The question of Buchanan's authorship was raised by Sidney Colvin in the pages of the* Athenaeum. *There was considerable confusion on this matter. Much of Rossetti's article is given over to a discussion of the hypocrisy in Buchanan's use of a* nom de plume *when the issue of authorial 'sincerity' is at stake in the relentless attack on the 'fleshly school'. It is for this reason that Rossetti refers to the strategies of Buchanan and the publishers of the* Contemporary Review, *Strahan, as 'stealthy'. Rossetti was vindicated when the* Athenaeum *printed two letters by Strahan and Buchanan which contradicted one another on the issue of authorship. Strahan declared that*

*Buchanan was not the author. Buchanan, however, confessed that the
article was his work. Unfortunately, Strahan and Buchanan did not
consult each other when writing to the* Athenaeum. *These letters were
placed at the close of Rossetti's article and are reprinted here*)

Your paragraph, a fortnight ago, relating to the pseudonymous
authorship of an article, violently assailing myself and other
writers of poetry, in the *Contemporary Review* for October last,
reveals a species of critical masquerade which I have expressed in
the heading given to this letter. Since then, Mr Sidney Colvin's
note,[11] qualifying the report that he intends to 'answer' that
article, has appeared in your pages; and my own view as to the
absolute forfeit, under such conditions, of all claim to honourable
reply, is precisely the same as Mr Colvin's. For here a critical
organ, professedly adopting the principle of open signature,
would seem, in reality, to assert (by silent practice, however, not
by enunciation), that if the anonymous in criticism was — as
itself originally inculcated — by an early caterpillar stage, the
nominate too is found to be no better than a homely transitional
chrysalis, and that the ultimate butterfly for a critic who likes to
sport in sunlight and yet to elude the grasp, is after all the
pseudonymous. But, indeed, what I may call the 'Siamese' aspect
of the entertainment provided by the *review* will elicit but one
verdict. Yet I may, perhaps, as the individual chiefly attacked, be
excused for asking your assistance now in giving a specific denial to
specific charges which, if unrefuted, may still continue, in spite of
their author's strategic *fiasco*, to serve his purpose against me to
some extent.

The primary accusation, on which this writer grounds all the
rest, seems to be that others and myself 'extol fleshliness as the
distinct and supreme end of poetic and pictorial art; aver that
poetic expression is greater than poetic thought; and, by inference, that the body is greater than the soul, and sound superior
to sense'. As my own writings are alone formally dealt with in the
article, I shall confine my answer to myself; and this must first
take unavoidably the form of a challenge to prove so broad a
statement. It is true, some fragmentary pretence at proof is put
here and there throughout the attack, and thus far an opportunity
is given of contesting the assertion.

A Sonnet, entitled 'Nuptial Sleep' is quoted and abused at
page 338 of the *Review*, and is there dwelt upon as a 'whole
poem', describing merely 'animal sensations'. It is no more a

whole poem, than is any single stanza of any poem throughout the book. The poem, written chiefly in sonnets, and of which this is one sonnet-stanza, is entitled 'The House of Life'; and even in my first published instalment of the whole work (as contained in the volume under notice) ample evidence is included that no such passing phase of description as the one headed 'Nuptial Sleep' could possibly be put forward by the author of 'The House of Life' as his own representative view of the subject of love. In proof of this, I will direct attention (among the love-sonnets of this poem) to Nos 2, 8, 11, 17, 28, and more especially 13, which, indeed, I had better print here.

LOVE-SWEETNESS

Sweet dimness of her loosened hair's downfall
   About thy face; her sweet hands round thy head
   In gracious fostering union garlanded;
Her tremulous smiles; her glances' sweet recall
Of love; her murmuring sighs memorial;
   Her mouth's culled sweetness by thy kisses shed
   On cheeks and neck and eyelids, and so led
Back to her mouth which answers there for all: —

What sweeter than these things, except the thing
   In lacking which all these would lose their sweet: —
   The confident heart's still fervour: the swift beat
And soft subsidence of the spirit's wing,
   Then when it feels, in cloud-girt wayfaring,
   The breath of kindred plumes against its feet?

Any reader may bring any artistic charge he pleases against the above sonnet; but one charge it would be impossible to maintain against the writer of the series in which it occurs, and that is, the wish on his part to assert that the body is greater than the soul. For here all the passionate and just delights of the body are declared — somewhat figuratively, it is true, but unmistakably — to be as naught if not ennobled by the concurrence of the soul at all times. Moreover, nearly one half of this series of sonnets has nothing to do with love, but treats of quite other life-influences. I would defy any one to couple with fair quotation of Sonnets 29, 30, 31, 39, 40, 41, 43, or others, to slander that their author was not impressed, like all other thinking men, with the responsibilities and higher mysteries of life; while Sonnets 35, 36, and 37, entitled 'The Choice', sum up the general view taken up in a manner only to be evaded by conscious insincerity. Thus much for 'The House of Life', of which the sonnet 'Nuptial Sleep' is one stanza, embodying, for its small constituent share, a beauty of natural universal function, only to be reprobated in art if dwelt on (as I have shown that it is not here) to the exclusion of those other highest things of which it is the harmonious concomitant.

At page 342, an attempt is made to stigmatise four short quotations as being specially 'my own property', that is, (for the context shows the meaning), as being grossly sensual; though all guiding reference to any precise page or poem in my book is avoided here. The first of these unspecified quotations is from the 'Last Confession', and is the description referring to the harlot's laugh, the hideous character of which, together with its real or imagined resemblance to the laugh heard afterwards from the lips of the one long cherished as an ideal, is the immediate cause which makes the maddened hero of the poem a murderer. Assailants may say what they please; but no poet or poetic reader will blame me for making the incident recorded in these lines as repulsive to the readers as it was to the hearer and beholder. Without this, the chain of motive and result would remain obviously incomplete. Observe also that these are but seven lines in a poem of some five hundred, not one other of which could be classed with them.

A second quotation gives the last two lines *only* of the following sonnet, which is the first of four sonnets in 'The House of Life' jointly entitled 'Willowwood': —

I sat with Love upon a woodside well,
    Leaning across the water, I and he;
    Nor ever did he speak nor looked at me,
But touched his lute wherein was audible
The certain secret thing he had to tell:
    Only our mirrored eyes met silently
    In the low wave: and that sound seemed to be
The passionate voice I knew; and my tears fell.

And at their fall, his eyes beneath grew hers;
And with his foot and with his white wing-feathers
    He swept the spring that watered my heart's drouth,
Then the dark ripples spread to waving hair,

> And as I stooped, his own lips rising there
> Bubbled with brimming kisses at my mouth.

The critic has quoted (as I said) only the last two lines, and he
has italicised the second as something unbearable and ridiculous. Of course the inference would be that this really was my
own absurd bubble-and-squeak notion of an actual kiss. The
reader will perceive at once, from the whole sonnet transcribed
above, how untrue such an inference would be. The sonnet
describes a dream of divided love momentarily re-united by the
longing fancy; and in the imagery of the dream, the face of the
beloved rises through deep dark waters to kiss the lover. Thus the
phrase, 'Bubbled with brimming kisses', &c, bears purely on the
special symbolism employed, and from that point of view will be
found, I believe, perfectly simple and just.

A third quotation is from 'Eden Bower', and says

> What more prize than love to impel thee?
> Grip and lip my limbs as I tell thee!

Here again no reference is given, and naturally the reader would
suppose that a human embrace is described. The embrace, on
the contrary, is that of a fabled snake-woman and a snake. It
would be possible still, no doubt, to object on other grounds to
this conception; but the ground inferred and relied on for full
effect by the critic is none the less an absolute misrepresentation.
These three extracts, it will be admitted, are virtually, though not
verbally, garbled with malicious intention; and the same is the
case, as I have shown, with the sonnet called 'Nuptial Sleep'
when purposely treated as a 'whole poem'.

The last of the four quotations grouped by the critic as
conclusive examples, consists of two lines from 'Jenny'. Neither
some thirteen years ago, when I wrote this poem, nor last year
when I published it, did I fail to foresee impending charges of
recklessness and aggressiveness, or to perceive that even some
among those who could really *read* the poem and acquit me on
these grounds, might still hold that thought in it had better have
dispensed with the situation that serves it for framework. Nor did
I omit to consider how far a treatment from without might here
be possible. But the motive powers of art reverse the requirement
of science, and demand first of all an *inner* standing-point. The
heart of such a mystery as this must be plucked from the very

world in which it beats or bleeds; and the beauty and pity, the self-questionings and all-questionings which it brings with it, can come with full force only from the mouth of one alive to its whole appeal, such as the speaker put forward in the poem, — that is, of a young and thoughtful man of the world. To such a speaker, many half-cynical revulsions of feeling and reverie, and a recurrent presence of the impressions of beauty (however artificial) which first brought him within such a circle of influence, would be inevitable features of the dramatic relation portrayed. Here again I can give the lie, in hearing of honest readers, the base or trivial ideas which my critic labours to connect with the poem. There is another little charge, however, which this minstrel in mufti brings against 'Jenny', namely, one of plagiarism from that very poetic self of which his tutelary prose does but enshroud for the moment. The question can, fortunately, be settled with ease by others who have read my critic's poems; and thus I need the less regret that, not happening myself to be in that position, I must be content to rank with those who cannot pretend to an opinion on the subject.

It would be humiliating, need one come to serious detail, to have to refute such an accusation as that of 'binding oneself by solemn league and covenant to extol fleshliness as the supreme end of poetic and pictorial art'; and one cannot but feel that here every one will think allowable merely to pass by with a smile the foolish fellow who has brought a charge thus framed against any reasonable man. Indeed, what I have said already is substantially enough to refute it, even did I not feel sure that a fair balance of my poetry must, of itself, do so in the eyes of every candid reader. I say nothing of my pictures; but those who know them will laugh at the idea. That I may, nevertheless, take a wider view than some poets or critics, of how much, in the material conditions absolutely given to man to deal with as distinct from his spiritual aspirations, is admissable within the limits of Art, — this, I say, is possible enough; nor do I wish to shrink from such responsibility. But to state that I do so to the ignoring or overshadowing of spiritual beauty, is an absolute falsehood, impossible to be put forward except in the indulgence of prejudice and rancour.

I have selected, amid much railing on my critic's part, what seemed the most representative indictment against me, and have, so far, answered it. Its remaining clauses set forth how others and myself 'aver that poetic expression is greater than poetic thought ... and sound superior to sense' — an accusation I elsewhere observe, expressed by saying that we 'wish to create form for its own sake'. If writers of verse are to be listened to in such arrangement of each other, it might be quite competent to me to prove, from the works of my friends in question, that no such thing is the case with them; but my present function is to confine myself to my own defence. This, again, it is difficult to do quite seriously. It is no part of my undertaking to dispute the verdict of any 'contemporary', however contemptuous or contemptible, on my own measure of executive success; but the accusation cited above is not against the poetic value of a certain work, but against its primary and (by assumption) its admitted aim. And to this I must reply that so far, assuredly, not even Shakespeare himself could desire more arduous human tragedy for development in Art than belongs to the themes I venture to embody, however incalculably higher might be his power of dealing with them. What more inspiring for poetic effort than the terrible Love turned to Hate, — perhaps the deadliest of all passion-woven complexities, — which is the theme of 'Sister Helen', and, in a more fantastic form, of 'Eden Bower', — the surroundings of both poems being the mere machinery of a central universal meaning? What, again, more so than the savage penalty exacted for a lost ideal, as expressed in the 'Last Confession'; — than the outraged love for man and burning compensations in art and memory of 'Dante at Verona'; — than the baffling problems which the face of 'Jenny' conjures up; — or than the analysis of passion and feeling attempted in 'The House of Life', and others among the more purely lyrical poems? I speak here, as does my critic in the clause adduced, of *aim* not of *achievement*; and so far, the mere summary is instantly subversive of the preposterous imputation. To assert that the poet whose matter is such as this aims chiefly at 'creating form for its own sake', is, in fact, almost an ingenuous kind of dishonesty; for surely it delivers up the asserter at once, bound hand and foot, to the tender mercies of contradictory proof. Yet this may fairly be taken as an example of the spirit in which a constant effort is here made against me to appeal to those who either are ignorant of what I write, or else belong to the large class too easily influenced by an assumption of authority in addressing them. The false name appended to the article must, as is evident, aid this position vastly; for who, after all, would not be apt to laugh at seeing one poet confessed come forward as aggressor against another in the field of criticism?

It would not be worth while to lose time and patience in

noticing how the system of misrepresentation is carried into points of artistic detail — giving us, for example, such statements as that the burthen employed in the ballad of 'Sister Helen' 'is repeated with little or no alteration through thirty-four verses', whereas the fact is, that the alteration of it in every verse is the very scheme of the poem. But these are minor matters quite thrown into the shade by the critic's more daring sallies. In addition to the class of attack I have answered above, the article contains, of course, an immense amount of personal paltriness; as, for instance, attributions of my work to this, that, or the other absurd derivative source; or again, pure nonsense (which can have no real meaning even to the writer) about 'one art getting hold of another, and imposing on it its conditions and limitations'; or, indeed, what not besides? However, to such antics as this, no more attention is possible than that which Virgil enjoined Dante to bestow on the meaner phenomena of his pilgrimage.

Thus far, then, let me thank you for the opportunity afforded me to join issue with the Stealthy School of Criticism. As for any literary justice to be done on this particular Mr Robert-Thomas, I will merely ask the reader whether, once identified, he does not become manifestly his own best 'sworn tormentor'? For who will then fail to discern all the palpitations which preceded his final resolve in the great question whether to be or not to be his acknowledged self when he became an assailant? And yet this is he who, behind his mask, ventures to charge another with 'bad blood', with 'insincerity', and the rest of it (and that where poetic fancies are alone in question); while every word on his tongue is covert rancour, and every stroke from his pen perversion of truth. Yet, after all, there is nothing wonderful in the lengths to which a fretful poet-critic will carry such grudges as he may bear, while publisher and editor can both be found who are willing to consider such means admissible, even to the clear subversion of first professed tenets in the *Review* which they conduct.

In many phases of outward nature, the principle of chaff and grain holds good, — the base enveloping the precious continually; but an untruth was never yet the husk of a truth. Thresh and riddle and winnow it as you may, — let it fly in shreds to the four winds, — falsehood only will be that which flies and that which stays. And thus the sheath of deceit which this pseudonymous undertaking presents at the outset insures in fact what will be found to be its real character to the core.

56 Ludgate Hill, Dec. 5, 1871

In your last issue you associate the name of Mr Robert Buchanan with the article 'The Fleshly School of Poetry', by Thomas Maitland, in a recent number of the *Contemporary Review*. You might with equal propriety associate with the article the name of Mr Robert Browning, or of Mr Robert Lytton, or of any other Robert.

Strahan & Co.

Russell Square, Dec. 12, 1871

I cannot reply to the insolence of Mr 'Sidney Colvin', whoever he is. My business is to answer the charge implied in the paragraph you published ten days ago, accusing me of having criticized Mr D.G. Rossetti under a *nom de plume*. I certainly wrote the article on 'The Fleshly School of Poetry', but I had nothing to do with the signature. Mr Strahan, publisher of the *Contemporary Review*, can corroborate me thus far, as he is best aware of the inadvertence which led to the suppression of my own name.

Permit to say further that, although I should have preferred not to resuscitate so slight a thing, I have now requested Mr Strahan to republish the criticism, with many additions but no material alterations, and with my name on the title-page. The grave responsibility of not agreeing with Mr Rossetti's friends as to the merits of his poetry, will be transferred, with all fitting publicity, to my shoulders.

Robert Buchanan

[Note by the editor of the *Athenaeum*.] Mr Buchanan's letter is an edifying commentary on Messrs Strahan's. Messrs Strahan apparently think that it is a matter of no importance whether signatures are correct or not, and that Mr Browning had as much to do with the article as Mr Buchanan. Mr Buchanan seems equally indifferent, but he now claims the critique as his. It is a pity the publishers of the Contemporary Review should be in such uncertainty about the authorship of the articles in that magazine. It may be only a matter of taste, but we prefer, if we are reading an article written by Mr Buchanan, that it should be signed by him, especially when he praises his own poems; and that little 'inadvertencies' of this kind should not be left uncorrected till the public find them out.

Passage 3.5

(from *Algernon Charles Swinburne, 'Notes on Poems and Reviews',
1866. Swinburne's* Poems and Ballads *caused much controversy when
they appeared in 1866. Most reviewers were outraged by Swinburne's erotic
interests. Here, Swinburne replies to his assailants by providing a commentary on three poems which were deemed particularly shocking: 'Anactoria',
'Dolores' and 'The Garden of Proserpine'. The following passage picks up
this discussion by vindicating another controversial poem, 'Faustine'.
Swinburne's polemic should be read in the light of the 'Fleshly School'
scandal surrounding the work of Rossetti: Passages 3.3 and 3.4)*

These poems thus disposed of are (I am told) those which have
given most offence and scandal to the venal virtue of journalists.
As I have not to review my reviewers, I need not be at pains to
relate at length every wilful error or conscious lie which a
workman that was inclined may drag into light. To me, as to all
others who may read what I write, the whole matter must
continue to seem too pitiable and trivial to waste a word or
thought on it which we can help wasting. But having begun this
task, I will add yet a word or two of annotation. I have heard that
even the little poem of *Faustine* had been to some readers a thing
to make the scalp creep and the blood freeze. It was issued with
no such intent. Nor do I remember that any man's voice or heel
was lifted against it when it first appeared, a new-born and virgin
poem, in the *Spectator* newspaper for 1862. Virtue, it would seem,
had shot suprisingly in the space of four years or less — a rank
and rapid growth, barren of blossom and rotten at the root.
Faustine is the reverie of a man gazing on the bitter and vicious
loveliness of a face as common and as cheap as the morality of the
reviewers, and dreaming of past lives in which this fair face may
have held a nobler or fitter station; the imperial profile may have
been Faustina's, the thirsty lips a Maenad's, when first she learnt
to drink blood or wine, to waste the loves and ruin the lives of
men; through Greece and again through Rome she may have
passed with the same face which now comes before us dishonoured and discrowned. Whatever of merit or demerit there
may be in the verses, the idea that gives them such life as they
have is simple enough: the transmigration of a single soul,
doomed as though by accident from the first to all evil and no
good, through many ages and forms, but clad always in the same
type of fleshly beauty. The chance which suggested to me this

poem was one which may happen any day to any man — the sudden sight of a living face which recalled the well-known likeness of another dead for centuries: in this instance, the noble and faultless type of the elder Faustina, as seen in coin and bust. Out of that casual glimpse and sudden recollection these verses sprang and grew.

Of the poem in which I have attempted once more to embody the legend of Venus and her knight, I need say only that my first aim was to rehandle the old story in a new fashion. To me it seemed that the tragedy began with the knight's return to Venus — began at the point which hitherto it seemed to have left off. The immortal agony of a man lost after all repentance — cast down from fearless hope into fearful despair — believing in Christ and bound to Venus — desirous of penitential pain, and damned to joyless pleasure — this, in my eyes, was the kernel and nucleus of a myth comparable only to that of the foolish virgins, and bearing the same burden. The tragic touch of the story is this: that the knight who has renounced Christ believes in him; the lover who has embraced Venus disbelieves in her. Vainly and in despair would he make the best of that which is the worst — vainly remonstrate with God, and argue on the side he would fain desert. Once accept or admit the least admixture of pagan worship, or of modern thought, and the whole story collapses into froth and smoke. It was not till my poem was completed that I received from the hands of its author the admirable pamphlet of Charles Baudelaire on Wagner's *Tannhäuser* [1861]. If anyone desires to see, expressed in better words that I can command, the conception of the medieval Venus which it was my aim to put into verse, let him turn to the magnificent passage in which M Baudelaire describes the fallen goddess, grown diabolic among ages that would not accept her as divine. In another point, as I then found, I concur with the great musician and his great panegyrist. I have made Venus the one love of her knight's whole life, as Mary Stuart of Chastelard's;[12] I have sent him, poet and soldier, fresh to her fierce embrace. Thus only both legend and symbol appear to me noble and significant. Light loves and harmless errors must not touch the elect of heaven and hell. The queen of evil, the lady of lust, will endure no rival but God; and when the vicar of God rejects him, to her only can he return to abide the day of judgement in weariness and sorrow and fear.

These poems do not seem to me condemnable, unless it be on

the ground of bad verse; and to any charge of that kind I should of course be as unable as reluctant to reply. But I certainly was less prepared to hear the batteries of virtue open fire in another quarter. Sculpture I knew was dead art, buried centuries deep out of sight, with no angel keeping watch over its sepulchre; its very grave-clothes divided by wrangling and impotent sectaries, and no chance anywhere visible of a resurrection. I knew that belief in the body was the secret of sculpture, and that a past age of ascetics could no more attempt or attain it than the present age of hypocrites; I knew that modern moralities and recent religions were, if possible, more averse and alien to this purely physical and pagan art than to the others; but how far averse I did not know. There is nothing lovelier, as there is nothing more famous, in later Hellenic art, than the statue of Hermaphroditus. No one would compare it with the greatest works of Greek sculpture. No one would lift Keats on a level with Shakespeare. But the Fates have allowed us to possess at once Othello and Hyperion, Theseus and Hermaphroditus. At Paris, at Florence, at Naples, the delicate divinity of this work has always drawn towards it the eyes of artists and poets. [Witness Shelley's version: —

> A sexless thing it was, and in its growth
>   It seemed to have developed no defect
> Of either sex, yet all the grace of both;
>   In gentleness and strength its limbs were decked;
> The bosom lightly swelled with its full youth,
>   The countenance was such as might select
> Some artist, that his skill should never die,
> Imaging forth such perfect purity.
>   *The Witch of Atlas*, 1820 (329-36)]

But Shelley had not studied purity in the school of reviewers. It is well for us that we have teachers able to enlighten our darkness, or Heaven knows into what error such as he, or such as I, might fall. We might even, in time, come to think it possible to enjoy the naked beauty of a statue or a picture without any virtuous vision behind it of a filthy fancy: which would be immoral. A creature at once foul and dull enough to extract from a sight so lovely, from a thing so noble, the faintest, the most fleeting idea of impurity, must be, and must remain, below comprehension and below remark. It is incredible that the meanest of men should derive from it any other than the sense of high and grateful pleasure.

Odour and colour and music are not more tender or more pure. How favourite and frequent a vision among the Greeks was this of the union of sexes in one body of perfect beauty, none need be told. In Plato the legend has fallen into a form coarse, hard, and absurd. The theory of God splitting in two the double archetype of man and woman, the original hermaphrodite which had to get itself bisected into female and male, is repulsive and ridiculous enough. But the idea thus incarnate, literal or symbolic, is merely beautiful. I am not the first who has translated into written verse this sculptured poem: another before me, as he says, has more than once 'caressed it with a sculptor's love'. It is, indeed, among statues as a lyric among tragedies; it stands below the Niobe as Simonides below Aeschylus, as Correggio beneath Titian.[13] The sad and subtle moral of this myth, which I have desired to indicate in verse, is that perfection once attained on all sides is a thing thenceforward barren of use and fruit; whereas the divided beauty of separate woman and man — a thing inferior and imperfect — can serve all turns of life. Ideal beauty, like ideal genius, dwells apart, as though by compulsion; supremacy is solitude. But leaving this symbolic side of the matter, I cannot see why this status should not be the text for yet another poem. Treated in the grave and chaste manner as a serious 'thing of beauty', to be for ever applauded and enjoyed, it can give no offence but to the purblind and the prurient. For neither of these classes have I ever written or will I ever write. 'Loathsome and abominable' and 'full of unspeakable foulnesses' must be that man's mind who could here discern evil; unclean and inhuman the animal which could suck from this mystical rose of ancient loveliness the foul and rancid juices of an obscene fancy. It were a scavenger's office to descend with torch or spade into such depths of mental sewerage, to plunge or peer into subterranean sloughs of mind impossible alike to enlighten or to cleanse.

I have now gone over the poems which, as I hear, have incurred most blame; whether deservedly or not, I have shown. For the terms in which certain critics have clothed their sentiments I bear them no ill-will: they are welcome for me to write unmolested, as long as they keep to simple ribaldry. I hope it gives them amusement; I presume it brings them profit; I know it does not affect me. Absolute falsehood may, if it be worthwhile, draw down contradiction and disproof; but the mere calling of bad names is a child's trick, for which the small fry of the press should have a child's correction at the hands of able editors;

standing as these gentlemen ought to do in a parental or peda-
gogic relation to their tender charges. They have, by all I see and
hear, been sufficiently scurrilous — one or two in particular.

> However, from one crime they are exempt;
> They do not strike a brother, striking *me*.
>> [Walter Savage Landor, 'Appendix to *Hellenics*',
>> 1847 (47-8)]

I will only throw them one crumb of advice in return; I fear
the alms will be of no avail, but it shall not be witheld: —

> Why grudge them lotus-leaf and laurel,
>   O toothless mouth and swinish maw,
> Who never grudged you bells and coral,
>   Who never grudged you troughs and straw?

> Lie still in kennel, sleek in stable,
>   Good creatures if the stall or sty;
> Shove snouts for crumbs below the table;
>   Lie still; and rise not up to lie.[14]

To all this, however, there is a grave side. The question at issue
is wider than any between a single writer and his critics, or it
might well be allowed to drop. It is this: whether or not the first
and last requisite of art is to give no offence; whether or not all
that cannot be lisped in the nursery or fingered in the schoolroom
is therefore to be cast out of the library; whether or not the
domestic circle is to be for all men and writers the outer limit and
extreme horizon of their world of work. For to this we have come;
and all students of art must face the matter as it stands. Who has
not heard it asked, in a final and triumphant tone, whether this
book or that can be read aloud by her mother to a young girl?
Whether such and such a picture can properly be exposed to the
eyes of young persons? If you reply that this is nothing to the
point, you fall at once into the ranks of the immoral. Never till
now, and nowhere but in England, could so monstrous an
absurdity rear for one moment its deformed and eyeless head. In
no past century were artists ever bidden to work on these terms;
nor are they now, except among us. The disease, of course,
afflicts the meanest members of the body with most virulence.

Nowhere is cant at once so foul-mouthed and so tight-laced as in the penny, twopenny, threepenny, or sixpenny press. Nothing is so favourable to the undergrowth of real indecency as this over-shadowing foliage of fictions, this artificial network of proprieties. *L'Arioste rit au soleil, l'Aretin ricane a l'ombre* [Ariosto laughs in the sun; Aretino sniggers in the shade].[15] The whiter the sepulchre without, the ranker the rottenness within. Every touch of plaster is a sign of advancing decay. The virtue of our critical journals is a dowager of somewhat dubious antecedents: every day that thins and shrivels her cheek thickens and hardens the paint on it; she consumes more chalk and ceruse than would serve a whole courtful of crones. 'It is to be presumed', certainly, that in her case 'all is not sweet, all is not sound' [Ben Jonson, *Epicoene, or The Silent Woman*, 1609-10 (I.i.92)]. The taint on her fly-blown reputation is hard to overcome by patches and perfumery. Litera-ture, to be worthy of men, must be large, liberal, sincere; and cannot be chaste if it be prudish. Purity and prudery cannot keep house together. Where free speech and fair play are interdicted, foul hints and vile suggestions are hatched into fetid life. And if literature indeed is not to deal with the full life of man and the whole nature of things, let it be cast aside with the rods and rattles of childhood. Whether it affect to teach or to amuse, it is equally trivial and contemptible to us; only less so than the charge of immorality. Against how few really great names has not this small and dirt-encrusted pebble been thrown! A reputation seems imperfect without this tribute also: one jewel is wanting to the crown. It is good to be praised by those whom all men should praise; it is better to be reviled by those whom all men should scorn.

Passage 3.6

(from *Alfred Austin, 'Mr Swinburne' in* The Poetry of the Period, *1870. Austin's essay appeared in an earlier form in* Temple Bar, *1869*)

In my essay on Mr Browning I have shown how dissatisfaction with the poetry of Mr Tennyson, as an exponent of his age, has driven even his once frantic admirers to hearken for yet another voice, and how, in their ignorance of what it is in Mr Tennyson that fails to satisfy them, they have pitched upon Mr Browning of all people to supply the omission. What Mr Tennyson wanted, I said, was loftiness; what Mr Browning possessed, I observed, was depth; and I added that, this distinction once made, it was obvious that the one could not possibly supplement the other, having no earthly affinity with it. But there exists another distinction between them, which, though in complete harmony with the one I have already drawn, sets the matter in another, and for my present purpose still more important, light. If I were asked to sum up the characteristics of Mr Tennyson's compositions in a single word, the word I should employ would be 'feminine', and if I had to do the same for Mr Browning's genius, the word inevitably selected would be 'studious'. The pen of the latter is essentially the pen of a student; the muse of the former is essentially — I must not the say the muse of a woman, for I should be rendering myself liable to misconception, but — a feminine muse. And in these two salient qualities are unquestionably representative men, and typify two of the prominent tendencies of the time. We have just had, from a much revered source, an essay [by J.S. Mill] on the Subjection of Women [1869]; but I think it would not be difficult to show that men, and especially in the domain of Art, are, and have for some time been, quite as subject to women, to say the least of it, as is desirable. In the region of morals, women, may, in modern times, have had a beneficent influence; though, as we shall see when we come to treat of Mr Swinburne's particular genius, recent phenomena have somewhat shaken the once favourable opinion on that score. But there can be no question that, in the region of Art, their influence has been unmitigatedly mischievous. They have ruined the stage; they have dwarfed painting till it has become little more than the representative of pretty little sentiment — much of it terribly false — and mawkish commonplace domesticities; and they have helped poetry to become in the hands of Mr Tennyson at least, and of his disciples, the mere handmaid of ther own limited interests, susceptibilities and yearnings. I do not say that Mr Tennyson is never by any chance and on occasion fairly manly, though I think no one can doubt who considers the matter, that he is not even fairly manly very often, and never conspicuously so; and the most unreasonable of his worshippers would not dare for one moment, in describing his supposed merits as a poet, to call him masculine. That feminine is the proper word to apply to his compositions, taken in their entirety, no impartial judge, I feel convinced, would dream of denying.

Between the essentially feminine genius and the genius of the

student there is an abyss; and it represents the enormous difference that there is between Mr Tennyson and Mr Browning. I am
not again going to discuss Mr Browning's studious quality, for I
have already fully insisted on the 'depth' of his genius in my past
paper — and between depth and studiousness there is so obvious
a similarity — that I may fairly assume the point is settled. What
I now wish to note is, that whilst, as I have said, not altogether
satisfied with Mr Tennyson's feminine, unlofty way of looking at
things, the critics, who are so enamoured of their age that they
are determined to find in it great poetry somewhere or other,
pitched upon the deep and studious Mr Browning, in hope that
he would afford them the satisfaction they required; they have, in
reality, failed, despite all their bravado and assurances to the
contrary, to find it in that quarter. It was simply impossible that
they should find it there. A studious writer is neither the complement nor the antithesis of a feminine one. When men say, 'This
poet is too feminine', what they want, of course, is a poet who
shall be masculine. A student, as far as sex is concerned, as far as
manly and womanly qualities are involved, is a nondescript. He
may be incidentally of a masculine or of a feminine turn, just as it
happens. He is in a neutral in the matter. It does so happen that
Mr Browning is certainly far more masculine than feminine in his
studiousness; but his masculinity is a mere sub-quality to that
one great predominating characteristic. He is, over and above all
things, an Analyser, and every other attribute is merged and lost,
so to speak, in its conspicuous supremacy. Little wonder, therefore, was it that these same critics, still sadly wanting an adequate
poet, for all their copious assurances that they already possessed a
couple, warmly welcomed Mr Swinburne's appearance, and,
enrolling him at once with the other two, have exultingly formed
for themselves a Trinity of Song. Mr Swinburne may thank Mr
Tennyson's imperfections and Mr Browning's shortcomings for
the reception he has met with; for let me hasten to say that, had a
really great, adequate poet been alive, Mr Swinburne would have
failed to attract much attention, save for those qualities which
even his admirers do not admire, but of which I may remark that
I shall be found very tolerant. But the existence of Mr Tennyson
and Mr Browning left ample room for Mr Swinburne, just as the
existence of Mr Tennyson, Mr Browning, and Mr Swinburne still
leaves ample room for another, or indeed many another, poetical
apparition.

It might be supposed, after what has been said, even though

Mr Swinburne should turn out, on examination, to be neither the one great poet we should all be so delighted to hail, nor even a poet bringing precisely those qualities which neither the feminine nor the studious temperament supplies, he would at any rate have contributed something strikingly distinct from what we have seen is contributed by the other two, and be as different from Mr Tennyson and from Mr Browning as they are from each other. Different in every respect he unquestionably is from Mr Browning, as every poet — and Mr Swinburne *is* a poet — necessarily must be; Mr Browning is not specifically a poet at all. It is with Mr Tennyson, therefore, we must compare or contrast him; and thus, once for all, we may dismiss Mr Browning to his own studious prose territory, having no further need of him in the poetical one.

Now, on first blush, it would seem as though Mr Swinburne's poetry were a genuine revolt against that of Mr Tennyson, and as though he had struck a distinct and antagonistic note. That Mr Swinburne himself thinks so is evident from some observatons dropped by him in his 'Notes on Poems and Reviews' [see passage 3.5]: a defence of his muse against the strictures of those who complained — in my opinion, with absurd extravagance — of its alleged indecency and profanity.

'In one thing', he says, 'it seems I have erred: I have forgotten to prefix to my work the timely warning of a great poet and humorist: —

> J'en préviens les mères des familles,
> Ce que j'écris n'est pas pour les petites filles
> Dont on coupe le pain en tartines; mes vers
> Sont des vers de jeune homme.
>
> [Théophile Gautier, *Albertus*, 1832 (98)]

'I have over looked the evidence which every day makes clear, that our time has room only for such as are content to write for children and girls ... Happily, there is no fear that the supply of milk for babes will fall short of the demand for some time yet. There are moral milkmen enough, in all conscience, crying their ware about the streets and byways.'

A few pages farther on Mr Swinburne adds: —

The question at issue is, whether or not all that cannot be lisped in the nursery or fingered in the school-room is therefore to be cast out of the library? whether or not the domestic circle is to be for all men and writers the outer limit and extreme horizon of their world of work? ... Literature, to be worthy of men, must be large, liberal, sincere; and if literature is not to deal with the full life of man and the whole nature of things, let it be cast aside with the rods and rattles of childhood. Against how few really great names has not this small and dirt-encrusted pebble been thrown! A reputation seems imperfect without this tribute also; one jewel is wanting to the crown ... With English versifiers now, the idyllic form is now in fashion ... We have idylls of the farm and the mill; idylls of the dining-room and the deanery ... The idyllic form is best for domestic and pastoral poetry. It is naturally on a lower level than that of tragic or lyric verse. Its gentle and maidenly lips are somewhat narrow for the stream, and somewhat cold for the fire of song. It is very fit for the sole diet of girls; not very fit for the sole sustenance of man.

The point could not be better or more clearly put. Neither could it possibly be made more apparent that Mr Swinburne here intends to protest against the excessive estimate usually paraded of the Laureate's poetry, both as regards its matter and its manner; and if the above is not an accusation, virtually embodying the distinction I have made, that Mr Tennyson's muse is essentially a 'feminine' one, and a trumpet-call to critics and the public to demand some more masculine stuff, and welcome it with open arms if it does appear, language must have lost all its uses. But of course it does embody such a protest against the feminine genius of Mr Tennyson's verse, and a bold, admirably written plea for what is more 'fit for the sustenance of man'.

The queston therefore arises, Has Mr Swinburne, acting up to his excellent theory, turned his back on the haunts of feminine muses, struck out a masculine strain, and wrung from strenuous chords nervous and extolling hymns worthy of men and gods? Alas! who shall say it? True, he has given us no more idylls of the farm and the mill, of the dining-room and the deanery; nor will any one pretend that his lyrics and ballards are fit for the sole or even for part of the diet of girls. But what have men — men brave, muscular, bold, upright, chivalrous — I will not say chaste, for that is scarcely a masculine quality ('I will find you twenty lascivious turtles ere one chaste man', says no less an authority than Shakespeare), but at any rate clean — men with 'pride in their port, defiance in their eye', men daring, enduring, short of speech, and terrible in action — what have these to do with Mr Swinburne's Venuses and Chastelards, his Anactorias and Faustines, his Dolores, his Sapphos, or his Hermaphroditus? If these be his Olympus, we prefer the deanery and the dining-room, or even the drawing-room. I do not say that they are not air, much less that they are illegitimate, subjects for the poet's pen; but are they masculine? That is the question. Mr Swinburne need fear no prudish or bigoted criticism from me. Venus or virgin, it is all one to me, provided he can make poetry out of either; though, of course, I should always reserve to myself the right of saying which I thought to be the nobler theme. He may take Priapus for his Apollo, if he will, so that he have dexterity and daintiness enough to handle a difficult matter becomingly, and extol a satyr into a Celestial. But it will not do to empty Olympus of its divinities, fill it with tipsy Bacchanals and mere-tricious Maenads, and then conceive that idylls of the earth, earthy — idylls of the farm and the mill — have been gloriously surpassed. Is this all that his hellenic culture has taught him? Were 'Kisses that burn and bite' the everlasting theme of Homer, of Pindar, or of the grand tragedians of their country? Who was it but an Athenian that declared that poetry should consist of nothing but hymns to the gods and praises of virtue, and in the severity of his wrath at lascivious strains and Lydian measures banished all bards from his ideal republic? We hear much of the puritanical spirit of Christianity; and in non-Catholic countries there has been at times considerably too much of this. But what about the occasional puritanism of Greek paganism? It too could revolt against literary excesses, and prove that in that respect, as in many another, it can compete with the creeds that helped over-throw it. If ever there was a thorough Christian poet, Wordsworth was surely that man. Yet so little did he associate paganism with what he at least, would have deemed profane and indecent, that, in his despair at the temper of his own times, he cried out: —

> Great God! I'd rather be
> A pagan suckled in a creed outworn
> So might I, standing on this pleasant lea,
> Have glimpses that would make me less forlorn;

Have sight of Proteus rising from the sea,
Or hear old Triton blow his wreathed horn.
[Wordsworth. 'The world is too much with us; late and
soon', 1807 (9-14)]

If Mr Swinburne be really anxious to see the fulfilment of his
prophecy in his 'Hymn to Proserpine' [1866] —

Though before thee the throned Cytherean be fallen, and
hidden her head,
Yet thy kingdom shall pass, Galilean; thy dead shall go
down with thee dead — (73-4)

it were surely desirable that he did not travesty the men and
women, the gods and goddesses, of that earlier time. And in what
way does he travesty them? By eliminating all that was masculine
— and what a masculine epoch it was! — and intensifying and
exaggerating what was not masculine by aid of his modern
feminine lens. For to this clear charge and distinct conclusion
must we come: that far from Mr Swinburne being more
masculine even than Mr Tennyson, he is positively less so. Where
has he given to us, to use his own words, 'Literature worthy of
men, large, liberal, sincere?' Where the 'literature that deals with
the full life of man and the whole nature of things?' I may readily
grant that the 'lilies and languors of virtue' do not constitute the
full life of man and the whole nature of things; but I must protest
that neither do 'the roses and raptures of vice'. Is that the sense in
which he reads the magnificent words of Schiller, when drenched
and suffused with the old classical temper he exclaimed, 'Man
has lost his dignity, but Art has saved it. Truth still lives in fiction,
and from the copy will the original be restored'.[16] What does Mr
Swinburne think is either the copy or original of man's dignity? Is
it represented in such lines as these? —

Ah that my lips were tuneless lips, but pressed
To the bruised blossom of thy scourged white breast!
Ah that my mouth for Muses' milk were fed
On the sweet blood thy sweet small wounds had bled!
That with my tongue I felt them, and could taste
The faint flakes from thy bosom to thy waist!
['Anactoria', 1866 (106-10)]

165

I do not shrink from quoting anything Mr Swinburne has written, and treating it with becoming critical fairness; but in quoting the above lines, I should like to know if their author thinks he is using art to save something man has lost or would otherwise lose? Is this the verse that is peculiarly 'fit for the sole sustenance of man'? Mr Tennyson, of whose extreme moral propriety some people have made such an absurd parade, has written something very similar, to the full as impassioned, and considerably better balanced: —

My whole soul waiting silently,
All naked in a sultry sky,
Droops blinded with his piercing eye:
I *will* possess him, or will die.
I will grow round him in his place;
Grow, live, die looking on his face;
Die, dying, clasp'd in his embrace.
                              [Tennyson, 'Fatima', 1832 (36-42)]

I distinctly remember lending the volume containing this poem to a young lady, and having it returned by her mamma, with the remark — I am indulging in no hackneyed joke, but narrating a simple fact — that she strongly objected to a volume containing such abomination as the foregoing, and preferred that her daughter should restrict her poetical reading to Mr [Martin] Tupper.[17] The man who wrote 'Vivien', and the parting scene between Guinevere and Lancelot, has not invariably been a moral milkman. Mr Tennyson has such immense skill as a craftsman, that he successfully passes off upon proper people what they would call shocking improprieties if proceeding from a less dextrous hand. Therefore, if all that Mr Swinburne is pleading for in his defence of something 'that cannot be lisped in the nursery and fingered in the school-room'; be it only the free delineation of sexual passion, I am bound to say that Mr Tennyson, in his more extreme moods, and the Hon Robert Lytton, in his ordinary ones, have both anticipated him, and thus blunted the force of his literary complaints.[18] It is true that neither of them has indulged in quite such warm language as Mr Swinburne; but that is an affair of relative colouring, not a matter of substance, or principle. As far as Mr Lytton is concerned, one has only to glance at [Lytton's] 'The Wanderer' [1857], *passim*, for a proof of the assertion; and surely such lines as —

O love! O fire! once he drew
With one long kiss my whole soul thro'
My lips, as sunlight drinketh dew (19-22)

from the 'Fatima', from which we have already quoted, or,

And then they were agreed upon a night
(When the good king should not be there) to meet
And part for ever. Passion-pale they met
And greeted. Hands in hands, and eye to eye,
Low on the border of her couch they sat
Stammering and staring

from the 'Idylls of the King' ['Guinivere' 1859, 95-101; Austin's
italics], are sufficient to exonerate Mr Tennyson from the
imputation of writing only for children and girls, and to prove
that he can compete — and in my opinion beat — Mr Swinburne
on his own special ground.

Passage 3.7

(*Walter Pater, 'Dante Gabriel Rossetti' in* Appreciations, *1889.
Rossetti's* Poems *and* Ballads and Sonnets *were published in 1881.
Before that date, some of his sonnets from 'The House of Life' had
appeared in* The Fortnightly Review *in 1869. Poems (1870) contained
well-known poems, such as 'Jenny', which sparked off the 'Fleshly
School' scandal: see Passages 3.3, 3.4, 3.5 and 3.6*)

It was characteristic of a poet who had ever something about him
of mystic isolation, and will still appeal perhaps, though with a
name it may seem now established in English literature, to a
special and limited audience, that some of his poems had won a
kind of exquisite fame before they were in the full sense
published. *The Blessed Damozel*, although actually printed twice
before the year 1870, was eagerly circulated in manuscript; and
the volume which it now opens came at last to satisfy a long-
standing curiosity as to the poet, whose pictures also become an
object of the same peculiar kind of interest. For these poems were
the work of a painter, understood to belong to, and to be indeed
the leader, of a new school then rising into note; and the reader of
to-day may observe already, in *The Blessed Damozel*, written at the

age of eighteen a prefigurement of the chief characteristics of that school, as he will recognise in it also, in proportion as he really knows Rossetti, many of the characteristics which are most markedly personal and his own. Common to that school and to him, and in both alike of primary significance, was the quality of sincerity, already felt as one of the charms of that earliest poem — a perfect sincerity, taking effect in the deliberate use of the most direct and unconventional expression, for the conveyance of a poetic sense which recognised no conventional standard of what poetry was called upon to be. At a time when poetic originality in England might seem to have had its utmost play, here was certainly one new poet more, with a structure and music of verse, a vocabularly, an accent, unmistakably novel, yet felt to be no mere tricks of manner adopted with a view to forcing attention — an accent which might rather count as the very seal of reality on one man's own proper speech; as that speech itself was the wholly natural expression of certain wonderful things he really felt and saw. Here was one, who had a matter to present to his readers, to himself at least, in the first instance, so valuable, so real and definite, that his primary aim, as regards form or expression in his verse, would be but its exact equivalent to those *data* within. That he had this gift of transparency in language — the control of a style which but did obediently shift and shape itself to the mental motion, as a well-trained hand can follow on the tracing-paper the outline of an original drawing below it, was proved afterwards by a volume of typically perfect translations from the delightful but difficult 'early Italian poets': such transparency being indeed the secret of all genuine style, of all such style as can truly belong to one man and not to another. His own meaning was always personal and even recondite, in a certain sense learned and casuistical, sometimes complex and obscure; but the term was always, one could see, deliberately chosen from many competitors, as the just transcript of that peculiar phase of soul which he alone knew, precisely as he knew it.

One of the peculiarities of *The Blessed Damozel* was a definiteness of sensible imagery, which seemed almost grotesque to some, and was strange, above all, in a theme so profoundly visionary. The gold bar of heaven from which she leaned, her hair yellow like ripe corn, are but examples of a general treatment, as naively detailed as the pictures of those early painters contemporary with Dante, who has shown a similar care for minute and definite imagery in his verse; there, too, in the very midst of profoundly mystic vision. Such definition of outline is indeed one among many points in which Rossetti resembles the great Italian poet, of whom, led to him at first by family circumstances, he was ever a lover — a 'servant and a singer', faithful as Dante, 'of Florence and of Beatrice' — with some close inward conformities of genius also, independent of any mere circumstances of education. It was said by a critic of the last century, not wisely though agreeably to the practice of his time, that poetry rejoices in abstractions. For Rossetti, as for Dante, without question on his part, the first condition of the poetic way of seeing and presenting things is particularisation. 'Tell me now', he writes, for Villon's

> Dictes-moy où, n'en quel pays,
> Est Flora, la belle Romaine —
>> ['The Ballad of Dead Ladies' (1-2) from
>> 'Three Translations from François Villon', 1450]

> Tell me now, in what hidden way is
> Lady Flora the lovely Roman:
>> ['Le Testament' (329-30)]

— 'way', in which one might actually chance to meet her; the unmistakably poetic effect of the couplet being dependent on the definiteness of that single word (though actually lighted on in the search after a difficult double rhyme) for which every one else would have written, like Villon himself, a more general one, just equivalent to place or region.

And this delight in concrete definition is allied with another of his conformities to Dante, the really imaginative vividness, namely, his personifications — his hold upon them, or rather their hold upon him, with the force of a Frankenstein, when once they have taken life from him. Not Death only and Sleep, for instance, and the winged spirit of Love, but certain peculiar aspects of them, a whole 'populace' of special hours and places, 'the hour' even; 'which might have been, yet might not be', are living creatures, with hands and eyes and articulat⸗ oices.

> Stands it not by the door —
> Love's Hour — till she and I shall meet;
> With bodiless form and unapparent feet
> That cast no shadow yet before,

Though round its head the dawn begins to pour
   The breath that makes day sweet?

                       Nay, why
Name the dead hours? I mind them well:
Their ghosts in many darkened doorways dwell
   With desolate eyes to know them by.
               ['The Stream's Secret' (163-9, 25-8)]

Poetry as a *mania* — one of Plato's two higher forms of 'divine' mania — has, in all its species, a mere insanity to it, the 'defect of its quality', into which it may lapse in its moment of weakness; and the insanity which follows a vivid poetic anthropomorphism like that of Rossetti may be noted here and there in his work, in a forced and almost grotesque materialising of abstractions, as Dante also became at times a mere subject of the scholastic realism of the Middle Ages.

In *Love's Nocturn* and *The Stream's Secret*, congruously perhaps with a certain feverishness of soul in the moods they present, there is at times a near approach (may it be said?) to such insanity of realism —

   Pity and love shall burn
     In her pressed cheek and cherishing hands;
And from the living spirit of love that stands
     Between her lips to soothe and yearn,
Each separate breath shall clasp me round in turn
     And loose my spirit's hands.
               ['The Stream's Secret' (109-14)]

But even if we concede this; even if we allow, in the very plan of those two compositions, something of the literary conceit — what exquisite, what novel flowers of poetry, we must admit them to be, as they stand! In the one, what delight in all the natural beauty of water, all its details for the eye of a painter; in the other, how subtle and fine the imaginative hold upon all the secret ways of sleep and dreams! In both of them, with much the same attitude and tone, Love — sick and doubtful Love — would fain inquire of what lies below the surface of sleep, and below the water; stream or dream being forced to speak by Love's powerful 'control'; and the poet would have it foretell the fortune, issue, and event of his wasting passion. Such artifices, indeed, were not unknown in the old Provencal poetry of which Dante had learned something. Only, in Rossetti at least, they are redeemed by a serious purpose, by that sincerity of his, which allies itself readily to a serious beauty, a sort of grandeur of literary workmanship, to a great style. One seems to hear there a really new kind of poetic utterance, with effects which have nothing else like them; as there is nothing else, for instance, like the narrative of Jacob's dream in *Genesis*, or Blake's design of the Singing of the Morning Stars, or Addison's Nineteenth Psalm.

With him indeed, as in some revival of the old mythopoeic age, common things — dawn, moon, night — are full of human or personal expression, full of sentiment. The lovely little sceneries scattered up and down his poems, glimpses of a landscape, not indeed of broad open-air effects, but rather that of a painter concentrated upon the picturesque effect of one or two selected objects at a time — the 'hollow brimmed with mist', or the 'ruined weir', as he sees it from one of the windows, or reflected in one of the mirrors of his 'house of life' (the vignettes for instance seen by Rose Mary in the magic beryl) attest, by their very freshness and simplicity, to a pictorial or descriptive power in dealing with the inanimate world, which is certainly also one half of the charm, in that other, more remote and mystic, use of it. For with Rossetti this sense of lifeless nature, after all, is translated to a higher service, in which it does but incorporate itself with some phase of strong emotion. Every one understands how this may happen at critical moments of life; what a weirdly expressed soul may have crept, even in full noonday, into 'the white-flower'd elder-thicket', when Godiva saw it 'gleam through the Gothic archways in the wall' [Tennyson, 'Godiva', 1842 (64-5)], at the end of her terrible ride. To Rossetti it was so always, because to him life is a crisis at every moment. A sustained impressibility towards the mysterious conditions of man's everyday life, towards the very mystery itself in it, gives a singular gravity to all his work: those matters never become trite to him. But throughout, it is the real intensity of love — of love based upon a perfect yet peculiar type of physical or material beauty — which is enthroned in the midst of those mysterious powers; Youth and Death, Destiny and Fortune, Fame, Poetic Fame, Memory, Oblivion, and the like. Rossetti is one of those who, in the words of Merimee, *se passionnent pour la passion*, one of Love's lovers.[19]

And yet, again as with Dante, to speak of his ideal type of beauty as material, is partly misleading. Spirit and matter, indeed, have been for the most part opposed, with a false contrast or antagonism by schoolmen, whose artificial creation those abstractions really are. In our actual concrete experience, the two trains of phenomena which the words *matter* and *spirit* do but roughly distinguish, play inextricably into each other. Practically, the church of the Middle Age by its aesthetic worship, its sacramentalism, its real faith in the resurrection of the flesh, has set itself against that Manichean opposition of spirit and matter, and its results in men's way of taking life; and in this, Dante is the central representative of its spirit. To him, in the vehement and impassioned heat of his conceptions, the material and the spiritual are fused and blent: if the spiritual attains the definite visibility of a crystal, what is material loses its earthiness and impurity. And here again, by force of instinct, Rossetti is one with him. His chosen type of beauty is one,

> Whose speech Truth knows not from her thought,
> Nor Love her body from her soul.

Like Dante, he knows no region of spirit which shall not be sensuous also, or material. The shadowy world, which he realises so powerfully, has still the ways and houses, the land and water, the light and darkness, the fire and flowers, that had so much to do in the moulding of those bodily powers and aspects which counted for so large a part of the soul, here.

For Rossetti, then, the great affections of persons to each other, swayed and determined, in the case of this highly pictorial genius, mainly by that so-called material loveliness, formed the great undeniable reality in things, the solid resisting substance, in a world where all beside might be but shadow. The fortunes of those affections — of great love so determined; its casuistries, its languor sometimes; above all, its sorrows; its fortunate or unfortunate collisions with those other great matters; how it looks, as the long day of life goes round, in the light and shadow of them: all this, conceived with an abundant imagination, and a deep, a philosophic, reflectiveness, is the matter of his verse, and especially of what he designed as his chief poetic work, 'a work to be called *The House of Life*', towards which the majority of his sonnets and songs were contributions.

The dwelling-place in which one finds oneself by chance or destiny, yet can partly fashion for oneself; never properly one's own at all, if it be changed too lightly; in which every object has its associations — the dim mirrors, the portraits, the lamps, the books, the hair-tresses of the dead and visionary magic crystals in the secret drawers, the names and words scratched on the windows, windows open upon prospects the saddest or the sweetest; the house one must quit, yet taking perhaps, how much of its quietly active light and colour along with us! — grown now to be a kind of raiment to one's body, as the body, according to [the Swedish philosopher and mystic, Emmanuel] Swedenborg, is but the raiment of the soul — under that image, the whole of Rossetti's work might count as a *House of Life*, of which he is but the 'Interpreter'. And it is a 'haunted' house. A sense of power in love, defying distance, and those barriers which are so much more than physical distance, of unutterable desire penetrating into the world of sleep, however 'lead-bound', was one of those anticipative notes obscurely struck in *The Blessed Damozel*, and, in his later work, makes him speak sometimes almost like a believer in mesmerism. Dream-land, as we said, with its 'phantoms of the body', deftly coming and going on love's service, is to him, in no mere fancy or figure of speech, a real country, a veritable expansion of, or addition to, our waking life; as he did well perhaps to wait carefully upon sleep, for the lack of it became a mortal disease with him. One may even recognise a sort of morbid and over-hasty making-ready for death itself, which increases on him; thoughts concerning it, its imageries, coming with frequency and importunity, in excess, one might think, of even the very saddest, quite unwholesome wisdom.

And indeed the publication of his second volume of *Ballads and Sonnets* preceded his death by scarcely a twelvemonth. That volume bears witness to the reverse of any failure of power, or falling-off from his early standard of literary perfection, in every one of his then accustomed forms of poetry — the song, the sonnet, and the ballad, was here at its height; while one monumental, gnomic piece, *Soothsay*, testifies, more clearly even than the *Nineveh* of his first volume, to the reflective force, the dry reason, always at work behind his imaginative creations, which at no time dispensed with a genuine intellectual structure. For in matters of pure reflection also, Rossetti maintained the painter's sensuous clearness of conception; and this has something to do with capacity, largely illustrated by his ballads, of telling some red-hearted story of impassioned action with effect.

Have there, in very deed, been ages, in which external conditions of poetry such as Rossetti's were of one spontaneous growth than in our own? The archaic side of Rossetti's work, his preferences in regard to earlier poetry, connect him with those who have certainly thought so, who fancied they could have breathed more largely in the age of Chaucer, or of Ronsard, in one of those ages, in the words of Stendhal — *ces siècles de passions où les âmes pouvaient se livrer franchement à la plus haute exaltation, quand les passions qui font la possibilité comme les sujets des beaux arts existaient* [those centuries of passions in which souls could surrender themselves freely to the highest exaltation, when those passions (which allowed this as a possibility) existed at the same time as the fine arts]. We may think, perhaps, that such old time as that has never really existed except in the fancy of poets; but it was to find it, that Rossetti turned so often from modern life to the chronicle of the past. Old Scotch history, perhaps beyond any other, is strong in matter of heroic and vehement hatreds and love, the tragic Mary herself being but the perfect blossom of them; and it is from that history that Rossetti has taken the subjects of the two longer ballads of his second volume: of the three admirable ballads in it, *The King's Tragedy* (in which Rossetti has dextrously interwoven some relics of James's own exquisite early verse) reaching the highest level of dramatic success, and marking perfection, perhaps, in this kind of poetry; which, in the earlier volume, gave us, among other pieces, *Troy Town*, *Sister Helen*, and *Eden Bower*.

Like those earlier pieces, the ballads of the second volume bring with them the question of poetic value of the 'refrain' —

Eden bower's in flower:
And O the bower and the hour!

— and the like. Two of those ballads — *Troy Town* and *Eden Bower*, are terrible in theme; and the refrain serves, perhaps, to relieve their bold aim at the sentiment of terror. In *Sister Helen* again, the refrain has a real, and sustained purpose (being here duly varied also) and performs the part of a chorus, as the story proceeds. Yet even in these cases, whatever its effect may be in actual recitation, it may fairly be questioned, whether, to the mere reader their actual effect is not that of positive interruption and drawback, at least in pieces so lengthy; and Rossetti himself, it would seem, came to think so, for in the shortest of his later ballads, *The White Ship* — that old true history of the generosity with which a youth, worthless in life, flung himself upon death —

he was contented with a single utterance of the refrain, 'given out' like the key note or tune of a chant.

In *The King's Tragedy*, Rossetti has worked upon motive, broadly human (to adopt the phrase of popular criticism) such as one and all may realise. Rossetti, indeed, with all his self-concentration upon his own peculiar aim, by no means ignored those general interests which are external to poetry as he conceived it; as he has shown here and there, in this poetic, as in pictorial, work. It was but that, in a life to be shorter even than the average, he found enough to occupy him in the fulfilment of a task, plainly 'given him to do'. Perhaps, if one had to name a single composition of his to readers desiring to make acquaintance with him for the first time, one would select *The King's Tragedy* — the poem so moving, so popularly dramatic, and lifelike. Notwithstanding this, his work, it must be conceded, certainly through no narrowness or egotism, but in the faithfulness of a true workman to a vocation so emphatic, was mainly of the esoteric order. But poetry, at all times, exercises two distinct functions: it may reveal, it may unveil to every eye, the ideal aspects of common things, after Gray's way (though Gray too, it is well to remember, seemed in his own day, seemed even to Johnson, obscure) or it may actually add to the number of motives poetic and uncommon in themselves, by the imaginative creation of things that are ideal from their very birth. Rossetti did something, something excellent, of the former kind; but his characteristic, his really revealing work, lay in the adding to poetry of fresh poetic material, of a new order of phenomena, in the creation of a new ideal.

Notes

1. Quotation unidentified.
2. Quotation unidentified.
3. The author of this work has not been traced.
4. It has not been possible to locate this edition.
5. Sulpicia, a Roman poet of the first century BC, belonged to the circle of Tibullus.
6. Erinna, a Greek poet of the fourth century BC, is known for 'The Distaff', of which only a few fragments remain.
7. Arthur O'Shaughnessy (1844-81), poet, attracted attention with *Epic of Women and Other Poems* (1870).
8. Simeon Solomon (1840-1905), painter, associated with the Pre-

Raphaelites, is perhaps best known for *The Meeting of Dante and Beatrice*, 1859-63.

9. Morris's review, 'Poems by Dante Gabriel Rossetti', appeared in the *Academy*, vol 1., no. 8 (1870), pp. 199-200. Swinburne's review, 'The Poems of Dante Gabriel Rossetti', appeared in the *Fortnightly Review*, NS vol. 7 (1870), pp. 551-79.

10. Presumably a name for the many Victorian penny papers. There was, of course, no *Day's Doings* as such.

11. Sidney Colvin participated in the 'Fleshly School' debate by publishing 'The Poetical Writings of Dante Gabriel Rossetti', *Westminster Review*, vol. 95 (1871), pp. 55-92.

12. Swinburne's tragedy, *Chastelard*, concerning Mary Queen of Scots, was published in 1865.

13. In Greek mythology, Niobe boasted of her superiority to Leto, mother of Artemis and Apollo. Leto's children killed the seven sons and seven daughters of Niobe, who wept until she became a column of stone. Simonides, Greek poet of the seventh century BC, is known for two poems: one a satire on women, the other a philosophical reflection on the unhappy lives of men. Aeschylus, of course, is the great Greek tragedian. Titian (1487/90-1576) is the outstanding Italian painter. Antonio Correggio (1489/94-1534) is one of Titian's lesser rivals.

14. According to Thomas J. Wise (the literary historian — and forger), these lines belong to Swinburne. See *A Swinburne Library* (1935).

15. Ariosto (1474-1533) is the Italian poet renowned for *Orlando Furioso*. Aretino (1492-1556) wrote obscene works.

16. Quotation unidentified.

17. Martin Tupper (1810-89), poet, gained popularity through his *Popular Philosophy* (1838-76), a collection of maxims in verse.

18. Robert Lytton (1831-91), poet, son of the popular novelist, Edward Bulwer-Lytton, published a number of poems under the pseudonym Owen Meredith. He served as Viceroy in India, 1876-80.

19. Prosper Merimee (1803-70), novelist, archaeologist and historian, is perhaps best known for his short stories.

4

The Study of Poetry

Passage 4.1

(from *Thomas Carlyle, 'Corn-Law Rhymes',* Edinburgh Review, *1832. This is a review of three volumes by Ebenezer Elliott:* Corn-Law Rhymes, Love: A Poem *and* The Village Patriarch, *all in their 1830 editions. Elliott's* Corn-Law Rhymes *were widely reviewed in the periodicals, notably by W. J. Fox, 'The Poor and Their Poetry',* Monthly Repository, *1832, and 'Christopher North' (John Wilson), 'Corn-Law Rhymes',* Blackwood's Magazine, *1832. The places mentioned in the extract from Elliott's 'The Ranter' are located in his native Yorkshire and nearby Derbyshire. In his attack on the Corn Laws, Elliott articulated widespread working-class discontent. Together with the debates around the first Reform Bill of 1832 and the extension of the franchise, the question of the repeal of the Corn Laws was at the centre of the Chartist movement. For the working-class context of Eliott's poetry, and his relation to Chartism and the many Chartist poets, see Martha Vicinus,* The Industrial Muse: A Study of Nineteenth-Century British Working-Class Literature *(London, 1974). Carlyle's polemical condemnation of Chartism is most fiercely expressed in* Past and Present *(1843))*

It used to be said that lions do not paint, that poor men do not write; but the case is altering now. Here is a voice coming from the deep Cyclopean forges, where Labour, in real soot and sweat, beats with a thousand hammers 'the red son of the furnace'; doing personal battle with Necessity, and her dark brute Powers, to make them reasonable and serviceable; an intelligible voice from the hitherto Mute and Irrational, to tell us at first-hand how it is with him, what in very deed is the theorem of the world and

177

of himself, which he, in those dim depths of him, in that wearied head of his, has put together. To which voice, in several respects significant enough, let good ear be given.

Here too be it premised, that nowise under the category of 'Uneducated Poets',[1] or in any fashion of dilettante patronage, can our Sheffield friend be produced. His position is unsuitable for that: so is ours. Genius, which the French lady declared to be of no sex, is much more certainly of no rank; neither when 'the spark of Nature's fire' has been imparted, should education take high airs in her artificial light, — which is too often but phosphorescence and putrescence. In fact, it now begins to be suspected here and there, that this same aristocratic recognition, which looks down with an obliging smile from its throne, of bound Volumes and gold Ingots, and admits that it is wonderfully well for one of the uneducated classes, may be getting out of place. There are unhappy times in the world's history, when he that is the least educated will chiefly have to say that he is the least perverted; and with the multitude of false eye-glasses, convex, concave, green, even yellow, has not lost the natural use of his eyes. For a generation that reads Cobbett's Prose, and Burns's Poetry, it need be no miracle that here also is a man who can handle both pen and hammer like a man.

Nevertheless, this serene-highness attitude and temper is so frequent, perhaps it were good to turn the tables for a moment, and see what look it has under that reverse aspect. How were it if we surmised, that for a man with natural vigour, with a man's character to be developed in him, more especially if in the way of Literature, as Thinker and Writer, it is actually, in these strange days, no special misfortune to be trained up among the Uneducated classes, and not among the Educated; but rather of two misfortunes the smaller?

For all men, doubtless, obstructions abound; spiritual growth must be hampered and stunted, and has to struggle through with difficulty, if not wholly stop. We may grant, too, that, for a mediocre character, the continual training and tutoring, from language-masters, dancing-masters, posture-makers of all sorts, hired and volunteer, which a high rank in any time and country assures, there will be produced a certain superiority, or at worst, air of superiority over the corresponding mediocre character of low rank: thus we perceive the vulgar Do-nothing, as contrasted with the vulgar Drudge, is in general a much prettier man; with a wider, perhaps clearer outlook into the distance; in innumerable superficial matters, however it may be when we go deeper, he has a manifest advantage. But with the man of uncommon character, again, in whom a germ of irrepressible Force has been implanted, and *will* unfold itself into some sort of freedom, altogether the reverse may hold. For such germs too, there is, undoubtedly enough, a proper soil where they will grow best, and an improper one where they will grow worst. True also, where there is a will, there is a way; where genius has been given, a possibility, a certainty of growing is also given. Yet often it seems as if the injudicious gardening and manuring were worse than none at all; and killed what the inclemencies of blind chance would have spared. We find accordingly that few Fredericks or Napoleons, indeed none since Great Alexander, who unfortunately drank himself to death too soon for proving what lay in him, were nursed up with an eye to their vocation; mostly with an eye quite the other way, in the midst of isolation and pain, destitution and contradiction. Nay, in our own times, have we not seen two men of genius, a Byron and a Burns; they both, by mandate of Nature, struggle and must struggle towards clear Manhood, stormfully enough, for the space of six-and-thirty years; yet only the gifted Ploughman can partially prevail therein: the gifted Peer must toil and strive, and shoot-out in wild efforts, yet die at last in Boyhood, with the promise of his Manhood still but announcing itself in the distance. Truly, as was once written, 'it is only the artichoke that will not grow except in gardens; the acorn is cast carelessly abroad into the wilderness, yet on the wild soil it nourishes itself, and rises to be an oak'. All woodmen, moreover, will tell you that fat manure is the ruin of your oak; likewise that the thinner and wilder your soil, the tougher, more iron-textured is your timber, — though unhappily also the smaller. So too with the spirits of men: they become pure from their errors by suffering for them; he who has battled, were it only with Poverty and hard toil, will be found stronger, more expert, than he who could stay at home from the battle, concealed among the provision-wagons, or even not unwatchfully 'abiding by the stuff'. In which sense, an observer, not without experience of our time, has said: Had I a man of clearly developed character (clear, sincere within its limits), of insight, courage and real applicable force of head and of heart, to search for; and not a man of luxuriously distorted character, with haughtiness for courage, and for insight and applicable force, speculation and plausible show of force, — it were rather among the lower than among the higher classes that I should look for him.

A hard saying, indeed, seems this same: that he, whose other wants were all beforehand supplied; to whose capabilities no problem was presented except even this, How to cultivate to best advantage, should attain less real culture than he whose first grand problem and obligation was nowise spiritual culture, but hard labour for his daily bread! Sad enough must the perversion be, where preparations of such magnitude issue in abortion; and so sumptuous an Art with all its appliances can accomplish nothing, not so much as necessitous Nature would of herself have supplied! Nevertheless, so pregnant is Life with evil as with good; to such height in an age rich, plethorically overgrown with means, can means be accumulated in the wrong place, and immeasurably aggravate wrong tendencies, instead of righting them, this sad and strange result may actually turn out to have been realised.

But what, after all, is meant by *uneducated*, in a time when Books have come into the world; come to be household furniture in every habitation of the civilised world? In the poorest cottage are Books; is one Book, wherein for several thousand years the spirit of man has found light, and calculate what it will amount to! Necessity, moreover, which we see here as the mother of Accuracy, is well known as the mother of Invention. He who wants everything must know many things, do many things, to procure even a few different enough with him, whose indispensable knowledge is this only, that a finger will pull the bell!

So that, for all men who live, we may conclude, this Life of Man is a school, wherein the naturally foolish will continue foolish though you bray him in a mortar, but the naturally wise will gather wisdom under every disadvantage. What, meanwhile, must be the condition of an Era, when the highest advantages there become perverted into drawbacks; when, if you take two men of genius, and put the one between the handles of a plough, and mount the other between the painted coronets of a coach-and-four, and bid them both move along, the former shall arrive a Burns, the latter a Byron: two men of talent, and put the one into a Printer's chapel, full of lamp-black, tyrannous usage, hard toil, and the other into Oxford universities, with lexicons and libraries, and hired expositors and sumptuous endowments, the former shall come out a Dr Franklin, the latter a Dr Parr! —[2]

However, we are not here to write an Essay on education, or sing *misereres* over a 'world in its dotage'; but simply to say that our Corn-Law Rhymer, educated or uneducated as Nature and art have made him, asks not the smallest patronage or compassion for his rhymes, professes not the smallest condition for them. Nowise in such attitude does he present himself; not supplicatory, deprecatory, but sturdy, defiant, almost menacing. Wherefore, indeed, should he supplicate or deprecate? It is out of the abundance of the heart that he has spoken: praise or blame cannot make it truer or falser than it already is. By the grace of God this man is sufficient for himself; by his skill in metallurgy can beat out a toilsome but a manful living, go how it may; has arrived too at that singular audacity of believing what he knows, and acting on it, or writing on it, or thinking on it, without leave asked of any one: there shall he stand, and work, with head and with hand, for himself and the world; blown about by no wind of doctrine; frightened at no reviewer's shadow; having, in his time, looked substances enough in the face, and remained unfrightened.

What is left, therefore, but to take what he brings, and as he brings it? Let us be thankful, were it only for the day of small things. Something it is that we have lived to welcome once more a sweet Singer wearing the likeness of a Man. In humble guise, it is true, and of stature more or less marred in its development; yet not without a genial robustness, strength and valour built on honesty and love; on the whole, a genuine man, with somewhat of the eye and speech and bearing that beseems a man. To whom all other genuine men, how different soever in subordinate particulars, can gladly hold out the right hand of fellowship.

The great excellence of our rhymer, be it understood, then, we take to consist even in this, often hinted at already, that he is *genuine.* Here is an earnest truth-speaking man; no theoriser, sentimentaliser, but a practical man of work and endeavour, man of sufferance and endurance. The thing that he speaks is not a hearsay, but a thing which he has himself known, and by experience become assured of. He has used his eyes for seeing; uses his tongue for declaring what he has seen. His voice, therefore, among the many noises of the Planet, will deserve its place better than the most; will be well worth some attention. Whom else should we attend to but such? The man who speaks with some half shadow of a Belief, and supposes, and inclines to think; and considers not with undivided soul, what is true, but only what is plausible, and will find audience and recompense: do we not meet him at every street-turning, on all highways and byways: is he not stale, unprofitable, ineffectual, wholly grown a weariness of the flesh? So rare is his opposite in any rank of Literature or of Life, so very rare, that even in the lowest he is precious. The authentic insight and experience of any human soul, were it but insight and experience in hewing of wood and drawing of water, is real knowledge, a real possession and acquirement, how small soever: *palabra* [such a word], again, were it a supreme pontiff's, is wind merely, and nothing, or less than nothing. To a considerable degree, this man, we say, has worked himself loose from cant and conjectural halfness, idle pretences and hallucinations, into a condition of Sincerity. Wherein, perhaps, as above argued, his hard social environment, and fortune to be 'a workman born', which brought so many other retardations with it, may have forwarded and accelerated him.

That a man, Workman or Idleman, encompassed, as in these days, with persons in a state of willing or unwilling Insincerity, and necessitated, as man is, to learn whatever he does traditionally learn by *imitating* these, should nevertheless shake off Insincerity, and struggle out from that dim pestiferous marsh-atmosphere, into a clearer and purer height, — betokens in him a certain Originality; in which rare gift, force of all kinds is presupposed. To our Rhymer, accordingly, as hunted more than once, vision and determination have not been denied: a rugged, homegrown understanding is in him; whereby, in his own way, he has mastered this and that, and looked into various things, in general honestly and to purpose, sometimes deeply, piercingly and with a Seer's eye. Strong thoughts are not wanting, beautiful thoughts; strong and beautiful expressions of thought. As traceable, for instance, in this new illustration of an old argument, the mischief of Commercial Restrictions:

These, O ye quacks, these are your remedies:
Alms for the Rich! — a bread-tax for the Poor!
Soul-purchased harvest on the indignant moor! —
Thus the winged victor of a hundred fights,
The warrior ship, bows low her banner'd head,
When through her planks the sea-born reptile bites
Its deadly way — and sinks in Ocean's bed,
Vanquish'd by worms. What then? The worms were fed.
Will not God smite thee black, thou whited wall?
Thy life is lawless, and they law a lie,
Or Nature is a dream unnatural.

Look on the clouds, the streams, the earth, the sky!
Lo, all is interchange and harmony!
Where is the gorgeous pomp which, yester morn,
Curtained yon Orb with amber, fold on fold?
Behold it in the blue of Rivelin, borne
To feed the all-feeding sea! The molten gold
Is flowing pale in Loxley's waters cold,
To kindle into beauty tree and flower,
And wake to verdant life hill, vale and plain.
Cloud trades with river, and exchange is power:
But should the clouds, the streams, the winds disdain
Harmonious intercourse, now dew nor rain
Would forest-crown the mountains: airless day
Would blast, on Kinderscout, the heathy glow;
No purply green would meeken into grey
O'er Don at eve; no sound of river's flow
Disturb the sepulchre of all below.

['The Ranter', 1831]

Nature and the doings of men have not passed by this man
unheeded, like the endless cloud-rack in dull weather; or lightly
heeded, like a theatric phantasmagoria; but earnestly inquired
into, like a thing of reality; reverently loved and worshipped, as a
thing with divine significance in its reality, glimpses of which
divineness she has caught and laid to heart. For his vision, as was
said, partakes of the genuinely Poetical; he is not a Rhymer and
Speaker only, but, in some genuine sense, something of a Poet.

Farther, we must admit him, what indeed is already herein
admitted, to be, if clear-sighted, also brave-hearted. A troublous
element is his; a Life of painfulness, toil, insecurity, scarcity; yet
he fronts it like a man; yields not to it, tames it into some subjection, some order; its wild fearful dinning and tumult, as of
devouring Chaos, becomes a sort of wild war-music for him;
wherein too are passages of beauty, of melodious melting
softness, of lightness and briskness, even of joy. The stout heart is
also a warm and kind one; Affection dwells with Danger, all the
holier and the lovelier for such stern environment. A working
man is this; yet, as we said, a man: in his sort, a courageous,
much-loving, faithfully enduring and endeavouring man.

What such a one, so gifted and so placed, shall say to a Time
like ours; how he will fashion himself into peace, or war, or
armed neutrality, with the world and his fellow-men; and work

out his course in joy and grief, in victory and defeat, is a question worth asking: which in these three little Volumes partly receives answer. He has turned, as all thinkers up to a very high and rare order in these days must do, into Politics; is a Reformer, at least a strewn Complainer, radical to the core: his poetical melody takes an elegiaco-tragical character; much of him is converted into hostility, and grim, hardly-suppressed indignation, such as right long denied, hope long deferred, may awaken in the kindliest heart. Not yet as a rebel against anything does he stand; but as a free man, and the spokesman of free man, not far from rebelling against much; with sorrowful appealing dew, yet also with incipient lightning, in his eyes; whom it were not desirable to provoke into rebellion. He says in Vulcanic dialect, his feelings have been *hammered* till they are *cold-short*; so they will no longer bend; 'they snap, and fly off', — in the face of the hammerer. Not unnatural, lamentable! Nevertheless, under all disguises of the Radical, the Poet is still recognisable: a certain music breathes through all dissonances, as the prophecy and ground-tone of returning harmony; the man, as we said, is of a poetical nature.

To his Political Philosophy there is perhaps no great mportance attachable. He feels, as all men that live must do, the dis-organisation, and hard-grinding, unequal pressure of our Social Affairs; but sees into it only a very little farther than far inferior men do. The frightful condition of a time, when public and private Principle, as the word was once understood, having gone out of sight, and Self-interest being left to plot, and struggle, and scramble, as it could and would, Difficulties had accumulated till they were no longer to be borne, and the spirit that should have fronted and conquered them seemed to have forsaken the world; — when the Rich, as the utmost they could resolve on, had ceased to govern, and the Poor, in their fast-accumulating numbers, and ever-widening complexities, had ceased to be able to do without governing; and now the plan of 'Competition' and '*Laissez-faire*' was, on every side, approaching its consummation; and each, bound-up in the circle of his own wants and perils, stood grimly distrustful of his neighbour, and the distracted Common-weal was a Common-woe, and to all men it became apparent that the end was drawing nigh: — all this black aspect of Ruin and Decay, visible enough, experimentally known to our Sheffield friend, he calls by the name of 'Corn-law', and expects to be in good part delivered from were the accursed Bread-tax repealed.

In this system of political Doctrine, even as here so emphatically set forth, there is not much of novelty. Radicals we have many; loud enough on this and other grievances; the removal of which is to be the one thing needful. The deep, wide flood of bitterness, and hope becoming hopeless, lies acrid, corrosive in every bosom; and flows freely enough through any orifice Accident may open; through Law-Reform, Legislative Reform, Poor-Laws, want of Poor-Laws, Tithes, Game-Laws, or, as we see here, Corn-Laws. Whereby indeed only this becomes clear, that a deep wide flood of evil does exist and corrode; from which, in all ways, blindingly and seeingly, men seek deliverance, and cannot rest till they find it; least of all till they know what part and proportion of it is to *be* found. But with us foolish sons of Adam this is ever the way: some evil that lies nearest us, be it a chronic sickness, or but a smoky chimney, is ever the acme or sum-total of all evil; the black hydra that shuts us out from a Promised Land; and so, in poor [Sterne's] Mr Shandy's fashion, must we 'shift from trouble to trouble, and from side to side; button up one cause of vexation, and unbutton another' [*Tristram Shandy*, 1760-7].

Thus for our keen-hearted singer, and sufferer, in itself a considerable but no immeasurable smoke-pillar, swoln out to be a world-embracing Darkness, that darkens and suffocates the whole earth, and has blotted out the heavenly stars. Into the merit of the Corn-Laws, which has often been discussed, in fit season, by competent hands, we do not enter here; least of all in the way of argument, in the way of blame, towards one who, if he read such merit with some emphasis 'on the scantier trenchers of his children', may well be pardoned. That the 'Bread-tax', with various other taxes, may ere long be altered and abrogated, and the Corn-trade become as free as the poorest 'bread-taxed drudge' could wish it, or the richest 'satrap bread-taxed' could fear it, seems no extravagant hypothesis: would that the mad Time could, by such simple hellebore-dose, be healed! Alas for the diseases of a world lying in wickedness, in heart-sickness and atrophy, quite another alcahest is needed; — a long, painful course of medicine and regimen, surgery and physic, not yet specified or indicated in the Royal-College Books!

But if there is little novelty in our friend's Political Philosophy, there is some in his political Feeling and Poetry. The peculiarity of the radical is, that with all his stormful destructiveness he combines a decided loyalty and faith. If he despise and trample under foot on the one hand, he exalts and reverences on the other; the 'landed pauper in his coach-and-four' rolls all the more glaringly, contrasted with the 'Rockinghams and Saviles' of the past, with the 'Lansdowns and Fitzwilliams', many a 'Wentworth's lord', still 'a blessing' to the present. This man, indeed, has in him the root of all reverence, — a principle of Religion. He believes in a Godhead, not with the lips only, but apparently with the heart; who, as has been written, and often felt, 'reveals Himself in parents, in all true Teachers and Rulers', — as in false Teachers and Rulers quite Another may be revealed! Our Rhymer, it would seem, is no Methodist: far enough from it. He makes 'the Ranter', in his hot-headed way, exclaim over

The Hundred Popes of England's Jesuitry

and adds, by way of note, in his own person, some still stronger sayings: How 'this baneful corporation, dismal as its Reign of Terror is, and long-armed its Holy Inquisition, must condescend to learn and teach what is useful, or go where all nuisances go' [Notes to 'The Ranter']. As little perhaps is he a Church-man; the 'Cadi-Dervish' seems nowise to his mind. Scarcely, however, if at all, does he show aversion to the Church as Church; or, among his many griefs, touch upon Tithes as one. But, in any case, the black colours of Life, even as here painted, and brooded over, do not hide from him that a God is the Author and Sustainer thereof; that God's world, if made a House of Imprisonment, can also be a House of Prayer; wherein for the weary and heavy-laden pity and hope are not altogether cut away.

It is chiefly in virtue of this inward temper of heart, with the clear disposition and adjustment which for all else results therefrom, that our Radical attains to be Poetical; that the harsh groanings, contentions, upbraidings, of one who has unhappily felt constrained to adopt such mode of utterance, become ennobled into something of music. If a land of bondage, this is still his Father's land, and the bondage endures not forever. As worshipper and believer, the captive can look with seeing eye: the aspect of the Infinite Universe still fills him with an infinite feeling; his chains, were it but for moments, fall away; he soars free aloft, and the sunny regions of Poesy and Freedom gleam golden afar on the widened horizon. Gleamings we say, prophetic dawnings from these far regions, spring up for him; nay, beams of actual radiance. In his ruggedness, and dim contractedness (rather of place than of organ), he is not without touches of a feeling and vision, which, even in the stricter sense, is to be named poetical.

Passage 4.2

(from *Rev. Fred W. Robertson, 'Two Lectures on the Influence of Poetry on the Working Classes, Delivered before the Members of the Mechanics' Institution'*, February 1852)

We proceed to the more direct business of this evening: the *influence* of Poetry of the Working Classes. But first, I disclaim the notion of treating this subject as if Poetry had a different sort of influence on them from that which it has on other classes. Very false is that mode of thought which recognises the souls as the classes who are not compelled to work as composed of porcelain: and of those who are doomed to work as made of clay. They feel, weep, laugh, alike: alike have their aspiring and their degraded moods: that which tells one human spirit, tells also upon another. Much, therefore, of what is said will belong to men of work, not specially, but only as human beings. If Poetry influences men, it must influence Working Men.

The influence of Poetry depends partly on the form: and aptly on the spirit which animates the form. I will consider the influence of form first.

We have defined Poetry to be a work of imagination wrought into form by art. Poetry is not imagination, but imagination shaped. Nor feeling; but feeling expressed symbolically: the formless suggested indirectly through form. Hence the form is an essential element of Poetry: and it becomes necessary to trace its influence.

The form in which poetical feeling expresses itself is infinitely varied. There may be a poetical act, or a poetical picture, or a variety of poetical words, to which last form we technically give the name of Poetry.

Take an example from the expression of countenance, which may be poetical. There are feelings which cannot be spoken out in words: therefore the Creator has so constituted the human countenance that it is expressive, and you only catch the meaning sympathetically by the symbolism of the features. We have all

seen such Poetry. We have seen looks inspired. We have seen
whole worlds of feeling at a glance: scorn, hatred, devotion,
infinite tenderness. This is what, in portraits, we call expression
as distinguished from similarity of feature. Innumerable touches
perfect the one: sometimes one masterly stroke will suggest the
other, so that nothing can add to it. This is Poetry. To such a look
the addition of a word would have spoilt it all —

> For words are weak, and most to seek,
>   When wanted fifty-fold;
> And then, if silence will not speak,
> And trembling lip, and changing cheek,
>   There is nothing *told.*

The form of Poetry, again, may be that of a symbolical action.
The Eastern nations express themselves abundantly in this way:
and if the subject were not too sacred, I might adduce many
examples from the significant actions of the Hebrew prophets.
But I will, instead, instance a case of modern history. Perhaps
you have read the anecdote, (I do not know on what historical
authority it rests), of the Earl of Warwick, in one of his last
battles, probably that of Barnet, when he found the day going
against him, dismounting from his favourite charger, and before
all his army plunging his sword into his heart, thereby cutting off
the possibility of escape, and expressing his resolve there to win
or fall. Conceive Warwick putting that into direct words.
Conceive his attempting to express all that was implied in that
act: the energy of despair, the resolve, the infinite defiance, the
untold words of *force* that must be in a man who could do an act
the whole terribleness of which none but a soldier could appreciate, slaying with his own hand the horse and friend that had
borne him through death and perils. And conceive the influence
upon the troops — how it must have said to any recreant waverer
in the ranks, 'Stand like a man, and dare to die!'

The next instance is a less dignified one; and I select it that we
may discern the manifold shapes and degrees of poetic form.
History tells us of a prince of France who asked permission to
offer a present to one much loved.The permission was given: the
gift chosen, a portrait: but with a stipulation annexed, in order to
prevent extravagance, that it should not be larger than could be
worn upon the finger, and that it should not be set in jewels. The
portrait was completed as agreed on; but, instead of glass, it was

covered with a single plate, cut out of the centre of an enormous diamond, which, of course, was sacrificed in the cutting. When the ingenious treachery was discovered, the picture was returned: whereupon the royal lover ground the diamond to powder, and dusted with it, instead of sand, his letter of reply. The use of this? It was useless. Had it been a matter of utility, it had not been one of Poetry. It was modified by French feeling, doubtless. Yet beneath it, you will discern something that was not merely French, but human, and which constituted the Poetry of the whole system of present giving. That which in the polite Frenchman was something more than gallantry, would have been in another, and in him, too, under more earnest or less successful circumstances the chivalrous feeling which desires to express itself in its true essence, as devotion to the weaker, through a sacrifice which shall be costly, (the costlier the more grateful, as the relief of feeling to the giver), and which shall be quite immeasurable by, and independent of the question of utility. The love of the base and plebian spirit is the desire to *take* all it can. The love of the nobler spirit is the desire to *give* all it can. Sacrifice is its only true expression; and every form of sacrifice in which the soul tries to express and relieve itself, whether it be in the lavish magnificence in which self and life can be freely spent, or the vulgar magnificence called princely, with which gold and jewels can be squandered, is a form of Poetry, more or less dignified.

It will now be clear, that in the large sense of the word Poetry, its proper form is always symbolism. The poet derives his power from the ardour of mankind to adopt symbols, and catch enthusiasm from them. Poetry is the language of symbolism.

Therefore we all are susceptible of its influences. Many a man thinks he has no taste for Poetry, because he does not chance to feel it in one of its forms, rhythmic words, is yet no stranger to its power. What is religious formalism, but an exaggeration or petrifaction of a true conviction — that outward forms and material symbols have a language of their own, fraught with a deeper, because infinite, religious significance to the heart than ever came from the poor rhetoric of the pulpit? Why is it that on the battle field there is ever one spot where the sabres glitter faster, and the pistol's flash is more frequent, and men and officers crowd together in denser masses? They are struggling for a flag, or an eagle, or a standard. — Strip it of its symbolism — take from it the meaning with which the imagination has invested it, and it is nothing but a bit of silk rag, torn with shot, and blackened with powder. Now go with your common sense and tell the soldier he is madly striving about a bit of rag. See if your common sense is as true to him as his Poetry, or able to quench it for a moment.

Take a case. Among the exploits of marvellous and almost legendary valour performed by that great chieftain, to whom not many years ago, when disaster after disaster left it uncertain whether the next mail would bring us news that we possessed any Indian Empire at all, the voice of England, with one unanimous impulse, cried 'There is one man in Britain who has the right of wisdom as well as courage to command in chief', — that daring warrior who, when the hour of danger was past, and the hour of safety had come, was forgotten by his country; to whom in the hour of fresh danger the people of England will look again, and his generous spirit will forget neglect; who has been laid aside uncoroneted and almost unhonoured because he *would* promote and distinguish the men of work in preference to the men of rank, and wealth, and titled idleness — amongst his achievements not the least wondrous was his subjugation of the robber tribes of the Cutchee hills, in the North of Scinde. Those warriors had been unsubdued for six hundred years. They dwelt in a crater-like valley, surrounded by mountains, through which there are but two or three narrow entrances, and up which there was no access but by goat paths, so precipitous that brave men grew dizzy and could not proceed. So rude and wild was the fastness of Trukkee, that the entrances themselves could scarcely be discovered amidst the labyrinth-like confusion of rocks and mountains. It was part of the masterly plan by which Sir Charles Napier had resolved to storm the stronghold of the robbers, to cause a detachment of his army to scale the mountain side. A service so perilous could scarcely be commanded. There was a regiment, the 64th Bengal infantry, which had been recently disgraced, in consequence of mutiny at Shikarpoor, their colonel cashiered, and their colours taken from them — a hundred of these men volunteered. 'Soldiers of the 64th', said the commander, who knew the way to a soldier's heart 'your colours are on the top of yonder hill!' I should like to have seen the precipice that would have deterred the 64th regiment, after words like those from the lips of the conqueror of Scinde!

And now, suppose that you had gone with common sense and economic science, and proved to them that the colours they were risking their lives to win back, were worth but so many shillings sterling value — tell me, which would the stern workers of the

64th regiment have found it easiest to understand, common sense or Poetry? Which would they have believed, Science, which said, 'It is manufactured silk'; or, Imagination, whose kingly voice had made it 'colours'?

It is in this sense that the poet has been called, as the name imports, creator, namer, maker. He stamps his own feeling on a form or symbol: names it, and makes it what it was not before: giving to feeling a local habitation and a name [*A Midsummer Night's Dream*, v.i.17], by associating it with form. Before, it was silk — so many square feet: now, it is a thing for which men will die.

And here we get at two distinctions. —

First, between the poet and the rhymster. A poet is one who creates and names: who interprets old or new thoughts by fresh symbolism. The rhymster repeats the accredited forms and phrases: and because he has got the knack of using metaphors and diction, which have been the living language of the makers of them, he is mistaken for a poet. Smooth writing, and facility of versification, and experiences in piecing together poetical words and images, do not constitute Poetry.

Next, a distinction between the poet and the mystic. The poet uses symbols, knowing that they are symbols. The mystic mistakes them for realities. Thus to Swedenborg a cloud, or a vine, or a cedar correspond throughout Scripture with one mystic spiritual truth; mean one thing, and but one. And thus to the mystical formalist, a sign or symbol is confused with the truth it symbolises: that symbol is *the* symbol of that truth; and to treat the symbol as Hezekiah treats the brazen serpent [2 Kings 18], is sacrilege. Now, the poet remains sane upon this point: his 'fine frenzy' never reaches the insanity which mistakes its own creations for fixed realities. To him a cloud or flower may express at different times a thousand truths: material things are types to him in a certain mood, of this truth or that; but he knows that to another person, or to himself in another mood, they are types of something else.

Tennyson has said this well —

But any man who walks the mead,
    In bud, or blade, or bloom may find,
According as his humours lead,
    A meaning suited to his mind.
For liberal applications lie

> In Art as Nature, dearest friend:
> So 'twere to cramp its use, if I
> Should hook it to some useful end.
> > ['Moral' in 'The Day-Dream', 1842 (9-16)]

And this will help us to discern how far there is truth in the opinion that Poetry belongs to the earlier ages, and declines with the advance of civilisation. Symbols perish — Poetry never dies. There was a time when the Trojan war, before Homer sang it, was what Milton says of the unsung wars of the Saxon Heptarchy, a conflict of kites and crows; the martyr's stake, a gibbet; Olympus and Parnassus, and a hill more holy still, common hills. The time may come when, as they were once without poetical associations, most of them shall be unpoetical again. And because of such a dying of the glory from the past, people begin to fancy that Poetry has perished. But is human courage lost, fidelity, imagination, honourable aims? Is the necessity of utterance gone, or the sufficiency of finite words for illimitable feeling greater? When the old colours of a regiment are worn out, it is sometimes the custom to burn them, and drink the ashes in wine, with solemn silence: before the consecration of new colours. Well — that is all we want. Let old forms and time-honoured words perish with due honour, and give us fresh symbols and new forms of speech to express, not what our fathers felt, but what we feel. Goethe says, 'The spirit-world is not fore-closed. *Thy* senses are dulled; *thy* heart is dead. Arise, become a learner; and bathe that earthly breast of thine, unwearied, in the dew of a fresh morning.'[3]

And this alone would be enough to show that the Poetry of the coming age must come from the Working Classes. In the upper ranks, Poetry, so far at least as it represents their life, has been worn out, sickly, and sentimental. Its manhood is effete. Feudal aristocracy with its associations, the castle and the tournament, has passed away. Its last healthy tones came from the harp of Scott. Byron sang its funeral dirge. But tenderness, and heroism, and endurance still want their voice, and it must come from the classes whose observation is at first hand, and who speak from nature's heart. What has Poetry to do with the Working Classes? Men of work! we want our Poetry from you — from men who will dare to live a brave a true life; not like poor Burns, who was fevered with flattery; manful as he was, and dazzled by the vulgar splendours of the life of the great, which he despised and still longed for; rather like Ebenezer Elliott, the author of the Corn Law Rhymes [see passage 4.1]. Our soldier ancestors told you the significance of high devotion and loyalty which lay beneath the smoke of battle fields. Now rise and tell us the living meaning there may be in the smoke of manufactories, and the heroism of perseverance, and the poetry of invention, and the patience of uncomplaining resignation.

Passage 4.3a

(from *Charles Kingsley, 'Burns and His School',* North British Review, *1851-2. Kingsley's article provides a survey of working-class poets. He claims that these 'uneducated' writers follow a tradition initiated by Burns. This essay examines the work of several poets: Ebenezer Elliott, John Bethune, William Thom and Thomas Cooper (the Chartist poet). This extract contains Kingsley's commentary on the writings of Robert Nicoll, and represents his tone and attitude to all the aforementioned writers in what is a lengthy essay. As his novel,* Alton Locke: Tailor and Poet *(1850) demonstrates, Kingsley's utopian Christian Socialism promoted the artisan poet as a figure instrumental to the reconciliation of the classes. In* Alton Locke, *Kingsley drew heavily on Carlyle's essays to outline a programme for spiritual reform. Compare Carlyle's response to the 'Corn-law Rhymer', Ebenezer Elliott, in Passage 4.1)*

The field in which Burns's influence has been, as was to be expected, most important and most widely felt, is in the poems of working men. He first proved it was possible to become a poet and a cultivated man, without deserting his class, either in station or in sympathies; nay, that the healthiest and noblest elements of a lowly born poet's mind might be, perhaps certainly must be, the very feelings and thoughts which he brought up with him from below, not those which he received from above, in the course of his artificial culture. From the example of Burns, therefore, many a working man, who would otherwise have 'died and given no sign', has taken courage, and spoken out the thought within him, in verse or prose, not always wisely and well, but in all cases, as it seems to us, in the belief that he had a sort of divine right to speak and be heard, since Burns had broken down the artificial ice-wall of centuries, and asserted, by act as well as song, that 'a man's a man for a' that'. Almost every volume of working men's poetry which we have read, seems to re-echo poor [Robert]

Nicoll's spirited, though somewhat over-strained address to the Scottish genius: —

This is the natal day of him,
  Who, born in want and poverty,
Burst from his fetters, and arose,
  The freest of the free.

Arose to tell the watching earth
  What lowly men could feel and do,
To shew that mighty, heaven-like souls
  In cottage hamlets grew.

Burns! thou hast given us a name
  To shield us from the taunts of scorn:
The plant that creeps amid the soil
  A glorious flower has borne.

Before the proudest of the earth
  We stand with an uplifted brow;
Like us, thou wast a toil-worn man,
  And we are noble now!

The critic, looking calmly on, may indeed question whether this new fashion of verse writing among working men has been always conducive to their own happiness. As for absolute success as poets, that was not to be expected of one in a hundred, so that we must not be disappointed if among the volumes of working men's poetry, of which we give a list at the head of our Article, only two should be found, on perusal, to contain writing of a very high order, althogh these volumes form a very small portion of the verses which have been written, during the last forty years, by men engaged in the rudest and most montonous toil. To every man so writing, the art, doubtless, is an ennobling one. The habit of expressing thought in verse not only indicates culture, but it is a culture in itself of a very high order. It teaches the writer to think tersely and definitely; it evokes in him the humanizing sense of grace and melody, not merely by enticing him to study good models, but by the very act of composition. It gives him a vent for sorrows, doubts, and aspirations, which might otherwise fret and canker within, breeding, as they too often do in the utterly dumb English peasant, self-devouring meditation, dogged melancholy, and fierce fanaticism. And if the effect of verse writing had stopped there, all had been well; but bad models have had their effect, as well as good ones, on the half-tutored taste of the working men, and engendered in them but too often a fondness for frothy magniloquence and ferocious raving, neither morally nor aesthetically profitable to themselves or their readers. There are excuses for the fault; the young of all ranks naturally enough mistake noise for awfulness, and violence for strength; and there is generally but too much, in the biographies of these working poets, to explain if not to excuse, a vein of bitterness which they certainly did not learn from their master, Burns. The two poets who have done most harm, in teaching the evil trick of cursing and swearing, are Shelley and the Corn-Law Rhymer; and one can well imagine how seducing the two models must be, to men struggling to utter their own complaints. Of Shelley this is not the place to speak. But of the Corn-Law Rhymer we may say here, that howsoever he may have been indebted to Burns's example for the notion of writing at all, he has profited very little by Burns's own poems. Instead of the genial loving tone of the great Scotchman, we find in Elliott a tone of deliberate savageness, all the more ugly, because evidently intentional. He tries to curse; 'he delights' — may we be forgiven if we misjudge the man — 'in cursing'; he makes a science of it; he defiles, of malice prepense, the loveliest and sweetest thoughts and scenes (and he can be most sweet) by giving some sudden, sickening revulsion to the reader's feelings; and he does it generally with a power that makes it at once as painful to the calmer reader as alluring to those who are struggling with the same temptations as the poet. Now and then, his trick drags him down into sheer fustian and bombast; but not always. There is a terrible Dantean vividness of imagination about him, perhaps unequalled in England, in his generation. His poems are like his countenance, coarse and ungoverned, yet with an intensity of eye, a rugged massiveness of feature, which would be grand but for the absence of love and of humour — love's twin and inseparable brother. Therefore it is, that although single passages may be found in his writings, of which Milton himself need not have been ashamed, his efforts at dramatic poetry are utter failures, dark, monstrous, unrelieved by any human vein of feeling or character. As in feature, so in mind, he has not even the delicate and graceful organization which made up in Milton for the want of tenderness, and so enabled him to write, if not in drama, yet still the sweetest masques and idyls.

Passage 4.3b

(from *Charles Kingsley, 'Burns and his School', 1851-2*)

The popular poetry of Germany has held that great nation together, united and heart-whole for centuries, in spite of every disadvantage of internal division, and the bad influence of foreign taste; and the greatest of their poets have not thought it beneath them to add their contributions, and their very best, to the common treasure, meant not only for the luxurious and the learned, but for the workman and the child at school. In Great Britain, on the contrary, the people have been left to form their own tastes, and choose their own modes of utterance, with great results, both for good and evil; and there has sprung before the new impulse which Burns gave to popular poetry, a considerable literature — considerable not only from its truth and real artistic merit, but far more so from its being addressed principally to the working-classes. Even more important is this people's literature question, about which we now hear such ado. It does seem to us, that to take every possible precaution about the spiritual truth which children are taught in school, and then leave to chance the more impressive and abiding teaching which popular literature, songs especially, give them out of doors, is as great *niaserie* [foolishness] as that of the Tractarians who insisted on getting into the pulpit in their surplices, as a sign that the clergy only had the right of preaching to the people, while they forgot that, by means of a free press, (of the license of which they too were not slack to avail themselves),[4] every penny-a-liner was preaching to the people daily, and would do, maugre their surplices, to the end of time. The man who makes people's songs is a true popular preacher. Whatsoever, true or false, he sends forth, will not be carried home, as a sermon often is, merely in heads, to be forgotten before the week is out: it will ring in the ears, and cling round the imagination, and follow the pupil to the workshop, and the tavern, and the fireside, even to the deathbed, such power is in the magic of rhyme. The emigrant, deep in Australian forests, may take down Chalmers's sermons on Sabbath evenings from the scanty shelf; but the songs of Burns have been haunting his lips, and cheering his heart, and moulding him unconsciously to himself, in clearing and in pasture all the weary week. True, if he be what a Scotchman should be, more than one old Hebrew psalm has brought its message to him during these week-days;

but there are feelings of his nature on which those psalms, not from defect, but from their very purpose, do not touch; how is he to express them, but in the songs which echo them? These will keep alive, and intensify in him, and in the children who learn them from his lips, all which is like themselves. Is it, we ask again, to be left to chance what sort of songs these shall be?

As for poetry written for the working-classes by the upper, such attempts as we yet have seen may be considered *nil*. The upper must learn to know more of the lower, and to make the lower know more of them — a frankness of which we honestly believe they will never have to repent. Moreover, they must read Burns a little more, and cavaliers and Jacobites a little less. As it is, their efforts have been as yet exactly in that direction which would most safely secure the blessings of undisturbed obscurity. Whether 'secular' or 'spiritual', they have thought proper to adopt a certain Tommy-good-child tone, which, whether to Glasgow artisans or Dorsetshire labourers, or indeed for any human being who is 'grinding among the iron facts of life', is, to say the least, nauseous; and the only use of their poematicula has been to demonstrate practically, the existence of a great and fearful gulf between those who have, and those who have not, in thought as well as in purse, which must be, in the former article at least, bridged over as soon as possible, if we are to remain one people much longer. The attempts at verse for children are somewhat more successful — a certain little 'Moral Songs' especially, said to emanate from the Tractarian School, yet full of a health, spirit, and wild sweetness, which makes its authoress, in our eyes, 'wiser than her teachers'.[5] But this is our way. We are too apt to be afraid of the men, and to take the children as our *pis aller*, covering our despair of dealing with the majority, the adult population, in a pompous display of machinery for influencing that very small fraction, the children. 'Oh, but the destinies of the empire depend on the rising generation!' Who has told us so? — how do we know that they do not depend on the risen gener-ation? Who are likely to do more work during our life-time, for good and evil, — those who are now between five and fifteen? Yet for those former, the many, and the working, and the powerful, all we seem to be inclined to do is parody Scripture, and say, 'He that is unjust, let him be unjust still; and he that is filthy, let him be filthy still'.

Not that we ask anyone to sit down, and, out of mere benevol-ence, to write songs for the people. Wooden, out of a wooden birthplace, would go such forth, to feed fires, not spirits. But if any man shall read these pages, to whom God has given a truly poetic temperament, a gallant heart, a melodious ear, a quick and sympathetic eye for all forms of human joy, and sorrow, and humour, and grandeur — an insight which can discern the outlines of the butterfly, when clothed in the roughest and most rugged chrysalis-hide; if the teachers of his heart and purposes, and not merely of his tastes and sentiments, have been the great songs of his own and of every land and age; if he can see in the divine poetry of David and Solomon, of Isaiah and Jeremiah, and, above all, in the parables of Him who spake as never man spake, the models and elemental laws of a people's poetry, alike according to the will of God and the heart of man; if he can welcome gallantly and hopefully the future, and yet know that it must be, unless it would be a monster and a machine, the loving and obedient child of the past; if he can speak of the subjects which alone will interest the many, on love, marriage, the sorrows of the poor, their hopes, political and social, their wrongs, as well as their sins and duties; and that with a fervour and passion akin to the spirit of Burns and Elliott, yet with more calm, more purity, more wisdom, and therefore with more hope, as one who stands upon a vantage ground of education and culture, sympathizing none the less with those who struggle behind him in the valley of the shadow of death, yet seeing from mountain peaks the coming dawn, invisible as yet to them. Then let man think it no fall, but rather a noble rise, to shun the barren glacier ranges of pure art, for the fertile gardens of practical and popular song, and write for the many, and with the many, in words such as they can understand, remembering that that which is simplest is always deepest, that the many contain in themselves the few, and that when he speaks to the wanderer and the drudge, he speaks to the elemental and primeval man, and in him speaks to all who have risen out of him. Let him try, undiscouraged by inevitable failures; and if at least he succeeds in giving vent to one song which will cheer hard-worn hearts at the loom and the forge, or wake one pauper's heart with the hope that his children are destined not to die as he died, or recall, amid Canadian forests or Australian sheep-walks, one thrill of love for the old country, and her liberties, and her laws, and her religion, to the settler's heart; — let her know that he has earned a higher place among the spirits of the wise and the good, by doing, in spite of the unpleasantness of self-denial, the duty which lay nearest him, than if he outrivalled Goethe on his own classic ground, and make all the cultivated and the comfortable of the earth desert, for the exquisite creations of his fancy, Faust, and Tasso, and Iphigenie.

Passage 4.4

(from *Matthew Arnold, 'The Study of Poetry', 1880. This essay prefaced an anthology edited by T.H. Ward,* The English Poets)

'The future of poetry is immense, because in poetry, where it is worthy of its high destinies, our race, as time goes on, will find an ever surer and surer stay. There is not a creed which is not shaken, not an accredited dogma which is not shown to be questionable, not a received tradition which does not threaten to dissolve. Our religion has materialised itself in the fact, in the supposed fact; it has attached its emotion to the fact, and now the fact is failing it. But for poetry the idea is everything; the rest is a world of illusion, of divine illusion. Poetry attaches its emotion to the idea the idea *is* the fact. The strongest part of our religion to-day is its unconscious poetry.'[7]

Let me be permitted to quote these words of my own, as uttering the thought which should, in my opinion, go with us and govern us in all our study of poetry. In the present work it is the course of one great contributory stream to the world-river of poetry that we are invited to follow. We are here invited to trace the stream of English poetry. But whether we set ourselves, as here, to follow only one of the several streams that make the mighty river of poetry, of whether we seek to know them all, our governing thought should be the same. We should conceive of poetry worthily, and more highly than it has been the custom to conceive of it. We should conceive of it as capable in higher uses, and called to higher destinies, than those which in general men have assigned to it hitherto. More and more mankind will discover that we have to turn to poetry to interpret life for us, to console us, to sustain us. Without poetry, our science will appear incomplete; and most of what now passes with us for religion and philosophy will be replaced by poetry. Science, I say, will appear incomplete without it. For finely and truly does Wordsworth call poetry 'the impassioned expression which is in the countenance of all science'; and what is a countenance without its expression?

Again, finely and truly, Wordsworth calls poetry 'the breath and finer spirit of all knowledge' [Preface to *Lyrical Ballads*, 1800]: our religion, parading evidence such as those on which the popular mind relies now; our philosophy, pluming itself on its reasonings about causation and finite and infinite being; what are they but the shadows and dreams and false shows of knowledge? The day will come when we shall wonder at ourselves for having trusted to them, for having taken them seriously; and the more we perceive their hollowness, the more we shall prize 'the breath and finer spirit of knowledge' offered to us by poetry.

But if we conceive thus highly of the destinies of poetry, we must also set our standard for poetry high, since poetry, to be capable of fulfilling such high destinies, must be poetry of a high order of excellence. We must accustom ourselves to a high standard and to a strict judgement. Sainte-Beuve relates that Napoleon one day said, when someone was spoken was spoken of in his presence as a charlatan: 'Charlatan as much as you please; but where is there *not* charlatanism?' — 'Yes', answers Sainte-Beuve, 'in politics, in the art of governing mankind, that is perhaps true. But in the order of thought, in art, the glory, the eternal honour is that charlatanism shall find no entrance; herein lies the inviolableness of that noble portion of man's being' [*Les Cahiers de Sainte-Beuve*, 1876]. It is admirably said, and let us hold fast to it. In poetry, which is thought and art in one, it is the glory, the eternal honour, that charlatanism shall find no entrance; that this noble sphere be kept inviolate and inviolable. Charlatanism is for confusing and obliterating the distinctions between excellent and inferior, sound and unsound or only half-sound, true and untrue or only half-true. It is charlatanism, conscious or unconscious, whenever we confuse or obliterate these. And in poetry, more than anywhere else, it is unpermissible to confuse or obliterate them. For in poetry the distinction between excellent and inferior, sound and unsound or only half-sound, true and untrue or only half-true, is of paramount importance. It is of paramount importance because of the high destinies of poetry. In poetry, as a criticism of life under the conditions fixed for such a criticism by the laws of poetic truth and poetic beauty, the spirit of our race will find, we have said, as time goes on and as other helps fail, its consolation and stay. But the consolation and stay will be of power in proportion to the power of the criticism of life. And the criticism of life will be of power in proportion as the poetry conveying it is excellent rather than inferior, sound rather than unsound or only half-sound, true rather than untrue or only half-true.

The best poetry is what we want; the best poetry will be found to have a power of forming, sustaining, and delighting us, as nothing else can. A clearer, deeper sense of the best in poetry, and of the strength and joy to be drawn from it, is the most precious benefit which we can gather from a poetical collection such as the present. And yet in the very nature and conduct of such a collection there is inevitably something which tends to obscure in us the consciousness of what our benefit should be, and to distract us from the pursuit of it. We should therefore steadily set it before our minds at the outset, and should compel ourselves to revert constantly to the thought of it as we proceed.

Yes; constantly, in reading poetry, a sense for the best, the really excellent, and of the strength and joy to be drawn from it, should be present in our minds and should govern our estimate of what we read. But this real estimate, the only true one, is liable to be superseded, if we are not watchful, by two other kinds of estimate, the historic estimate and the personal estimate, both of which are fallacious. A poet or a poem may count to us historically, they may count to us on grounds personal to ourselves, and they may count to us really. They may count to us historically. The course of development of a nation's language, thought, and poetry, is profoundly interesting; and by regarding a poet's work as a stage in this course of development we may easily bring ourselves to make it of more importance as poetry than in itself it really is, we may come to use a language of quite exaggerated praise in criticising it; in short, to over-rate it. So arises in our poetic judgements the fallacy caused by the estimate which we may call historic. Then, again, a poet or a poem may count to us on ground personal to ourselves. Our personal affinities, likings, and circumstances, have great power to sway our estimate of this or that poet's work, and to make us attach more importance to it as poetry than it itself really possesses, because to us it is, or has been, of high importance. Here also we over-rate the object of our interest, and apply to it a language of praise which is quite exaggerated. And thus we get the source of a second fallacy in our poetic judgements — the fallacy caused by an estimate which we may call personal.

Both fallacies are natural. It is evident how naturally the study of history and development of a poetry may incline a man to pause over reputations and works once conspicuous but now obscure, and to quarrel with a careless public for skipping, in obedience to mere tradition and habit, from one famous name or work in its national poetry to another, ignorant of what it misses, and of the reason for keeping what it keeps, and of the whole process of growth in its poetry. The French have become diligent students of their own early poetry, which they long neglected; the study makes many of them dissatisfied with their so-called classical poetry, the court-tragedy of the seventeenth century, a poetry which [Paul] Pellisson long ago reproached with its want of true poetic stamp, with its *politesse sterile et rampante*, but which nevertheless has reigned in France as absolutely as if it had been the perfection of classical poetry indeed. The dissatisfaction is natural; yet a lively and accomplished critic M. Charles d'Hericault, the editor of Clement Marot, goes too far when he says that 'the cloud of glory playing round a classic is a mist as dangerous to the future of literature as it is intolerable for the purposes of history'. 'It hinders', he goes on, 'it hinders us from seeing more than one single point, the culminating and exceptional point; the summary, fictitious and arbitrary, of a thought and of a work. It substitutes a halo for a physiognomy, it puts a statue where there was once a man, and hiding from us all trace of the labour, the attempts, the weaknesses, the failures, it claims not study but veneration; it does not show us how the thing is done, it imposes upon us a model. Above all, for the historian this creation of classic personages is inadmissable; for it withdraws the poet from his time, from his proper life, it breaks historical relationships, it blinds criticism by conventional admiration, and renders the investigation of literary origins unacceptable. It gives us a human personage no longer, but a God seated immovable amidst His perfect work, like Jupiter on Olympus; and hardly will it be possible for the young student, to whom such work is exhibited at such a distance from him, to believe that it did not issue ready made from that divine head.'[6]

All this is brilliantly and tellingly said, but we must plead for a distinction. Everything depends on the reality of a poet's classic character. If he is a dubious classic, let us sift him; if he is a false classic, let us explode him. But if he is a real classic, if his work belongs to the class of the very best (for this is the true and right meaning of the word *classic, classical*), the great thing for us is to feel and enjoy his work as deeply as ever we can, and to appreciate the wide difference between it and all work which has not the same high character. This is what is salutary, this is what is formative; this is the great benefit to be got from the study of poetry. Everything which interferes with it, which hinders it, is injurious. True, we must read our classic with open eyes, and not with eyes blinded by superstition; we must perceive when his work comes short, when it drops out of the class of the very best, and we must rate it, in such cases, at its proper value. But the use of this negative criticism is not in itself, it is entirely in its enabling us to have a clearer sense and a deeper enjoyment of what is truly excellent. To trace the labour, the attempts, the weaknesses, the failures of a genuine classic, to acquaint oneself with his time and his life and his historical relationships, is mere literary dilettantism unless it has that clear sense and deeper enjoyment for its own end. It may be said that the more we know about a classic the better we shall enjoy him; and, if we lived as long as Methusalah and had all of us heads of perfect steadfastness, this might be true in fact as it is plausible in theory. But the case here is much the same as the case with the Greek and Latin studies of our schoolboys. The elaborate philological groundwork which we require them to lay is in theory an admirable preparation for appreciating the Greek and Latin authors worthily. The more thoroughly we lay the groundwork, the better we shall be able, it may be said, to enjoy the authors. True, if time were not so short, and schoolboys' wits not so soon tired and their power of attention exhausted; only, as it is, the elaborate philological preparation goes on, but the authors are little known and less enjoyed. So with the investigator of 'historic origins' in poetry. He ought to enjoy the true classic all the better for his investigations; he often is distracted from the enjoyment of the best, and with the less good he overbusies himself, and is prone to over-rate it in proportion to the trouble which it has cost him.

The idea of tracing historic origins and historical relationships cannot be absent from a compilation like the present. And naturally the poets to be exhibited in it will be assigned to those persons for exhibition who are known to prize them highly, rather than those who have no special inclination towards them. Moreover the very occupation with an author, and the business of exhibiting him, disposes us to affirm and amplify his importance. In the present work, therefore, we are sure of frequent temptation to adopt the historic estimate, or the personal estimate, and to forget the real estimate; which latter, nevertheless, we must employ if we are to make poetry yield us its full benefit. So high is that benefit, the benefit of clearly feeling and of deeply enjoying the really excellent, the truly classic in poetry, that we do well, I say, to set it fixedly before our minds as our object in studying poets and poetry, and to make the desire of attaining it the one principle to which, as the *Imitation* says, whatever we may read or come to know, we always return.

Notes

1. In the early 1830s, two major articles on 'Uneducated Poets' appeared in the periodicals. These focused on John Jones's *Attempts in Verse* (1831), which were furnished with a preface by Robert Southey. See T.H. Lister, 'Southey's *Uneducated Poets*', *Edinburgh Review*, vol. 54 (1831), pp. 69-84; and J.G. Lockhart, 'John Jones's *Attempts in Verse*', *Quarterly Review*, vol. 44 (1831), pp. 52-82.

2. Benjamin Franklin (1706-90), inventor and politician, is a key figure in eighteenth-century American history. Samuel Parr (1747-1825) is remembered for his wit and scholarship. Eight volumes of his works, *Parriana*, were pubished in 1828-9.

3. Quotation unidentified.

4. Probably Alice Cary whose Tractarian songs came out in 1852.

5. Arnold's opening paragraph closes his 'Introduction on Poetry' in *The Hundred Greatest Men* (1879).

6. See Charles d'Hericault's introduction to *The Works of Clement Marot* (Paris, 1867).

Select Bibliography

Specialised studies of individual Victorian poets do not appear in this bibliography except where such books include an account of nineteenth-century poetic theory.

Abrams, M.H. *The Mirror and the Lamp: Romantic Theory and the Critical Tradition* (New York, Oxford University Press, 1953)

Altick, Richard D. *The English Common Reader: A Social History of the Mass Reading Public, 1800-1900* (Chicago, University of Chicago Press, 1957)

Armstrong, Isobel, ed. *The Major Victorian Poets: Reconsiderations* (London, Routledge and Kegan Paul, 1969)

—— ed. *Victorian Scrutinies: Reviews of Poetry, 1830 to 1870* (London, Athlone Press, 1972)

—— *Language as Living Form in Nineteenth-Century Poetry* (Brighton, Harvester Press, 1982)

Buckley, Jerome *The Victorian Temper: A Study in Literary Culture* (Cambridge, Mass., Harvard University Press, 1951)

—— *The Triumph of Time: A Study of the Victorian Concepts of Time, History, Progress, and Decadence* (Cambridge, Mass., Harvard University Press, 1966)

Christ, Carol T. *The Finer Optic: The Aesthetic of Particularity in Victorian Poetry* (New Haven, Yale University Press, 1975)

—— *Victorian and Modern Poetics* (Chicago, Unversity of Chicago Press, 1984)

Dale, Peter Allen *The Victorian Critic and the Idea of History: Carlyle, Arnold, Pater* (Cambridge, Mass., Harvard University Press, 1977)

DeLaura, David J. *Hebrew and Hellene in Victorian England: Newman, Arnold, Pater* (Austin, Texas, University of Texas Press, 1969)

—— 'The Future of Poetry: A Context for Carlyle and Arnold' in *Carlyle and His Contemporaries: Essays in Honour of Charles Richard Sanders*, ed. John Clubbe (Durham, NC, Duke University Press, 1976)

Faverty, Frederic E., ed. *The Victorian Poets: A Guide to Research*, 2nd edn (New York, MLA, 1968)

Fleishman, Avrom 'Notes for a History of Victorian Poetic Genres', *Genre* 18 (1985), pp. 362-72

Fraser, Hilary *Beauty and Belief: Aesthetics and Religion in Victorian Literature* (Cambridge, Cambridge University Press, 1986)

Fredeman, William E. *Pre-Raphaelitism: a Bibliocritical Study* (Cambridge, Mass., Harvard Unversity Press, 1965)

—— and Ira B. Nadel, eds *Dictionary of Literary Biography: Volume 32: Victorian Poets Before 1850* (Detroit, Gale Research Corporation, 1984)

—— *Dictionary of Literary Biography: Volume 35: Victorian Poets After 1850* (Detroit, Gale Research Corporation, 1985)

Helsinger, Elizabeth K., Robin Lauterbach Sheets and William Veeder, eds *The Woman Question*, 3 vols (Manchester, Manchester University Press, 1983)

Houghton, Walter E. and G. Robert Strange *Victorian Poetry and Poetics*, 2nd edn (Boston, Houghton Mifflin, 1968)

Johnson, E.D.H. *The Alien Vision of Victorian Poetry* (Princeton, NJ, Princeton University Press, 1952)

Knights, Ben *The Idea of the Clerisy in the Nineteenth Century* (Cambridge, Cambridge University Press, 1978)

Mermin, Dorothy *The Audience in the Poem: Five Victorian Poets* (New Brunswick, NJ, Rutgers University Press, 1983)

Murray, Christopher D. 'D.G. Rossetti, A.C. Swinburne, and R.W. Buchanan: The Fleshly School Revisited', Parts 1 and 2, *The Bulletin of the John Rylands Library*, vol 65., no. 1 (1982), pp. 206-34 and vol 65., no. 2 (1983), pp. 176-207

Prickett, Stephen *Romanticism and Religion: The Tradition of Coleridge and Wordsworth in the Victorian Church* (Cambridge, Cambridge University Press, 1976)

Shaw, W. David *The Lucid Veil: Poetic Truth in the Victorian Age* (London, Athlone Press, 1987)

Sinfield, Alan *Alfred Tennyson* (Oxford, Basil Blackwell, 1986)

Tennyson, G.B. *Victorian Devotional Poetry: The Tractarian Mode* (Cambridge, Mass., Harvard University Press, 1981)

Thesing, William B. *The London Muse: Victorian Poetic Responses to the City* (Athens, Ga, University of Georgia Press, 1982)

Vicinus, Martha *The Industrial Muse: A Study of Nineteenth-Century British Working Class Literature* (London, Croom Helm, 1974)

Warren, Alba H. Jr. *English Poetic Theory, 1825-1865* (Princeton, NJ, Princeton University Press, 1950)

Weinstein, Mark A. *William Edmonstoune Aytoun and the 'Spasmodic Controversy'* (New Haven, Yale University Press, 1968)

Woolford, John 'Periodicals and the Practice of Literary Criticism, 1855-64' in *The Victorian Periodical Press: Samplings and Soundings*, eds Joanne Shattock and Michael Woolf (Leicester, Leicester University Press, 1982)

Index

Since classical writers are alluded to so frequently in Victorian criticism of poetry, this name index is restricted to modern authors.

207